The How and Why
of Home Schooling

The How and Why of Home Schooling

Ray Ballmann

CROSSWAY BOOKS • WHEATON, ILLINOIS
A DIVISION OF GOOD NEWS PUBLISHERS

The How and Why of Home Schooling

Copyright © 1987 by Ray Ballmann

Second Edition, Copyright © 1995 by Ray Ballmann

Published by Crossway Books
a division of Good News Publishers
1300 Crescent Street
Wheaton, Illinois 60187

Cover illustration: Jessie Wilcox Smith

Cover design: Cindy Kiple

First printing, 1987

First revised edition, 1995.

Printed in the United States of America

ISBN 0-89107-859-2

Unless otherwise indicated, Scripture is taken from Holy Bible: New International Version, copyright © 1973, 1978, 1984 by International Bible Society. Used by permission of Zondervan Publishing House. All rights reserved.

The "NIV" and "New International Version" trademarks are registered in the United States Patent and Trademark Office by International Bible Society. Use of either trademark requires the permission of International Bible Society.

04		03		02		01		00					
19	18	17	16	15	14	13	12	11	10	9	8	7

*Dedicated
to the dear family
God has entrusted to me*

Table of Contents

ACKNOWLEDGMENTS   ix

FOREWORD
by Dick Armey, Member of Congress, Majority Leader   xi

FOREWORD
by Mike Farris, President, Home School Legal Defense Association   xiii

PREFACE
by Samuel Blumenfeld   xv

ONE
Home Schooling: The Return to a Biblical and Historical Model
of Education   17

TWO
Is Home Schooling For You?   27

THREE
Public Education:Retarding America and Imprisoning Potential   39

FOUR
Why Home Schooling Is the Best Alternative   77

FIVE
The "How" of Home Schooling   103

SIX
Why Fathers Should Be Involved in the Home School   141

SEVEN
How to Begin   153

EIGHT
Why Grandparents Should Support Home Schooling   163

NINE
How to Win Over Friends and Relatives to a Point of Understanding   169

TEN
Reasons to Home School through High School   175

ELEVEN
Common Questions Asked about Home Schooling   183

APPENDIX   193

NOTES   207

SELECT BIBLIOGRAPHY   215

Acknowledgments

The author gratefully acknowledges those who graciously gave of their time and energy toward the complete revision of this book. Special thanks is due my wife Cindy for her many hours of help and support; to Leonard Goss and Steve Hawkins for their editorial suggestions; and to home schoolers everywhere for their input, thoughts, and suggestions on what should be included in a home schooling primer. Further, I'd like to thank the Home School Legal Defense Association and the National Home Education Research Institute for their assistance in supplying and tracking down information.

Also I would like to recognize and thank those who provided the fine illustrations and chart used in the book: Chuck Asay of the *Colorado Springs Gazette Telegraph*; Matt Arnold; *Congressional Quarterly*; and Theodore E. Wade, Jr., et al. *The Home School Manual: For Parents Who Teach Their Own Children.*

Foreword

The *How and Why of Home Schooling* is an invaluable treatise on the most important educational movement of the past 150 years.

For the first quarter-millennium of our history, from Plymouth Rock to the 1850s, virtually all Americans were home schooled. Government schooling has actually been the exception, not the rule, in our four and a half centuries on this continent.

Sadly, government schooling has been accompanied by a seemingly irresistible movement toward ever greater centralization and bureaucratic control. Last year, this trend culminated in an alarming, and thankfully unsuccessful, proposal in Congress to bring all teachers, including home schooling parents, under federal certification—a key to control.

In fighting that provision, I had the honor and privilege to act as the "champion" of parents across the nation who placed more than one million concerned phone calls to Capitol Hill. To this day, home schoolers stop me in the street to thank me. But the truth of the matter is I was merely the vessel of their concerns. It was they who acted with dispatch to preserve their most precious possession, their freedom. It is they who deserve the respect and gratitude of parents everywhere.

Why do home schooling families care so passionately for freedom? The answer to this is ably provided in the pages of this excellent book. But it might also be summarized in the words of President Calvin Coolidge, who in his famous address on the 150th anniversary of the Declaration of Independence, said:

> If we are to maintain the great heritage which has been bequeathed to us, we must be like-minded as the fathers who created it . . . . We must cultivate the reverence which they had for the things that are holy. We must follow the spiritual and moral leadership which they showed. We must keep replenished—that they may glow with a more compelling flame—the altar fires before which they worshipped.

In home schooling their children, more and more American families are choosing to replenish the ancient altar fires of our freedom beside the warming hearths of their own homes. I can think of few activities more hopeful for the future of our democracy.

DICK ARMEY
Member of Congress
Majority Leader

Foreword

Home schooling is America's educational growth industry. The number of children who are being taught by their own parents is doubling every three to four years. As a consequence, almost everyone in our country now knows at least one family who is home schooling its children.

There are external reasons home schooling is growing so rapidly. The decline of academics, morality, discipline, and even personal safety in the public schools is well known to all. The rise of Outcome Based Education with its legendary reliance on strategies to coerce children to adopt politically-correct values has done more recently than any other single program to cause parents to doubt that the public schools are right for their children.

But the problems in public schools only raise questions about educational alternatives; recognition of these problems does not give affirmative direction to enable parents to choose what is best for their child.

More and more parents are choosing home schooling because of what I call the *Great Kid/Average Parent Syndrome*. They look at children who are being home schooled and say, "Boy, those are great kids. I'd sure like my kids to turn out like that." Then they look at the parents and say, "They're just average parents. If they can be successful so can I."

After thirteen years as a home schooling dad, and twelve years as the lead litigator for home schoolers in the nation, I am convinced that any parent who is willing to work hard can be very successful at home schooling their child. They can have success with their children on every front: academics, spiritual development, family relationships, and social development.

But this kind of success does not come automatically. Some strategies work better than others (although God seems to delight in creating people who constantly prove that there is yet another way to be successful).

For those considering home schooling or who are in your first few years of this lifestyle, advice from a seasoned, wise, home schooling pioneer is of extraordinary value.

Ray Ballmann is just that kind of home schooling pioneer. This book is a unique blend of factual information and down-to-earth practicality. The insights you can gain from his writing can help you get going in the right way. You can also get the encouragement you need to keep going.

Children are not raised in thirty minutes. Home schooling will not change your life in thirty days or your money back. While you may well see some immediately positive results, the real treasure is at the end of the road when you have a child who is spiritually mature, academically solid, poised, and able to win the favor of God and man.

You want that for your children? Well, this books tells you the how and why of this wonderful story.

MIKE FARRIS
President,
Home School Legal Defense Association

Preface

Home schooling is the fastest growing educational phenomenon in America today. And with good reason! The public schools, with few exceptions, have so badly deteriorated that they are no longer safe for children. In fact, children are at risk in four ways in the public schools—academically, spiritually, morally, and physically. Academically, because of widespread educational malpractice which turns perfectly normal children into learning-disabled cripples. Spiritually, because the schools are doing all in their power to destroy the religious faith of the children. Morally, because of such programs as values clarification and sex education that undermine the biblical concept of moral absolutes. And physically, because of rampant crime and violence among public school children.

What are the alternatives? Private schools or home schools. I prefer the home school because it is by far the superior form of education. And Ray Ballmann proves it in this very thorough and illuminating book on home education. Ray has assembled in this one volume an enormous amount of useful and sometimes astonishing information about the home school movement. All of it is the result of Ray's intensive and detailed knowledge of the home school movement gathered over the last eight years. If you are seriously thinking of educating your children at home, a reading of this book will convince you that home schooling is the right choice.

I know this from my own experience with the home school movement. I have spoken at many home school conventions, visited many home school families and read enough home school publications to know that for the Christian family, home schooling is the only choice that makes sense. For home schooling is not only good for the children's education, it is good for the family as a whole. The strengthening of the Christian family is indeed as important an outcome of the home school movement as the education of the children, for in home schooling the parents learn more than the children. The result is that they become better parents and better citizens. And this bodes well for the future of America.

I believe that the home school movement will do more to restore America as a God-fearing, righteous nation than any other social phenomenon presently in ferment. And the faster it spreads, the sooner we shall see the American people living in accordance with God's law and reaping the blessing and benefits of His bounty and benevolence.

SAMUEL L. BLUMENFELD
Author and Lecturer

ONE

Home Schooling: The Return to a Biblical and Historical Model of Education

Home schooling has become one of the most exciting and explosive movements of the century. Already it is the signpost of a profound social and educational shift at the grassroots level. Public education has for years been losing its glitter, and its fractured foundation is crumbling on every side. In the wake of massive youth illiteracy, immorality, and rebellion against domestic authority, concerned parents all across America are exercising their right to teach their children at home. The thriving home schooling movement has become one of the most encouraging and hope-inspiring developments in our country today.

Perhaps, like many people today, you are asking, What is home schooling all about? Is it a fundamentalist fringe of society? Are home schoolers a mixture of fanatics, radicals, and escapists? Or is it a legitimate movement? Why are people in ever growing numbers starting to home school? These are legitimate questions. It is my hope that these and other questions will be answered in the pages that follow. If you have an interest in knowing more about the emergence, growth, and purpose of the home schooling movement, this book was written with you especially in mind. Further, I hope to demonstrate why *you* should personally consider home schooling and how to begin.

Who's Who of Home Schooling

Some of the greatest names in history were educated at home. Home schooling has helped forge some of the world's best leaders—exceptional men and women with sound character, emotional stability, and intellectual genius. Here is a partial hall of fame list of those who have been educated at home.

Abigail Adams	James Madison
John Quincy Adams	Cyrus McCormick
Hans Christian Andersen	John Stuart Mill
Alexander Graham Bell	Claude Monet
Pearl Buck	James Monroe
Andrew Carnegie	Wolfgang Mozart
George Washington Carver	Florence Nightingale
Charlie Chaplin	Blaise Pascal
Agatha Christie	George Patton
Winston Churchill	William Penn
George Rogers Clark	Franklin Delano Roosevelt
Noel Coward	Theodore Roosevelt
Pierre Curie	George Bernard Shaw
Charles Dickens	Albert Schweitzer
Pierre DuPont	Leo Tolstoy
Thomas Edison	Mark Twain
Albert Einstein	George Washington
Benjamin Franklin	Martha Washington
Alexander Hamilton	Daniel Webster
Bret Harte	John Wesley
Patrick Henry	Phyllis Wheatley
Stonewall Jackson	Woodrow Wilson
Robert E. Lee	Orville Wright
Abraham Lincoln	Wilbur Wright
C. S. Lewis	Andrew Wyeth[1]
Douglas MacArthur	

As you can see, presidents (at least ten were substantially taught at home), patriots, delegates to the constitutional convention, famous generals, ministers, lawyers, scientists, businessmen, authors, composers, educators, economists, inventors, and many others have been taught at home.

The home is mankind's first and most basic school. Home-centered education is as old as civilization itself, commencing long before public schools were organized or even conceived. Throughout much of American history, the primary center of instruction was found in the family. Parents were frequently the sole instructors of their offspring.

Today however, educational bureaucrats, the NEA teacher's

union, and the uninformed have charged that home educators are unqualified to teach and are depriving their children of vital socialization. But the history of our nation clearly demonstrates otherwise. Home schoolers constitute the very flower of human potential, leadership, and ability. Most of those listed were persons of compassion, intelligence, skill, adeptness, and self-sufficiency. And the common root that cultivated these unique qualities was home tutoring.

Until just after World War I, family schools were the principle form of education in America. The home served as the social center of influence, the root of moral and spiritual guidance, and the primary academic instructor. The only exceptions to this general rule were during those periods following major wars or immediately prior to societal collapse, when the education of children was largely given over to slaves or public agencies. The chilling consequences of these exceptional times were that children grew up without having received a solid base of values and morality. Hence, after 1812, 1865, 1918, and 1945, the United States suffered from epidemic crime and moral breakdown.[2] Today, once again, public institutions have begun to replace the home in vital areas, often becoming the predominant source for forming and transmitting values in our nation's youth, with the same devastating results.

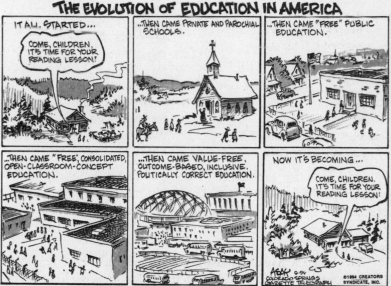

Synopsis of American Education

The following succinct review of American education shows a slow, cancerous growth of anti-Christian philosophies in the school system, along with the appropriate response by concerned Christian families nationwide.

1620—*Christian education.* Schools taught the Bible, and colleges like Harvard, Princeton, and Yale were founded to train young men to preach the gospel.

1837—*Public education begins.* The first public school was established. Horace Mann, a Unitarian, worked for a state-controlled educational system. The Bible was still taught in the public schools.

1905—*Progressive education.* John Dewey, the father of progressive education, introduced Socialistic, anti-Christian philosophy in the schools. The Bible was separated from academic studies.

1925—*Supreme Court rules on home schooling.* In *Pierce v. Society of Sisters* it says Oregon parents can't be denied their own schools, noting, "The child is not the mere creature of the state."

1933—*Humanistic education.* The *Humanist Manifesto*, written by John Dewey and thirty-three other signers enunciates the doctrines of secular humanism. God and the supernatural are rejected and replaced with man's reason and science.

1963—*Anti-Christian education.* Bible reading in public schools is declared unconstitutional. The vacuum is quickly filled with curriculum materials that promote immorality, rebellion against parents, the occult, and other teachings contrary to Scripture.

1960s—*Rise of Christian education.* There are now over ten thousand Christian schools to combat the destructive education of religious humanism. A Christian school is started every seven hours.[3]

1980s—*Rise of home education.* Desiring to return to the biblical model, concerned parents all across America begin reclaiming their right and responsibility for the education of their children. Number of home schoolers rises from 60,000 in 1983 to 244,000 by 1988.

1983—*A Nation At Risk.* Education Department releases study critical of U.S. education, *A Nation At Risk.* Formation of the Home School Legal Defense Association.

1990s—*Home schooling flourishes.* There are between five hundred thousand and one million school-age, home-schooled children nationwide. Home schooling is now active in all fifty states. Home schoolers have become a political force.

Public education has been taken over by proponents of anti-Christian, anti-family values. The reason why is obvious. Education is the means by which the next generation forms its outlook on the world. Young hearts and minds are especially vulnerable, having an amazing ability to absorb large amounts of teaching innocently, naively, without judgment, prejudice, or bias. Since those opposed to Christianity and traditional values hold the reigns of educational power, they have gone a long way toward molding the next generation in their own image.

But the jig is up. More and more parents, concerned with preserving and transmitting traditional moral and educational values, are opting out of the public schools. The home school movement is a direct consequence of the increasing de-Christianization of our nation's classrooms and textbooks, combined with the secular worldview that saturates the American educational process. Concerned parents are outraged at today's appalling educational environment. Hence, in a massive protest against the public schools, they are pulling their children out and saying, "Enough is enough." At the same time, they are rediscovering their own educational calling. Vigilant Christian parents in all fifty states are responding to the numerous biblical Injunctions that hold them ultimately accountable for child training and instruction.

Growing numbers of Christian parents are refusing to lay down in docile compliance to the massive public educational system. No longer are they recoiling in intimidation and fear or waffling helplessly in uncertainty of action. Instead, many are beginning to fight back. They are putting on their spiritual armor and hoisting the battle flag for combat and struggle "against the rulers, against the authorities, against the powers of this world and against the spiritual forces of evil in the heavenly realms" (Eph. 6:12). They are retaking the mantle of educational duties upon themselves and forging ahead into victory for their children and their families.

Why the Home Schooling Movement is Exploding

The home schooling movement is growing very rapidly. In light of research performed by Patricia Lines and the annual growth rate reports from national home school leaders, it is reasonable to assume that there may be approximately one million home schoolers nationwide. (That's a ratio of approximately one home schooler for every forty-five public school students.) There are only eleven states in the United States that have a public school enrollment of more than one million students. Further, the movement is evidencing an annual growth rate of between fifteen and forty percent, according to Dr. Brian Ray of the National Home Education Research Institute. The only limiting factor to sustained growth is the number of parents who are willing to stay home and live on one income. Michael Farris, founder and president of the Home School Legal Defense Association, predicts that ultimately the movement will grow to five to seven percent of the nation's school-age population, aided by the sophisticated communications technology increasingly available in the home.[3]

There are several reasons why home schooling is growing all across our land. First and foremost, the movement has grown because *it has God's blessing.* There is no doubt that God's hand is upon it. No nationwide parental and familial effort could grow as fast and as successful as this one has, clear the vast majority of legal hurdles that it has, unless divine providence is on its side.

Second, home schooling is growing because parents are realizing and affirming Bible truth with their lives. Scripture clearly states that *educational responsibility lies firmly in the hands of parents.* Home schooling is the biblical model of education. Christian homeschoolers believe that God has given them the charge and the authority to educate their children. The home school movement is profoundly Christian for the most part. God's Word clearly establishes that the mental and spiritual development of children is to be a parent's highest priority. The injunction in Proverbs, "Train up a child in the way he should go . . . ." was not given to public school teachers but to parents. It is an awesome responsibility. Parents are charged with the duties and held accountable for their child's education. Scripture is replete with biblical counsel regarding parental responsibility for their children's education such as Deuteronomy chapters 4 and 6, and Proverbs 22. Educational duties can be delegated to public or private school teachers but not the final responsibility for what they are taught. Public and private teachers are but proxies, substitutes, surrogates for those ultimately responsible—the parents.

A third reason home schooling is growing is because *parents are realizing the value of instilling Christian values.* True education integrates faith in Jesus Christ and the content and process of learning. True education seeks to train not just the mind but also the heart and soul. This is what we call character training. Balanced education cannot take place in a spiritual vacuum. This is one of several areas where public education is failing and failing miserably. Contrary to what the public schools relate, there is no such thing as academic neutrality.

Development of character is critical to the proper growth and maturation of a young child. Home educators are returning to the crucial responsibility of developing and nurturing character. The most important task of the educator is to prepare students for life. And the best way to prepare a student for life is to teach, model, and promote the development of godly character. Character development is the most important and most laudable activity for a student and teacher to be engaged in. If a student is taught nothing else save character alone, he will still be better prepared for life than an academic egghead without character. Commenting on the absence of character training in American schools, child-development expert Dr. Urie Bronfenbrenner says:

> In terms of content, education in America, when viewed from a cross-cultural perspective, seems peculiarly one-sided, emphasizing subject matter to the exclusion of another fundamental aspect of the child's development for which there is no generally accepted term in our educational vocabulary: what the Germans call *erziehung*, the Russians *vospitanie* and the French *education*. Perhaps the best equivalents are "upbringing" or "character education," expressions that sound outmoded and irrelevant to us.[4]

Christian parents understand exactly what the missing element is that Dr. Bronfenbrenner speaks about. Character development should be at the core of American education. It is the essential ingredient so grievously lacking in many young people today. It is the teaching and development of Christlike qualities such as love, kindness, forgiveness, honesty, service, dependence on God, enthusiasm and hunger for the Word of God, and fervent prayer. It is also the nurturing of highly valued practical virtues such as cleanliness, dependability, neatness, and hard work. Students who are taught these qualities will more likely become the model citizens and future leaders of our society. They will exhibit traits such as industry and ingenuity instead of laziness and negligence; self-leading and independence instead of peer-manipulation and control; giving instead of taking; serving instead of selfishness. This, in turn, will go a long way toward giving the child a sense of high self-respect and purpose for living. Are these not the qualities every responsible parent wants to see in his or her child? Because of the environmental conditions and consistent modeling advantage unique to home educators, parents can successfully seize the opportunity of building godly character in their children.

Fourth, home schooling is growing because more and more parents are becoming aware of *the historic and highly effective track record of home schooling*. Home schooling was the momentous tool of early American education.

Public education as we know it today did not exist in colonial

America or in the first decades after the adoption of the Constitution. Education of children was left strictly to parents, who provided the necessary instruction at home or through private, parochial schools.[5] Therefore, home education, along with some 21,000 Christian schools in our country today, have deep roots in America's history.

Home-schooling families tend to be practical and self-sufficient. These parents wish to develop a strong family that is self-reliant but not isolated from society. Such a do-it-yourself perspective harmonizes with the invincible spirit which made America great.

In historical perspective, public schools are the newcomers on the block. Instruction of children away from home is a relatively new tradition. Processes of urbanization and standardization began to herald the arrival of formalized educational institutions and, with them, free public education. In 1837, the Massachusetts state senate began the first state-wide system of public education in the United States. However, it wasn't until the mid-1870s that teaching took on the appearance of an accepted profession. It must not be forgotten, however, that the institution is the substitute. The home school is the original.

What was the literacy record in America like under home schools? Historical evidence indicates that prior to the introduction of public education and compulsory attendance laws, Americans were probably the most literate people in the world. Remember, many of the greatest leaders in America such as Patrick Henry, Daniel Webster, Thomas Edison, Mark Twain, George Patton, Douglas MacArthur, and at least nine United States presidents were all home schooled.

For all these reasons, home schooling is a growing phenomenon in America and Canada. Homeschoolers are not fanatics, radicals, or escapists but loving parents who want the very best for their children. The broad picture of the movement indicates that home schooling is primarily a Christian revival taking place through the education of our youth. Most home school parents do so for religious reasons. All revival movements start somewhere. For the past two or three decades there has been a massive de-Christianization of our public schools. Since religion and academics have been separated in the public schools, children receive substantially different values than pastors and parents can unteach on weeknights or weekends. Consequently, many parents have decided to shelter their children from a learning environment that is ineffective and morally repugnant and replace it with one that is wholesome and Christ-centered. This has inadvertently helped create a revival in the church—a revival that is beginning at the earliest ages through the subculture comprised of home schooled students. The spawning of this revival is the consequence of parents returning to a biblical model of education.

Conclusion

When confronted with the scriptural interrogative, "How can a young man keep his way pure?" parents and Christian educators take refuge in the divinely provided solution: "by living according to Your Word" (Ps. 119:9). But if the purifying light and influence of God's Word is removed from public classrooms, as has been done, then humanistic forces have gained the upper hand. Wise Christian parents do not ignore this fact and hide their heads in the sand, nor can they assume the damaging effects from being in a humanistic institution forty hours a week, nine months a year, can be effectively countered and neutralized by a couple of hours a week in Sunday school or church. Instead, they are open to seriously examine their educational alternatives. And one of the solutions many have arrived at is home schooling, which is a return to a biblical and historical model of education.

TWO

Is Home Schooling For You?

Consider seriously these questions. Do you believe that your child is a gift of God and your greatest earthly blessing? Do you want the very best that life has to offer your child? Do you cherish your child's love, attention, and respect? Are you concerned about the present course of public education in America? Is the development of your child's moral character, academic competency, responsibility, discipline, and social grace important to you? Are you concerned about your child's spiritual growth? Do you want your child to be a success in life? Finally, are you open to explore a very old and yet refreshingly new concept in alternative education? If so, then perhaps *you* are a prime candidate for home schooling.

Far too long now parental value and worth has been belittled by the educational bureaucracy and its cronies. Over the years parents have been deceptively led to believe that they are unqualified to teach and unable to adequately impart sound values. Parents have been made to feel inept in every way when it comes to educating their own children. A barrage of disinformation from the educational establishment, the media, and antifamily proponents has reinforced these views. As a result, parents have slowly come to believe that public schools can do a far better job than they in instructing their children.

This is simply not so. The truth is, if you are a literate, responsible, loving, and interactive parent, you not only qualify to raise your child but to teach him as well. Teaching is as natural for parents as learning is for children. Education always begins in the home. Here children learn their first language—a most impressive task. Do parents suddenly become inadequate as the child turns five or six? Must the state march in, rescue the young ones from their families, and then institutionalize the poor mortals? Children belong to parents, not the state. Children inherit characteristics from their parents, not from the government.

Is home schooling for *you*? The answer to that question could be **YES** if you agree with six basic beliefs. These beliefs are enunciated below in the form of seven questions.

WHO IS RESPONSIBLE FOR OUR CHILDREN?

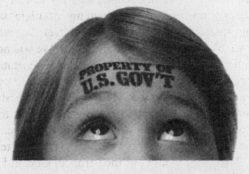

Belief #1
Do you believe that God has given parents the responsibility for their child's upbringing? Scripture clearly charges parents with educational accountability for how and what their children are taught. Parents are to be the key educational superintendent of their children. This is more than a just a privilege; it is a scriptural injunction of sweeping magnitude. Children are a gift of God placed completely under parental charge. Holy Writ gives parents the educational reins. Below is a review of a few relevant Scriptures that pertain to parental duty in this area:

Deuteronomy 4:9—Only be careful, and watch yourselves closely so that you do not forget the things your eyes have seen or let them slip from your heart as long as you live. Teach them to your children and to their children after them.
Deuteronomy 6:1,2,6,7—These are the commandments, decrees and laws the Lord your God directed me to teach you to observe in the land you are crossing the Jordan to possess, so that you, your children and their children after them may fear the Lord as long as you live by keeping all his

decrees and commands that I give you, and so you may enjoy long life. . . .These commandments that I give you today are to be upon your hearts. Impress them on your children. Talk about them when you sit at home and when you walk along the road and when you lie down and when you get up.

Deuteronomy 11:18,19—Fix these words of mine in your hearts and minds; tie them as symbols on your hands and bind them on your foreheads. Teach them to your children, talking about them when you sit at home and when you walk along the road, and when you lie down and when you get up.

1 Samuel 1:28; 2:2—So now I (Hannah) give him to the Lord. For his whole life he will be given over to the Lord. . . . And the boy Samuel continued to grow in stature and in favor with the Lord and with men.

Psalm 78:1-7—O my people, hear my teaching; listen to the words of my mouth. I will open my mouth in parables, I will utter things hidden from of old—things we have heard and known, things our fathers have told us. We will not hide them from their children; we will tell the next generation the praiseworthy deeds of the Lord, his power, and the wonders he has done. He decreed statutes for Jacob and established the law in Israel, which he commanded our forefathers to teach their children, so the next generation would know them, even the children yet to be born, and they in turn would tell their children. Then they would put their trust in God and would not forget his deeds but would keep his commands.

Proverbs 4:3-5—When I was a boy in my father's house, still tender, and an only child of my mother, he taught me and said, "Lay hold of my words with all your heart; keep my commands and you will live. Get wisdom, get understanding; do not forget my words or swerve from them."

Proverbs 22:6—Train a child in the way he should go, and when he is old he will not turn from it.

Galatians 4:2—He (a child) is subject to guardians and trustees until the time set by his father.

Ephesians 6:1—Children, obey your parents in the Lord, for this is right. "Honor your father and mother"—which is the first commandment with a promise—"that it may go well with you and that you may enjoy long life on the earth." Fathers, do not exasperate your children; instead, bring them up in the training and instruction of the Lord.

1 Thessalonians 2:11,12—We dealt with each of you as a father deals with his own children, encouraging, comfort-

ing and urging you to live lives worthy of God, who calls you into his kingdom and glory.

Many other Scriptures teach by inference the same thing. The Apostle Paul commended Timothy's mother and grandmother who "from infancy" taught him the "holy Scriptures" (2 Tim. 3:15). The local pastor/overseer was to meet certain qualifications that were to serve as a model to other fathers in the church. Two of these qualifications stipulated that he was "able to teach" and "to manage his own family well and see that his children obey him with proper respect" (1 Tim. 3:2,4). Young mothers were called on to "love their children" and be "busy at home" (Titus 2:4,5). Scripture reminds parents of the awesomeness of looking after their children's spiritual, educational, emotional, and physical needs, by warning, "If anyone does not provide for his immediate family, he has denied the faith and is worse than an unbeliever" (1 Tim. 5:8). Hence, our own spirituality is measured by what we do with those educational reins. It is an awesome responsibility!

This monumental task of teaching and training our children in the ways of God cannot be done by going to church once or twice a week. Nor can it be relegated to Sunday school teachers, Vacation Bible Schools, nor summer Bible camps. We must have a daily, ongoing commitment to steep our children in the Word of God. Deuteronomy 6:7 makes clear that it requires comprehensive, full-life training from the parents. How can parents keep their children in a humanistic educational system, eight hours a day, five days a week, and fulfill this requirement?

God is the bestower of every good gift. Apart from salvation, children are the most important gifts this side of heaven (Ps. 127:3-5). We are called to be good stewards of that gift. Children belong to God but are "loaned" to us in this life to raise for His purposes. We cannot do with them as we will. We cannot raise them any way we see fit. That is blatant irresponsibility. Instead, we must raise them to love, honor, respect, and obey God. But how can they be raised to serve God if they are subject to an educational system and textbooks that are anti-God and saturated with the religion of humanism? Can Christian parents in good conscience sacrifice their "loaned-from-God" children on the altar of humanism?

Home schooling should be entered upon with the heartiest of Christian conviction. But what is Christian conviction? Unlike a preference, which is a religious belief subject to change, a conviction rests on an unshakable truth that you believe is ordained by God. A conviction is a strongly held, personal belief rooted in Christian values and biblical principles that guides every aspect of your thinking and decision-making. Christian convictions compel you unto a distinctive lifestyle. You must do it! You must follow your conviction—for example, the belief that God ordained parents, not government, to be responsible for the education of their children. A conviction, therefore, is entwined in the very fabric of one's belief system. It is an unalterable biblical truth you firmly believe is of divine origin.

Studies show that those who home school merely out of preference have a much higher attrition rate. That is, they start the process but soon quit in frustration or apathy. Why? Simple. They lack genuine Christian conviction!

Belief #2

Are you willing to embrace your constitutional rights? The Constitution of the United States along with it's amendments guarantees every citizen certain inalienable rights. One of those rights is the freedom to teach your own children because of religious convictions. This is a fundamental constitutional right. Regarding parental liberty, the Supreme Court in *Yoder* tenaciously held:

> This case involves the fundamental interest of parents, as contrasted with that of the state, to guide the religious future and *education of their children.* The history and culture of Western civilization reflect a strong tradition of parental concern for the nurture and upbringing of their children. This primary role of the parents in the upbringing of their children is now *established beyond debate as an enduring American tradition.*
>
> The fundamental theory of liberty upon which all governments in this union repose excludes any general power of the state to standardize its children by forcing them to accept instruction from public teachers only. The child is not the mere creature of the state; those who nurture him and direct his destiny have the right, coupled with the high duty, to recognize and prepare him for additional obligations.[6](emphasis mine)

The Supreme Court made clear in *Pierce v. Society of Sisters* that the child "is not the mere creature of the state." Now more than ever we need to empower parents with respect to the education of their children. This must include affording them an array of educational alternatives and letting them choose wisely.

In these days of big government, with its ever-expanding power and influence over family life, free citizens must guard their constitutional rights with utmost care. Infringement of our precious constitutional rights lay in the balance. History vividly records how easy it is to lose them and how difficult it is to get them back. Are you willing to embrace your constitutional rights as parents?

Belief #3

Do you believe that God and patriotism should still hold a central place in the classroom? Is there anything more important to your child than his spiritual development and maturation? The Bible says, "Seek *first* [God's] kingdom and his righteousness, and all these things will be given to you" (Matt. 6:33). What shapes your child's development more than his daily environment? In public school, love of God has been substituted with self-centeredness and worldly, anti-family values. Traditional morality is shunned while immorality is condoned. Regrettably, the cancerous anti-Christian bias prevalent in public schools today is demoralizing the soul of millions of our young children. God and traditional morality have been forced out the front school-door. What used to be commonplace is now considered taboo. The God who blessed us with life, liberty, and the ability to pursue happiness should never have been expelled from our public schools. Do you believe that it has helped the children of America?

Patriotism and national pride are also eschewed. Why are the Pledge of Allegiance and patriotism absent in many of our public classrooms? Why are they avoided or left out altogether? It is not only in what is said but also in what is left unsaid. Some textbooks are silent on many of the heroic efforts of brave, freedom-loving men and women in American history, as we shall see in Chapter 3. These same texts overlook facts that build patriotism, independence, and national sovereignty and pride—the bedrock of our freedom and democracy. A proper love of country seems absent among many school's of today.

It is my firm conviction that God and a patriot mentality still *belong* in the classroom. The home schooling families I know cherish their national and religious heritage and endeavor to impart that same knowledge to their children. Is it important to you that God and patriotism once again find a central place in the classroom?

Belief #4

Is the development and growth of your child's delicate self-respect—that he or she is made in the image of God—very important to you? Many parents feel the battle for healthy self-respect is being lost in the public school classroom. Every year thousands of young, impressionable children are being sacrificed to the beast of institutional arrogance and insensitivity. The powerful public educational system feeds this beast daily with a growing diet of immoral, violence-prone, anti-family, evolutionary textbooks coupled with a side dish of behavior modification and value clarification techniques. Add to this a daily seasoning of worldly peer pressure, and what do you have? A confused child with a mounting problem of self-respect. Worse yet, by the time it becomes noticeable, irreparable damage has likely occurred.

Mel and Norma Gabler, specialists in critiquing public school textbooks, have found that much public school literature follows a pattern of "depressive, negative themes." Below are twelve categories of negative themes they have found nationwide in textbook reviews:

1) Alienation	7) Hate
2) Death and suicide	8) Disrespect
3) Degradation or humiliation	9) Low goals
4) Depression	10) Lack of motivation
5) Discontentment	11) Problems stressed
6) Fear and horror	12) Skepticism[7]

Are these the themes that come from an all-loving God? Do they build and promote godly character and self-respect, or do they destroy it? Why do these pervasive themes appear to run through the heart of our public school textbooks? How can a Christian foundation be fostered with such literature being shoved down the throats of our children? An extensive study by Professor Paul Vitz of New York University proves conclusively that the textbooks typically used in public education exclude Christianity and traditional values. Vitz concluded:

> Are public school textbooks biased? Are they censored? The answer to both is yes. And the nature of the bias is clear: Religion, traditional family values, and conservative political and economic positions have been reliably excluded from children's textbooks. This exclusion is particularly disturbing because it is found in a system paid for by taxpayers and one that claims, moreover, to be committed to impartial knowledge and accuracy.[8]

Your child's self-respect is important to his success in life. His whole personality and effectiveness in the future is made or broken within the confines of proper self-esteem. It is a child's self-respect that makes him view the world as either cold and cruel or challenging and adventuresome. A healthy self-respect is one of the priceless gifts that you can help your child develop.

A comprehensive study on the subject was carried out by Dr. Stanley Coopersmith. The conclusion of his intensive study revealed that parents have a powerful influence on a child's self-image. Parents can give their child the ability to withstand societal pressure by bolstering his confidence or they can leave him practically defenseless. How parents respond and interact with their growing child will mold him one way or the other. A child who feels the warmth, love, attention, and respect of his parents will most likely grow up with a high degree of self-worth. Says Dr. Coopersmith:

> Children—young children especially—are vulnerable and dependent upon their parents . . . they survive and thrive largely by accommodating themselves to parental standards . . . . Parental acceptance has an enhancing effect upon self-esteem in particular and psychosocial development in general. Parental rejection, the other extreme, presumably results in an impoverished environment and a diminished sense of personal worthiness.[9]

Do you think government schools are as concerned about your child's self-respect as you are? No way! Do you think they will reinforce in your child that he is made in the image of God? Far from it! On occasion there may be individual teachers who show a special interest in their students, but rarely as comprehensively as a loving mother and father. Concerned parents are the crucial element in a child's emotional development. Only you can consistently explain to your son or daughter their worth as a child of God. No one can build your child's self-respect or prepare him for life quite like loving parents.

Belief #5
Do you want to continue a special bond of closeness between you and your child? Every parent does. Yet, beginning with a child's first year away in school, a distancing often develops between a parent and child that increases every year the child remains in the public system. It may be unnoticeable at first, but as the years go by a rebellious, anti-parent, philosophical indoctrination will reveal its indelible mark.

Children learn early in school that they must compete for teacher approval, instead of having instant access to Mom or Dad. In the early grades, they must compete for toys before they are emotionally ready to share. Worst still, they begin quickly to compete for the attention of their age-mates, absorb their language and manners and habits and principles, and become dependent on their approval.[10]

When parents try to explain why children should not say certain things, their children often do not understand, for they are not yet cognitively ready—they do not understand fully the "why" of Mom or Dad's explanation. And since "all the kids are doing it," they give the backs of their little hands to their parents' cherished values and become dependent upon their peers for their value systems. Thus, little by little, *parents lose control, their authority usurped by the school authorities* to whom they delegated responsibility for their children.[11]

In spite of the overwhelming propaganda to the contrary, a child need not be kicked out of his loving nest at age five to be "socialized." Home schooled children have an opportunity to develop a unique bond of closeness with their parents. The reason is that they can spend priceless time being nurtured by a physical, emotional, and spiritual closeness to Mom and Dad. And that bonding also extends to sibling relationships. Brothers and sisters are closer and have deeper interrelationships when they are home schooled. Because they share more childhood experiences apart from school peer pressure, they develop a refreshing dependence on the family. Home schooling is a sane response to the impersonality of mass education and an excellent way to restore community and family life.

Peer pressure at an early age should be of grave concern to parents. In elementary years in particular, a child is not mature enough to develop values independently. He struggles to find an example, someone to give him desperately needed guidance. He looks for a model in the one thing available in quantity: his school environment. Unfortunately, it is difficult for him to delineate between right and wrong. Further still, he is extremely susceptible to the mannerisms, language, attitudes, and values of his age-mates. Scripture warns parents not to let their children run with a companion of fools. Since he is not old enough to resist ridicule from those he works and plays with, he unknowingly caves into peer conformity. This, in turn, weakens the parental bonds and values cherished and loved by so many.

Belief #6
As a parent do you have more of your child's best interest at heart than anyone else? Your answer to this question is of paramount importance. Many parents believe they have more of their child's interest at heart than a nine-month-a-year public teacher. First, a teacher's student interest can wax and wane with mood, group size, and classroom conditions. This mood can change day to day, week to week, and year to year. Usually a teacher must develop rapport not only with a new class but with each individual child as well. This would be a monumental undertaking for the best professional adolescent psychiatrist, much less a teacher. Every year pupils change teachers. Instructors come and go. Does such teacher transience serve the young child's best interest?

Even if rapport is built, a further question must be raised. How much individual attention does the average teacher give to his students? How many teachers take time to meet each child's personal requirements? Dr. John Goodlad, graduate dean of education at UCLA, did a comparative study of over a thousand schools and found that the average amount of time spent in one-on-one responses between teachers and students amounted to seven minutes a day.[12] Does your child need more than seven minutes a day of individual attention to learn? Under such circumstances, how is a child's desperate need for recognition and self-approval fulfilled? Without question, there is no replacement for personal attention to young, emotionally delicate students that parents can give.

Developmental psychologist Dr. Raymond Moore has made the following vital observations in the area of classroom deficiency.

> In the typical school, children cannot be treated with partiality—individually or personally—but only as an integral part of the class. In spite of the fact that children of the same age vary greatly in ability, achievement, background, and personality, they must more or less go through the same assembly line—doing the same thing at the same time and fitting roughly into the same mold as the others. In truth, the partiality needed by the young child brings the feeling that he is special to his parents—loved and cherished as a unique individual. These forced omissions and most schools' overwhelming concern for subject matter greatly interfere with free exploration and the child's development as a unique person.

Contrast the school routine with the opportunities your youngster has in a reasonably well-regulated, loving home. Here he experiences relative quiet and simplicity in his daily program; one-to-one responses to his questions, needs, and interests, practically on call; and the opportunity for solitude. As he is allowed to associate closely with his parents in their daily activities of work, play, rest, and conversation, the child shares responsibility and feels that he is part of the family team—needed, wanted, and depended upon. And thereby he develops a sense of self-worth, the cornerstone of positive socialization.[13]

Dr. Moore further states:

> For the first eight to ten years at least—until their values are formed, most parents, even average parents, are by far the best people for their children. And those that are not, usually can and should be . . . Most mothers and fathers can provide deeper security, sheerer closeness, sharper instincts, longer continuity, warmer responses, more logical control

and more natural examples than the staff of the best care center or kindergarten.[14]

In the modern public school classroom, little time is given to actual instruction. Management, busywork, waiting, leaving and arriving, and other diversions reduce gross instructional time to around ninety minutes a day. According to Dr. David Elkind, attention in class to single students may average, per student, only six hours per year.[15] To cover the material, teachers need responses from students able and willing to give it, and so they pay attention to about a third of the class, largely ignoring those who need instruction most, who may be written off as failures in the early weeks of the semester. A high percentage of failure is expected and accepted.

There are some things about your child only you as a parent can know. For example, your child might be in a poor frame of mind for learning if his dog died the night before. Knowing this will help you as a parent to be more understanding of your child's emotional requirements. Only a parent knows that his child's eating habits have dropped off, or that he has been preoccupied with some physical defect or condition and is supersensitive to ridicule. Only a parent can truly know his child's heart and respond to it.

Parents love their children to a depth no teacher can match. Teaching at home is an act of love before it is anything else. Unquestionably, the interest that parents have in their child not only has the weightier motivation of parental love and affection, but it also spans a more diverse spectrum of overall concern. Unlike public schools that are concerned only with your child's mental development, Christian parents take an interest in their physical, psychological, emotional, and spiritual well-being. Do you agree that you have more of your child's interest at heart than an institutional instructor?

Conclusion

Home schoolers are not odd, but they are different in that they desire to raise their children with a godly view of life. They choose morality, academic excellence, and family commitment instead of a worldly, humanistic mold of depravity, illiteracy, and peer dependency. They want to be close to their children throughout all their growing years. They do not want to wake up one day and find out they are strangers to their own children. This is often the regrettable plight of well-intentioned public school parents. Could this happen to you? It certainly could! How? By allowing a slow but deeply instilled rebellious spirit to be seeded and nurtured in your child in humanistic classrooms. Those who think it can't happen to their children are being naive.

Christian parents want children who are taught godly character, morality, traditional values, and respect for life. But this is not automatic. It only comes to those who are willing to affirm their biblical, parental, and constitutional rights and exercise them. It comes to those who are willing to pay the price and invest their time in their greatest earthly gift: their children.

How about you? What kind of children do you want to raise? What do you desire them to be like in five years? In ten? In fifteen? The law of the farmer applies: you reap what you sow. If you let the world feed, water, and cultivate your child, expect the appropriate results. If you entrust your child for seven hours a day, five days a week, into a government school setting, expect him to absorb and emulate his environment. But remember this, your child's delicate spirit and personality are entrusted to your care for only a brief time, and then the opportunity is gone. I know of no better way to develop and nurture an endearing relationship with your child than through home schooling. What kind of child do you want to raise?

If you can share the following six beliefs, then home schooling may very well be right for you: 1) I believe that God has given parents the responsibility for their children's upbringing. 2) I am willing to embrace my constitutional rights regarding the education of my children. 3) I believe that God and patriotism should still hold a central place in the classroom. 4) The development and growth of my children's delicate self-respect—that he or she is made in the image of God-is very important to me. 5) I want to continue a special bond of closeness between me and my children. 6) As a parent, I have more of my child's best interest at heart than anyone else.

THREE

Public Schools: Retarding America and Imprisoning Potential

Little Johnny goes to school. He can't read or write. He can't add or subtract. But he knows all about sex, condoms, and AIDS. He knows how to use a knife and a gun. And he thinks his parents' faith is foolish. Johnny is the modern product of America's public school system.

Many parents are waking up to the fact that public classrooms have dramatically changed since the days when they were in school. It's natural for us to reminisce and to remember things as being basically the same. Of course, candy bars used to cost a nickel and people used to get by without locks on their front door too, but it is a whole different environment these days. Nowhere is this more true than in the area of educational evolution in American public schools.

Picture this: your state enacts legislation requiring your child to enroll in a series of government-sponsored swimming classes. Swimming is an important skill to master, so you have no objections. Instruction is given daily for twelve consecutive summers, and you are promised tremendous results. The lessons are supported by the taxpayers at a considerable rate. You tolerate the taxation since your child is promised to learn the fine art of swimming. The taxes also generate enough revenue to provide the finest swimming facilities in the world.

Several months after classes begin, you ask your child to demonstrate what he has learned. You find out that your child has developed a fear of the water and a hatred of the classes themselves. The instructor tells you it's natural and will pass with time. The next year you again ask your child to demonstrate what he has learned. He reluctantly lowers himself into the water and soon begins to panic. He tries to dog paddle but quickly abandons this basic yet unmastered technique. The teacher tells you he is a slow learner, but they will work with him as best they can.

Years pass by. You hear other parents remark about the swimming difficulties their children are experiencing. You ask your son to show you how well he can swim. Your son says, "I swim as well as the other kids. Besides, my teacher says I'm doing fine." You kindly ask again, "Would you please show me?" He says, "It's none of your business." Taken back by that surly remark you become extremely concerned. You make a surprise poolside visit to your son's class. You observe some bizarre things: an instructor incompetent to teach swimming; however, he is showing the boys and girls how to use a prophylactic device. By an empty, graffiti-laden pool, many of the students are simultaneously screaming obscenities and displaying rowdy behavior; some are flirting seductively near the changing rooms, while others are buying and selling drugs near the diving board. When you ask the pool director what is going on, he at first says you have no business being there. However, you continue to press your question, and he eventually responds with a barrage of lame excuses. He forcefully tells you about the low pay the instructors receive and the resulting inability to attract good ones, about uncaring parents, and about insufficient funding.

It sounds like a terrible nightmare, yet many feel the analogy relates to modern public education. In this chapter we want to take a hard but realistic look at public education as it is today. In order to do this objectively, we must shed our skins of defensiveness and hyper-sensitivity. We must not try to excuse or rationalize any failures of the system that we may uncover. The time has arrived to remove the fog, be intellectually honest, and see the system for what it really is. Nostalgic views of yesteryear's public school do not apply. As long as we do not project our perception of the past into the present, it is alright to reminisce. But we must keep in mind that what may have been true then is probably not true today.

Why You Should Be Concerned About Public Education

There are those who ask, "Why should I be concerned about public education and its direction? Why not let the educators handle their own problems?" There are at least four good reasons why we should concern ourselves with public education.

First, the bloated public education bureaucracy is extremely expensive. It digs deeply into the pockets of our working population. Taxpayers do not want to see their hard-earned dollars squandered and frivolously spent. We have a right to want a good return on our educational investment. Considering that public education is the second-largest industry in America, with well over two million classroom teachers, the largest union in the world, and the second-largest budget in government, why should we settle for an inferior job?

Second, we should be concerned because many of the recent products of our educational system are apparently illiterate and ill-equipped to handle even the most basic demands of life. Consider these appalling facts:

> Twenty-five million adults cannot read the poison warnings on a can of pesticide, a letter from their child's teacher, or the front page of a daily paper. An additional thirty-five million read only at a level which is less than equal to the full survival needs of our society. Together, these sixty million people represent more than one third of the entire population.
>
> Given a paycheck and the stub that lists the usual deductions, 26 percent of adult Americans cannot determine if their paycheck is correct. Thirty-six percent, given a W-4 form, cannot enter the right number of exemptions in the

proper places on the form. Forty-four percent, when given a series of "Help Wanted" ads, cannot match their qualifications to the job requirements. Twenty-two percent cannot address a letter well enough to guarantee that it will reach its destination. Twenty-four percent cannot add their own correct return address to the same envelope. Twenty percent cannot understand an "Equal Opportunity" announcement. Over 60 percent, given a series of "For Sale" advertisements for products new and used, cannot calculate the difference between prices for a new and used appliance. Over 20 percent cannot write a check that will be processed by their banker—or will be processed in the right amount. Over 40 percent are unable to determine the correct amount of change they should receive, given a cash register receipt and the denomination of the bill used for payment.[16]

With results like these how can anyone not be concerned? If this trend continues, where will our nation be in a few short years? Students who graduate illiterate and ill-equipped to face life not only hurt themselves, but they also adversely affect those around them.

American society pays dearly, not just in money we spend on education, but the cost to our country in those things which are intangible and yet essential. For example, illiteracy robs our citizenry of the ability to understand and analyze current events. "Forty-five percent of adult citizens do not read newspapers. Only 10 percent abstain by choice. The rest have been excluded by their inability to read."[17] Newspapers are already written on an estimated tenth grade level or lower, but even that biased crutch is unable to help those who cannot read.

Illiteracy and academic inferiority affect our ability to compete in international markets. Corporate executives from all across our land are complaining about the intellectual caliber, work ethic, and values of the young people now entering the workforce. Illiteracy affects our productivity. There's a growing crescendo of criticism from the business world that our high school graduates don't measure up to industry personnel standards. In some cases, American industry can't keep up with foreign competition in steel, electronics, optics, textiles, and other areas. For example, how many cameras do you own that are made in the United States? Did you know that the presses printing the American currency in your purse or wallet are not made in the United States, but in Germany?

Third, educational deficiencies affect an individual's self-esteem and hopes of making something of his or her life. The cost to society of inadequately educating our future leaders, scientists, mathematicians, and our workforce in general is indeed high. A sound education is essential to our country's health and well-being. Americans know this. That is why a recent Gallup Poll shows that we feel that public education contributes more to national strength than either industrial might or military power.[18]

Fourth, we should be concerned because a wayward educational system helps lead to a moral and spiritual decline of our society at large. When children are trained in values-free, government classrooms where anti-God views are discussed and encouraged, it leads to the moral breakdown of our whole populace. This, in turn, effects everyone who lives in society. There is no place one can hide. When public schools become the handmaiden of self-centeredness, anti-nomianism, God-hatred, and hedonism, any society is headed for disaster.

Parents in ever increasing numbers are responding defensively to protect their children from wave after wave of public school-generated problems, peer pressure, and foundering educational standards. But why should they be forced into a defensive posture when their children are in a tax-supported institution? This is one of the regrettable ironies of modern education in America.

Common Excuses for Keeping Children in Public School

Some parents defend their public education decision using erroneous assumptions or excuses. Here are a few common excuses people give for not looking at their educational alternatives:

1) Public schools aren't all that bad.
2) We just happen to be in a good school district.
3)My child's teacher is the exception; she/he is excellent.
4) My child needs the extracurricular activities that public school offers.
5) I believe in teaching by certified teachers.
6) I believe a child needs competition to help him learn.
7) My child doesn't seem to be having any problems.
8) My child needs the socialization that schools provide.
9) I don't have the time or money to do anything else.
10) I need time alone during the day.
11) My child would not obey me. (relevant to home schooling)
12) I am not organized enough. (relevant to home schooling)
13) I'm not qualified to teach. (relevant to home schooling)

Before making any more excuses, consider some facts. Maybe you should know what the teachers know.

Revelation Of A Well-Guarded Secret

Who knows better than public school teachers how ineffective the teaching environment of public classrooms are? Perhaps this explains why so many teachers send their own children the private school. According to a study performed by the American Enterprise Institute for the United States Department of Education, teachers are more likely to send their children to private school than any other occupational group. The study notes that the percentages of teachers sending their children to private school in cities around the country is consistently higher than that of the general population.[19] What do they know that you don't?

Outcome-Based Education—Where Public Education Is Going

With the signing into law of *Goals 2000*, American educational failure was virtually guaranteed well into the future. *Goals 2000* was the most sweeping federal education legislation in decades. Using *Goals 2000* as the engine, a massive restructuring of American education is underway. If you hardly recognize education today compared to when you were in school, you won't believe what's unfolding. The net effect of the *Goals 2000* law is the federalizing of the educational system, which is forcing Outcome-Based Education (OBE) upon every school district in the nation. (Note: Outcome-Based Education in the past has traveled under other names like: Outcome-based learning; Mastery learning; Performance-based education; Core curriculum; and Value-added curriculum/testing).

So what is Outcome-Based Education? In a nutshell, it is the dumbed-down educational method of the New World Order. It calls for a complete change in the way children are taught, graded, and graduated, K-12th grade. Previously called "mastery learning," Outcome-Based Education is the Skinnerian pigeons-pecking-for-pellets model of schooling. Children must perform a task over and over until they produce the required "outcome." If they cannot give the government-desired answer, they will be remediated over and over until they deliver it. OBE shifts a school's focus from how much students know (cognitive outcomes) to how well they're socialized (affective outcomes). It holds smart children back to the pace of the slowest learners. It weans children from their parents' values to instill in them politically correct, secular-left values.[20] Academic and factual matter are being replaced by politically-correct attitudes and vague and subjective learning outcomes such as world citizenship, United

Nations supremacy, population control, multiculturalism, social conformity, tolerance of differing values, radical environmentalism, attitudinal compliance, gun control, homosexuality and the ability to fit in with governmental planning. These are the learning nuggets of OBE. Classrooms are to be value-free and non-directive. As someone said, "Public school parents start buying the Tums; cause whether you want OBE or not, here it comes!"

Outcome-Based Education ensures that reading abilities will continue to fall, since it is wholly committed to the "whole language" or "look-say" word-guessing method rather than the phonics method. Under OBE, teachers are cautioned not to correct spelling and syntax errors because it could be damaging to the student's self-esteem and creativity. OBE stresses political correctness at the expense of the 3 R's of Reading, Riting and Rithmetic.

Outcome-Based Education offers no method of accountability to students, parents, teachers, or taxpayers. OBE includes no objective standards of achievement that are measurable. Goodbye Stanford Achievement, Iowa Basic Skills, and California Achievement Testing, at least as most of us know them. Instead, universal testing to measure and correct the attitudes, values, and religious beliefs of our young people are replacing them. Lack of conventional norm-referenced testing will hide OBE's failures. OBE sets up a computer file that tracks each child's learning outcomes. These electronic portfolios take the place of traditional assessments and results of a new kind of testing become the basis for the school's efforts to remediate whatever attitudes and behaviors the school deems unacceptable. Many parents are surprised to learn that the computer files include all school, psychological, and medical records and will be made available to prospective employers upon graduation.[21] Planned are government-assigned identification numbers for all school children. This barcoded ID number will track students for the rest of their lives and will allow government data banks to pass information on to other states, schools, colleges, the federal government, and future employers. Outcome-Based Education sounds like the creation of an educational Frankenstein, doesn't it?

Furthermore, the educational establishment has prepared "A Do-It-Yourself Kit For Educational Renewal" to help manipulate public acceptance of phony OBE reforms. The educational bureaucracy fully expects a reluctant citizenry not to like it, so the public is being re-educated, using your tax dollars of course, to see the value of OBE. The "toolkit" provides detailed instruction on how to change the attitudes and behaviors of the community so that the National Education Goals via Outcome-Based Education will be accepted.

Track Record of Public Education—A Report Card

That American public education is in trouble is an understatement. What is going on in our public classrooms today that is causing such horrendous results? That is the crucial question at hand concerning public education. As we dive into the facts, let's remember that we are not embarking on some kind of an anti-public school campaign. Our objective here is personal enlightenment of what is currently taking place in modern public education. Then, after we analyze the facts, we want to ask ourselves: Is public school where I want my child to be? What are my educational alternatives? More specifically, is home schooling a viable option for me?

Now, if we were to honestly evaluate the public school system today and give it a report card, it might look something like this:

> F in Academics
>
> F in Morality
>
> F in Socialization
>
> F in Discipline
>
> F in Manners
>
> F in the Promotion of Democratic Ideals

If we use the socially popular pass/fail method, the F would stand for failure. As we consider each of these areas one by one, ask yourself, is this the environment I really want my child in?

F in Academics

The failure of our public school system in the area of academics is both regrettable and unnecessary. Why should the children of America, living in the greatest and most powerful nation on earth, be sinking to the bottom of the academic barrel? There is no justifiable excuse for the United States to rank 49th among 158 member nations of the U.N. in its literary levels.[22] A director of Human Engineering Laboratory recently said that young people today know less than their parents. The director went on to explain that they have recorded a 1 percent drop in vocabulary per year. Consider the devastating impact. It doesn't take much to figure out what a drop in knowledge of 1 percent a year for thirty years will do to America.[23]

The academic decline in America has not gone unnoticed. Back in 1983 the National Commission on Excellence in Education gave its report to Congress serving notice of the conditions in American schools. Among other things, it revealed the following shocking facts about the academic environment in America:

> Our society and its educational institutions seem to have lost sight of the basic purposes of schooling, and of the high expectations and disciplined effort needed to attain them . . . .
>
> International comparisons of student achievement, completed a decade ago, reveal that on nineteen academic tests American students were never first or second and; in comparison with other industrialized nations, were last seven times.
>
> Some twenty-three million American adults are functionally illiterate by the simplest tests of everyday reading, writing, and comprehension.
>
> About 13 percent of all seventeen-year-olds in the United States can be considered functionally illiterate. Functional illiteracy among minority youth may run as high as 40 percent.
>
> Average achievement of high school students on most standardized tests is now lower than 26 years ago when Sputnik was launched.

The College Board's Scholastic Aptitude Tests (SAT) demonstrate a virtually unbroken decline since 1963 (which, the author would like to point out, was the year Bible-reading was taken out of the schools). Average verbal scores fell over 50 points and average mathematics scores dropped nearly 40 points.[24]

So Congress and the country it represents were given ample official notice of our national academic decline. Top educational professionals have also been warning us about it for years as well. Declares John I. Goodlad, former dean of the UCLA Graduate school of Education, after completing an eight-year study: "American schools are in trouble. In fact, the problems of schooling are of such crippling proportions that many schools may not survive. It is possible that our entire public education system is nearing collapse."[25] Researcher Paul Hurd charges that "we are a generation of Americans that is scientifically and technologically illiterate."[26] Former director of the National Science Foundation John Slaughter warns of "a growing chasm between a small scientific and technological elite and a citizenry ill-informed, indeed uninformed, on issues with a scientific component."[27]

SAT scores are being re-normed to cover government school failure. SAT scores have dropped in recent years between 25 and 78 points. So the College Board is re-norming the SAT to make the new lower scores the average. The SAT gives scores between 200 and 800. The average for students until the late 1960s had been 500 points. The average now has dropped to 475 for math and 422 for verbal, showing that modern students are performing much worse than their predecessors did. So the College Board is simple going to adjust the SAT norm.[28] What this means is that the results are being skewed.

Why is it that the United States is falling way behind other industrialized nations in basic and yet vital areas such as math and science? Japanese students, for example, start specializing in math, physics, and biology in the sixth grade. Students in Russia start learning basic algebra and geometry in elementary school. Why is it that Japan, with a population half our size, graduates more engineers than we do? Why is it that the Russians are producing almost five times as many engineers as the United States? Something is decidedly wrong!

The dismal academic performance among public school students can be attributed to a minimum of four areas: 1) abandonment of God in the classroom, 2) teacher incompetence and failed methodology, 3) ineffective textbooks, and 4) grade inflation and automatic passage.

Abandonment of God in the Classroom

Many schools, if not most, have stopped scheduling spring break around Easter to avoid the appearance of advancing religion. In Kanawha County, West Virginia, school officials ordered all Bibles to be removed from school premises and dumped in an incinerator.[29] The fact that these things are happening in America show the degree of ideological transition that has taken place.

It is a fact that since the Supreme Court decision to remove prayer and the Bible from the public schools, there has been an almost unbroken decline in the SAT scores. The Scriptures say, "Do not be deceived, God cannot be mocked," (Gal. 6:7). God has been thrown out of the public schools, but He has not been mocked. The academic scores show it.

Consider the Supreme Court decisions that have orchestrated the removal of God from public education. In 1954, in *Gideons International v. Tudor*, the Supreme Court let stand a New Jersey law that declared Bible distribution in public schools unconstitutional. The Gideons have a long history of providing free Bibles to students, servicemen, prisoners, nurses, etc. In 1962, in *Engel v. Vitale*, the Court held unconstitutional nonsectarian school prayer. One year later came the landmark decision of *Schempp/Murray*, which was a catastrophic setback for Christianity in America. This 8-1 Supreme Court decision declared devotional reading of the Bible and school-sponsored prayer (in this case, the Lord's Prayer) unconstitutional. Madalyn Murray O'Hair and her cohorts won a major victory for national atheism and the humanizing of public schools. To further demonstrate the Court's tenacious drive to root out every hint of Christian influence, we merely look at *Netcong*. This 1971 decision ruled that prayer reading in school before formal opening of classes violated the First Amendment, even though (in this case) the prayers were taken from the Congressional Record and *attendance was voluntary*. Incredible, isn't it? Even if voluntary prayer is allowed back in the public schools by means of a constitutional amendment, which is a step in the right direction, it will not solve the wider problem of anti-Bible, value-free education.

The Supreme Court has made repeated rulings on the public classrooms that undermine and repudiate the biblical basis of American society. The teaching of a Comprehensive Christian worldview, which was the norm of early American education, has been thoroughly eradicated in the name of academic neutrality in a pluralistic society. One day those justices will have to answer to God.

But the question for you is this: do you want to keep your child in an educational environment that has been morally neutered by the Supreme Court?

Teacher Incompetence

Teacher incompetence is another area of serious academic concern. Though teachers have been getting more training in the past few decades than ever before, many are nevertheless grossly deficient. Perhaps this explains why the average achievement of high school graduates has been steadily declining over the same period of time. Consider the following:

- An Oregon kindergarten teacher who had received A's and B's at Portland State University was found to be functionally illiterate.
- A third-grade teacher in Chicago wrote on the board: "Put the following words in alfabetical order." Another Chicago teacher told a T.V. journalist, "I teaches English."
- A local school board in Wisconsin was outraged with teacher curriculum proposals which were riddled with bad grammar and spelling. Teachers misspelled common words: dabate for debate, documant for document, woud for would, seperate for separate.
- A fifth-grade Alabama teacher with a Master's degree sent a note home to parents which read in part, "Scott is dropping in his studies he acts as if he don't care. Scott want pass in his assignment at all, he a had a poem to learn and he fell to do it."
- Houston teachers shocked the school board when the results of a teacher competency test showed that 62 percent failed a standard reading skills test, 46 percent flunked in math, 26 percent in writing. But worst of all, of the 3,200 teachers who were tested, *it was discovered that 763 had cheated.*[30]

According to the National Council of Supervisors of Mathematics, "Twenty-six percent of all math positions are filled by teachers uncertified to teach math."[31] In the crucial area of science, "the National Science Teachers Association estimates that as many as 40 percent of science classes across the nation are being taught by unqualified instructors."[32] A study by the Carnegie Commission on Science, Technology, and Government found more than 80 percent of math teachers deficient in math themselves, and two-thirds of elementary science teachers inadequately prepared to teach science.[33]

Furthermore, those students seeking teaching degrees in our nation's colleges and universities are, on the average, testing below normal on the Scholastic Achievement Test. The average SAT verbal score for students contemplating a major in education is 406 (national average is 422), and their math score is 441 (national average is 475).[34] As you can see, these teachers of tomorrow are falling well below national averages. It is difficult for incompetent teachers to impart to students that which they themselves have not attained.

The incompetence of many public school teachers is a national disgrace. I am not attempting to sound anti-teacher. That is not my objective here. But parents with children in public school should be cognizant of growing teacher incompetence. It is important to expose those tools, methods, philosophies, and even teachers which potentially harm young minds. It must be acknowledged, however, that there are still good teachers who are instructing their students in the best way they know how. Many very dedicated teachers strive valiantly to give their charges the best education they can within a deficient educational system. Others, equally dedicated, are corrupted at our teachers colleges—with liberal humanist theories of education described as progressive education. Such brainwashed victims of our high educational system—a system controlled by secular humanists for over one hundred years—are dangerous to the mental health of our children.

Failed methodology should also concern us. Consider the "whole-language" method of reading instruction or what used to be called the "look-say" method. Whole-language, the reading method of Outcome-Based Education, produces crippled readers because it trains a child to view words holistically by their configurations instead of phonetically by their syllabic structure. We have an alphabetic writing system in which letters stand for speech sounds. The way you become a proficient reader is to develop an automatic association between letters and sounds. That's how you develop a *phonetic reflex*.[35]

On the other hand, whole-language forces children to look at written English as if it were Chinese, an ideographic writing system rather than an alphabetic one. A child is taught to look at words holistically, as if they were little pictures to be figured out by a variety of strategies, thus creating a *holistic reflex*. Whole-language teaches children to memorize words in context using pictures or clues. If you asked a whole-language teacher if she teaches phonics or not, she would say yes because some of the cues they use refer to letter sounds, usually beginning consonants. But that is not the same as intensive, systematic phonics in which a child learns to read phonetically with little need for other cues. What it does do is create a block against seeing words phonetically. In other words, it causes dyslexia or reading disability.[36]

That illiteracy is a national problem of crisis proportions is an established fact. When you study the results of this methodology you will know why the problem persists. Whole-language is a grossly ineffective reading method used by the majority of our public elementary schools. That is the primary culprit behind widespread reading problems and illiteracy. Extensive research by reading experts Dr. Jeanne Chall and Dr. Rudolph Flesch and others has demonstrated that phonics is vastly superior to whole language or look-say methodology. This had been known for over thirty years when the late Dr. Flesch wrote his first eye-opening work, *Why Johnny Can't Read*. In that book Dr. Flesch reported the results of 124 studies which all confirmed the superiority of phonics. The results were confirmed years later in his sequel, *Why Johnny Still Can't Read*.

Most children are ready to read by first grade and, when formal instruction begins, the teaching method is of great significance. For decades the "whole language" method, used under one name or another, has prevailed in American elementary schools and has relied on memorizing the meaning and appearances of entire words. But consistent research has confirmed what experience and common sense tell us: that children learn to read more effectively when they first learn the relationship between letters and sounds. This is known as *phonics*.

Whole-language has never compared favorably with phonics. Not surprisingly, as authorities like Drs. Chall and Flesch have spoken out against it, they have been quickly denounced by the mammoth and unwieldy educational establishment and promoters of whole-language reading techniques. Moreover, whole-language advocates quickly hire their own "experts" who attempt to divert attention from the overwhelming evidence by discrediting their critics and rushing to assure the public that people like Flesch are twisting the facts. Some publishers have seemingly accepted the overwhelming evidence, only to alter their material into a quasi-phonics or phony phonics that still has the debilitating pull of "whole language" undercurrents.

Research supports a cognitive edge when students learn phonics. A study by neurologists at Washington University in St. Louis found that the brain is better designed for phonics instruction than for whole-word recognition. The researchers used a PET scan which identifies brain activity as subjects read single words. When subjects viewed a string of non-sense letters without vowels, such as "przntb" the word-recognition area of brain did not activate. When, however, subjects were shown combinations of letters which had vowels in the right place, but which were not words (poozy, floop) the word-recognition parts of the brain activated. The results rule out the theory behind whole-word—that the mind recognizes the shape of the word—and supports the foundations of phonics. Words are recognized by spelling rules which are based on phonics. In order to determine if a set of letters are recognized as a word, the brain must be trained in spelling rules, that is, in phonics.[37]

A crucial question is, why are the majority of our public elementary schools still using the ineffective whole-language methodology? And why are most private schools and home schools teaching phonics? Obviously, because it has much higher literacy results! Then why do the public schools persist in using this horribly ineffective method? It is either a determined effort to undermine our nation's youth or else our educators with all of their doctoral degrees literally don't know what they are doing. After all, teaching children to read is no big mystery. Teachers have been doing it for the last 3,000 years. The U.S. government's own statistics show they were teaching reading quite well until the big switch took place in teaching methods.[38]

On the other hand, the literacy record in America from early home schools is unparalleled. Historical evidence indicates that prior to the introduction of public education and compulsory attendance laws, Americans were probably the most literate people in the world.[39] John Adams in 1765 remarked that "A native of America, especially of New England, who cannot read and write is as rare a phenomenon as a comet." A study performed in 1800 revealed that literacy was universal in early America.[40] Remember, there were no public schools then. Clearly, modern government education has produced results a long way from that.

Then there are the Outcome-Based Education math standards recommended by the National Council of Teachers of Mathematics. According to the NCTM,

> In grades K-4, the mathematics curriculum should include two-and-three-dimensional geometry so that students can develop spatial sense . . .
> Spatial understandings are necessary for interpreting, understanding, and appreciating our inherently geometric world . . .
> Children who develop a strong sense of spatial relationships and who master the concepts and language of geometry are better prepared to learn number and measurement ideas as well as other advanced mathematical topics.
> There is no rote memorization, no cut-and-dry drill.[41]

This simply means that children will learn geometry before they learn number ideas. This new math encourages no memorization of the arithmetic facts. However, our ten-symbol, Arabic-Hindu place-value system requires memorization of the arithmetic facts if the child is to become proficient in using that system. These standards recommended by the National Council of Teachers of Mathematics are going to deny children the key mental exercise that only rote memorization provides and will deny them a full understanding of our abstract counting system. No parent with any common sense would want his child taught math using this absurd method.[42] Yet the plan is to press ahead even if it defies good sense.

Ineffective Textbooks

School textbooks, too, can embody either quality methods or academic shoddiness. It is no secret that many of our textbooks have been "dumbed down." That is, they have to be made less difficult because students cannot handle the harder material.[43] Dr. Paul Copperman in his book *The Literacy Hoax* describes this in greater detail.

> . . . most of the major textbook publishers have instituted a conscious policy of rewriting their textbooks in order to reduce their readability to a level two years below the grade for which they are intended. Thus, eleventh-grade American History books are being rewritten to a ninth-grade level, and twelfth-grade American Government texts are being rewritten to a tenth-grade level. This movement to reduce the readability levels of textbooks is widely known and accepted among secondary-school teachers and administrators, yet most parents have not been informed of it.[44]

A Cornell University professor has developed a scale to rate the literacy levels of most texts. Starting at "0" point for the average difficulty of a large daily newspaper, Dr. Donald Hayes' LEX scale went from plus-58 points for a highly technical article in a science publication to minus-56 points for the language used by farmers to address dairy cows. Using this scale, Hayes found that contemporary honors high school texts are no more difficult than standard eighth-grade readers were before World War II.[45]

What kind of commentary is this on public education? The old saying goes, "If you can't bring Muhammad to the mountain, then bring the mountain to Muhammad." This is apparently what American textbook publishers are doing, and the public schools are buying them. Instead of lowering our textbook levels, why not raise our student's intellectual capacities? Why not stretch their minds? Accommodating student academic laziness should not be tolerated.

Numerous factual errors have been found in textbooks as well. For example, critiquers Mel and Norma Gabler report how they discovered fourteen errors on one page in a World Geography book. Conveniently, eight of the mistakes favored Marxist countries and five of the other six mistakes were unfavorable to non-Marxist countries.[46] In one year the Gablers found thousands of errors in the textbooks publishers were trying to peddle to Texas. Since Texas is one of the largest textbook purchasers, the state has the clout needed to force changes from the publishers. Texas required corrections of over seven thousand errors in the text of ten history books and fined the publishers $860,000. The next year the companies offered "the cleanest books in the history of books." However, the Gablers found an additional 582 errors in these "clean books." The errors included such items as: the House of Representatives voted to impeach Nixon (it never did); George Washington bombarded Boston (he never did); the War Powers Act requires the president to consult Congress before committing troops (it doesn't); and the U.S. won the War of 1812 (it was a draw). The Gablers said the "corrected" United States government texts were even worse than the history books, with a higher per-page error rate. Errors included such blunders as missing the year the Constitution was adopted, claiming the Senate can hold elections to fill vacant seats of members which is, in fact, a power given to the individual state governments.[47] Year after year the Gablers have been documenting hundreds of falsities in Texas school books that are printed by major textbook publishers. Most of the flaws are too blatant to be believed.

The third area of textbook concern is the stressing of nonessentials and rewriting history. Let me cite two brief examples of stressing non-essentials. A fifth-grade history book gave seven pages to Marilyn Monroe, while mentioning George Washington only eight times (and without telling about his accomplishments). George Washington and his accomplishments have been censored out by the humanists. One eighth-grade history text leaves out altogether crucial historical figures such as Ethan Allen, Nathan Hale, John Paul Jones, David Farragut, and George Washington Carver. That same text, however, makes note of Bob Dylan, Janis Joplin, Gertrude Ederle, Bobby Jones, Joan Baez, and DuBois.[48] Is Janis Joplin a more crucial historical figure than John Paul Jones? Schools on all levels are teaching trivia. If you doubt this, don't take my word for it. Visit classroom after classroom in widely separated regions of this country, as I have done.

History is being rewritten as well. For example, the true meaning of the first Thanksgiving is largely ignored or revised. Many texts comment that the pilgrims were giving thanks to the Indians instead of to God. By censoring and leaving out important facts and Christian events in American history, they are declared insignificant. For example, you'd be hard-pressed to find George Washington's farewell address in most history textbooks. Did you also know that most textbooks have had Patrick Henry's stirring speech before the House of Burgesses in Virginia expunged right out of them? This is the speech where he said, "Give me liberty or give me death!" Why has it been left out? Because the burning passion for liberty that so inflamed Henry's soul and helped form this country is inconsistent with the new world order. So, the humanists have just taken his speech out of the textbooks, and we have a whole generation of people who have never heard those inspiring words of a Christian man who was called "the tongue of the revolution." Patrick Henry was a man who, perhaps more than any other, was responsible for igniting the sparks that caused the independence of this nation to come to pass. Without his burning passion for liberty and his willingness to pay the ultimate price for it, perhaps you and I would not know the blessings of liberty today. The absence of Patrick Henry's speech is intended to communicate to students that it is not important. That which is important to the liberal, educational establishment finds its way into the textbooks, and what is not important (from their perspective) is left out or rewritten.

The integrity and reliability of textbooks have slipped badly. This in turn has contributed to the overall academic decline of our students. Most parents do not want their children to be led astray or deceived by what is printed or left out of their school textbooks. Do you?

Grade Inflation and Automatic Passage

The grave state of academic deficiency is also attributed to grade inflation and automatic passage. Grade inflation is the deceiving technique of academic leniency which alters a student's grade upwards, making it appear that his ability is higher than what it really is. Experts have confirmed that students today get at least *25 percent more A's and B's* than they did fifteen years ago, but at the same time they *know less.*[49] It is ironic that while courses are getting easier, and reading and writing assignments are being reduced, high school grades are moving upwards. In other words, not only are class requirements getting easier, but so are grading standards. Grades are threatening to become almost meaningless due to teachers dropping traditional standards of academic quality and, instead, dispersing A and B marks offhandedly to a growing number of students. Sooner or later, however, there comes a a day of reckoning.

For example, one tragic consequence of grade inflation was a valedictorian of Western High School in Washington, D.C. He was refused admission to George Washington University because of a low SAT score in both the math and verbal sections. Because his teachers were giving him excellent grades, he was deceived into thinking he was a real scholar. The unfortunate reality, however, was that he was not up to par with other acceptable collegiate applicants. The admissions dean at George Washington University exclaimed, "My feeling is that a kid like this has been conned; he's been deluded into thinking he's gotten an education."[50] The culprit of the con game? Grade inflation!

Grade inflation is a serious problem. In a study of high school students, Sanford Dornbusch polled a large number of metropolitan high school students about the grading methods of their teachers. About half felt that if they did poor work or did not try, they would still receive average or above-average grades.[51] What is this teaching our young people? It is teaching them mainly that good work and hard work are essentially pointless. Throughout their secondary schooling they learn that there is only a very tenuous relationship between effort and reward.

What this can mean for parents with children in public school is this: your child's grades may not truly reflect his academic performance or skill. He may be the victim of grade inflation and might not be aware of it until after he takes his college entrance exams. How disappointing for a high school senior to discover after high school graduation that he had been strung along for years with a false sense of academic security.

Coupled with grade inflation is automatic passage—the practice of advancing students automatically from grade to grade no matter how deficient their academic performance. You need not look very far to find out how extensive the problem of automatic passage is. The shame of this practice comes when a graduate is hired based upon his completion of twelve grades but then shows little of the skill and competency that should accompany a high school diploma. The victim of automatic passage will be in for rough sailing for the rest of his life.

The fruit of public school educational malpractice is becoming manifest. About one-third of public high school seniors are poorly prepared for the basics once they reach college. A survey of 826 college campuses in fifteen states by the Southern Regional Education Board found that one-third of entering freshman require remedial training in math, reading, or writing and are not ready to begin college courses.[52] Facts don't lie! Public schools are retarding American children and imprisoning the potential of our country's future citizens. Are these the kind of academic results you want for your child? If not, consider taking them out. The public schools receive a grade of F in the area of academics.

F in Morality

It is important to remember that when we speak of education, we are not exclusively referring to the intellect. A child also learns morality and value judgment, whether it is formally taught or not. A child is constantly in a state of learning. Many educational bureaucrats would have us believe that they hold a neutral academic position. But who are they kidding? A child who is publicly schooled will inevitably learn value judgments from both his teachers and his peers. The question is: What kind of morality or immorality is your child learning? And how is it affecting his character?

Consider what is happening to traditional family values in the public schools. Students attending are force-fed a steady diet of anti-Christian, anti-family points of view. Biblical creationism is treated as a mythological joke. Traditional marriage, the sanctity of a human life, love and respect for parents, and family integrity are often distorted or rejected. When this happens, public schools do not compliment the family—they subvert it, contributing to rebellion, sexual promiscuity, drug usage, delinquency, and violence among our nation's youth!

Dr. Paul C. Vitz of New York University, after an extensive study regarding religion and traditional values in public school textbooks concluded:

> When one looks at the total sample of 670 pieces in these basal readers the following findings stand out. Serious religious motivation is featured nowhere. References to Christianity or Judaism are uncommon and typically superficial. In particular, Protestantism is almost entirely excluded. At least for whites. Patriotism is close to nonexistent in the sample. Likewise, any appreciation of business success is essentially unrepresented. Traditional roles for both men and women receive virtually no support, while feminist portrayals regularly show women engaged in activities indistinguishable from those of men. Indeed, clear attacks on

traditional sex roles, especially traditional concepts of manhood, were common.

The above characteristics taken together make it clear that these basal readers are so written as to represent a systematic denial of the history, heritage, beliefs, and values of a very large segment of the American people.[53]

Testifying in a federal district classroom in Alabama, Professor Timothy L. Smith, a distinguished historian of American religion at Johns Hopkins, said he was "profoundly shocked" by the almost total lack of religious references in the state's eleventh-grade history texts. He pointed out that there was little mention of religion's role in the development of American pluralism or the "absolute central role" of Christians in the abolition of slavery.[54] In the same courtroom, Dr. William Coulson, a professor of psychology at the United States International University in San Diego, criticized public schools for substituting psychology for hard moral reasoning. He cited a course on decision-making in family life in which never once "is it suggesting that [what is morally] right can be known."[55]

Consider the dramatic and far-reaching impact of a 1985 Supreme Court ruling on an Oklahoma state law. Their decision restrains public schools from firing any teacher who advocates, promotes, or encourages homosexuality as a legitimate lifestyle. Bizarre, isn't it? Would it bother you if a homosexual teaches your child, perhaps even a sex education class, knowing that he/she can legally promote his/her lifestyle? It no longer matters what you think, for you have little choice in the matter. The Supreme Court ruling remains the law of the land and has widespread implications for public schools in every state. Homosexuals, no matter how deviant and perverse one considers their lifestyle, can now teach children and mingle with them in the halls and classrooms. Will their teaching, influence, and presence promote traditional family values or be destructive to them?

Consider further some of the things being taught in public schools these days that instruct a gutter morality: explicit sex education; texts that have lessons in violence, hate, and despair; values clarification; relativism; and death education. These are but a few specifics out of many that could be chosen. These five areas should suffice in illustrating the immorality that is often being taught in today's public classrooms.

Regarding *explicit sex education*, a father gave testimony before a United States Department of Education hearing in Seattle,

Washington, in which he described his son's fifth-grade health class. On the day he visited, he testified:

> A plastic model of female genitalia with a tampon insert was passed around to the boys so they might understand how tampons fit. Birth control pills were also passed around and explained. Anal intercourse was described. At no time was there any mention of abstinence as a desirable alternative for 5th graders. The morality that was taught in the classroom that day was complete promiscuity.[56]

In a similar hearing held in Concord, New Hampshire, another confused father testified:

> When my wife spoke to the school nurse about the health education program at school, the nurse told her that she delivers female students' urine samples to family planning clinics for pregnancy testing. I never thought that schools work to educate therapeutically and test young girls for pregnancy. I always thought that schools had to do with developing learning skills and knowledge.[57]

These are not isolated examples, nor are they the worst. Much of what I have researched in this area is unprintable. Many textbooks are saturated with explicit sexual lingo. Here are some actual examples taken from textbooks.

> Adolescent petting is an important opportunity to learn about sexual response and to gratify sexual and emotional desires without a more serious commitment.
> In many societies, premarital intercourse is expected and serves a useful role in the selection of a spouse. In such societies, there are seldom negative psychological consequences.[58]

One student health book had a caption underneath a picture of two young men embracing in a section titled "family health," which read: "Research shows that homosexuals can lead lives that are as full and healthy as those of heterosexuals."[59] Without a doubt, repeated sexual suggestions and fantasies in textbooks teach promiscuity, immorality, and homosexuality.

Under the guise of AIDS awareness education, children from the first grade level up are being taught safe sex, condom education, and explicit information about heterosexual and homosexual relationships. No health and hygiene program is considered complete without it.

Because of AIDS this whole concept of sex education has gone wild, like a fire out of control. Children are not only being taught graphic details of heterosexual activity, but in many instances, homosexual activity as well. Many states have mandatory courses in which they are teaching fourth graders in mixed company how to use condoms. We are talking about nine-year-old boys and girls in a mixed classroom setting. If your nine-year-old is in there, and they are slipping condoms over bananas, cucumbers, or plastic sex organs, the devastation to their modesty, decency, and purity would be horrendous. Many parents become livid when they find out their children are being taught graphic, explicit details of sexuality and homosexual sodomy, as well as how to use condoms. They are infuriated at the suggestion that their children be exposed to ungodly sodomite activity and especially when the Surgeon General's office coerces and promulgates it at the lowest grade possible. They don't want their child's modesty and purity ruined in such a manner and at such an early age. Remember, innocence can never be reclaimed or re-established.

Recently, a Chicago high school student who asked to be excused from the showing of pornographic films in an English literature course was denied that right by the school. Scott K., who took a film studies course to learn film history and camera technique, discovered that his teacher had another idea. The teacher showed his class both homosexual and heterosexual X-rated porno films as an "experiment to see the students' reaction." Apparently the teacher did not like the reaction he got from Scott. The student asked to be excused from the sections, saying they made him "feel like going home and taking a shower." He offered to do substitute activities such as submit an extra research paper but to no avail. School officials sided with the teacher. The Bible says, "It is shameful even to mention what the disobedient do in secret" (Eph. 5:12). I ask you, what place does this have in the classroom?[60]

To make matters worse, children with AIDS will be attending school along with all the others who don't carry the AIDS virus. And according to the Surgeon General's office, some children will develop brain disease which will produce changes in mental behavior. Though we want to be compassionate to those who have acquired the dreaded disease, seriously and soberly ask yourself, Do I want my child exposed to those inflicted with and suffering from the lethal AIDS contagion, some of whom will likely be manifesting signs of dementia—a state of brain deterioration resulting from the AIDS virus? In answering that question, keep in mind that this is perhaps the most devastating disease ever to ravage our population. There is no known cure in sight for this biological scourge. It is 100 percent fatal. Further, there remains considerable question and debate on some of the possible means of transmitting the deadly disease in school settings, like biting, coughing, kissing, and sweat. Medical analysts simply need more time to make absolute determinations about AIDS and all its possible means of transmission.

Another development affecting public schools is the travesty known as school-based clinics (SBCs). Since the first one opened at Mechanics High School in St. Paul, Minnesota, dozens and dozens have been established in high schools across America. Their function includes dispensing contraceptives, family planning, abortion referrals, laboratory and diagnostic screening, immunizations, nutrition and weight reduction programs, child care, and drug and alcohol abuse programs. However, though SBCs are being marketed as comprehensive health clinics, their main purpose appears to be the development of a contraceptive delivery mechanism into the schools. SBCs are being pushed by Planned Parenthood and other self-appointed advocates of teen sexual liberation who have consistently resisted efforts to require parental consent or notification for adolescent abortions and birth control counseling. Once a parent signs a "blank check" consent form for his son or daughter to receive a free sports physical, the SBC has the freedom to distribute contraceptives and engage in birth control counseling without parental notification or consent.

Statistics reveal that approximately 75 percent of all females lose their virginity by the age of nineteen.[61] Do SBCs help stem the tide of unwanted teen pregnancies through sex education and liberal contraceptive distribution as promoters intimate? To the contrary, they may have exacerbated the problem. A study of premarital, sexually active females aged fifteen to nineteen found that as sexual activity increases, the probability of pregnancy also increases—even when contraceptives are used consistently.[62] A House Select Committee on Children, Youth, and Families found that despite sex education and contraceptive distribution programs, "there has been no change in the percentage of sexually active teens who become pregnant, but there has been a huge increase in the percentage of teens who are sexually active. And this increase in sexual activity has led to a proportionate increase in pregnancies to unmarried teens."[63] Even Planned Parenthood's own journal states that "more teenagers are using contraceptives and using them more consistently than ever before. Yet the number and rate of premarital pregnancies continues to rise."[64]

In light of the fact that school-based clinics fail to reduce the pregnancy rate, will be involved in diagnosis rather than treatment, and offer services already available in most communities through private physicians and public agencies, wasteful expenditures to initiate and sustain the school-based clinic program is totally unjustifiable from a moral and fiscal standpoint. If anything, they help corrupt America's school age youth. Yet SBCs continue to grow in number each year, expanding their influence and their immorally suggestive activity.

Another moral disaster that has been unleashed in the public schools is drug availability and trafficking. Americans have consistently named drug use among the top problems confronting the nation's schools. A Department of Education report revealed that the United States has the highest rate of teenage drug use of any industrialized nation. The drug problem in this country is ten times greater than in Japan, for example. Sixty-one percent of high school seniors have used drugs.[65] A study by the University of Michigan found that the trend of increasing drug use is skyrocketing among younger children. Twenty-five percent of eighth-graders acknowledge use of illicit drugs. That figure rises to 35 percent when inhalants are included.[66] That's one out of three!

What makes the problem so heart-wrenching is where they are getting them—at school. A study of teenagers who contacted a cocaine hotline revealed that 57 percent of the respondents bought most of their drugs at school.[67] Our nation's schools more often resemble drug dens instead of hallowed halls of learning. Despite stepped-up law enforcement activity, the problem continues to mushroom.

Cocaine usage is the fastest growing drug problem in America. What makes it particularly alarming is its recent availability in a cheap but potent form called crack. Crack is a purified form of cocaine that is smoked. Here are some startling facts surrounding the mounting crack epidemic:

1. *Crack is inexpensive to try*—Crack is available for as little as ten dollars. As a result, the drug is affordable to many new users, including high school and even elementary school students.

2. *Crack is easy to use*—It is sold in pieces resembling small white gravel or soap chips and is sometimes pressed into small pellets. Crack can be smoked in a pipe or put into a cig-

arette. Because the visible effects disappear within minutes after smoking, it can be used at almost anytime during the day.

3. *Crack is extremely addictive*—crack is far more addictive than heroin or barbiturates. Because crack is smoke, it is quickly absorbed into the bloodstream. It produces a feeling of extreme euphoria, peaking within seconds. The desire to repeat this sensation can cause addiction within a few days.

4. *Crack leads to crime and severe psychological disorders*—Many youths, once addicted, have turned to stealing, prostitution, and drug dealing in order to support their habit. Continued use can produce violent behavior and psychotic states similar to schizophrenia.

5. *Crack is deadly*—Cocaine in any form can cause cardiac arrest and death by interrupting the brain's control over the heart and respiratory system.[68]

If your child is in a public school, he/she will not only be exposed to drugs, but will witness the illicit trafficking and casual usage of drugs. Powerful peer pressure will entice him/her to "fit in" or be socially ostracized. The Attorney General of one state said, "It is a sad and sobering reality that trying drugs is no longer the exception among high school students. It is the norm." Such environment is hardly conducive to moral stability and soundness of character.

Some textbooks exacerbate the problem by teaching *violence, hate, and despair*. Perhaps this is one reason why every month some 282,800 persons are physically attacked in schools, 204 million high school students have something stolen from them, and six hundred million dollars are spent yearly on repairing vandalism.[69] Here is a violent poem found in a textbook used in many public schools:

> *Jack be nimble, Jack be quick*
> *Snap the blade, and give it a flick*
> *Grab the purse, it's easily done*
> *Then just for kicks, just for fun*
> *Plunge the knife, and cut and run. . . .*[70]

How about this narration in a textbook depicting a girl waiting to kill her brother:

> She picked up a long knife which one of the boys had used to cut bread and looked at its sharp-scraped edge. She would kill him. She sat straight in her chair, one hand resting on the table, the other holding the knife between her knees, concealing it in the folds of her nightgown. She kept her eyes steadily on the door, and Len came in. He started to walk

around the table. "In a minute," she thought, "he'll pass me, and then his back will be turned. Then I'll kill him." Her fingers tighten on the handle of the knife.[71]

Other school readers have been found to have graphic accounts of gang fights, raids by wild motorcyclists, violent demonstrations against authority, murders of family members, and rape. Are these the kinds of textbooks you want your child to read? Is it the kind of literature that impressionable young minds should read? Do your religious convictions allow you to accept such ungodly indoctrination? What responsible parent can condone the teaching of violence, hate, and despair?

A fourth area that undermines morality in our youth is *relativism*. Relativism is a dangerous practice which assumes that all values are situational. It teaches that the surrounding circumstances at any given time determine what is right and what is wrong. As we all know, situations and public opinion are constantly in a state of change. Hence, while the Ten Commandments have not changed in several thousand years, the relativist teaches that what was "wrong" yesterday may very well be "right" today.

The term "situation ethics" was coined by a man named Joseph Fletcher. Fletcher, a professor at the Episcopal Theological Seminary, believed that Christian doctrine was weird and utterly untenable and so "de-Christianized" himself. His moral guide for judging all situations in life came to be based on its relevance to perceived human benefit. In other words, moral decisions should not be based on the absolutes of God's Word but on human feelings and judgments in any given situation.

An example of this becomes clear when we look at the wording in one sex education text. It says, "In a society where values are constantly shifting, the young adult may often be confused by which set of values he or she is to follow."[72] Really? This would lead a youngster to believe that there are no absolute morals which are applicable to every generation. Instead, it implies that each generation must develop its own values. That is outright antinomianism and rugged, individual paganism. It creates a feeling of "do whatever is right in your own eyes." What parent wants his child subjected to such moral chaos prevalent in our public schools or the "thought police" of the liberal, New World Order educational bureaucracy?

There is also a technique called *values clarification*. This is a very subtle procedure that combines group sensitivity training and peer pressure. It rapidly exerts a very powerful hold on the moral development of young children. A much more accurate term for values clarification would be *morals modification* because that is exactly what it is: the most poisonous technique ever devised for turning forty-some million school children away from the traditional moral values of their parents and country.

This evil technique is applied in a very controlled environment, where preselected concepts and questions are coupled with peer pressure and are usually far too advanced for those involved. It doesn't take long for the group to reprobate itself and arrive at debased conclusions when no moral absolutes are permitted in the discussion. This in turn creates in impressionable young minds an amoral attitude towards life. For example, imagine these actual textbook questions being debated where no moral absolutes apply:

- How many of you think there are times when cheating is justified?
- How many of you have ever had problems so bad you wished you could die so you wouldn't have to face them?
- How many would like to have different parents?
- How many would approve of a young couple trying out marriage by living together for six months before actually getting married?
- How many think a suspected homosexual should be allowed to teach in the public schools?
- How many think their parents should teach their children to masturbate?
- How many of you would choose to go to Heaven if it meant playing harps all day?[73]

William Kilpatrick, a professor of education at Boston College, wrote the illuminating book *Why Johnny Can't Tell Right from Wrong*. Kilpatrick aptly points out that the reason why schools are producing so many moral illiterates is due to the shift away from morality-based character education to nonjudgmental values clarification and decision making. Children go to school to learn usable skills, not how to question morality. The bottom line for parents is this: whom do you want determining the values in your children— you or the school system?

A fifth area of moral concern in the public classroom comes from *death education*. As the name implies, this is the practice of exposing your youngster to death. Now that you are getting a feel for the content of many of our public textbooks, how many of these texts do you think present the Christian's firm belief in life after death? You guessed it!

One mother testified in a United States Department of

Education hearing in Orlando, Florida, that first-graders were required to make their own coffins out of shoe boxes. In the same hearing, another mother testified that her daughter was given a list of ten ways to die, some of them violently. Her daughter was instructed to choose the most and least preferred. She was also asked what she wanted done to her if she was terminally ill. Two of the five preselected choices were mercy killing.[74]

All death education tactics have the same morbid goal of focusing attention on death and dying from a Christless perspective. Do you want your child taught death from an anti-Christian perspective?

In each of these five areas: explicit sex education; lessons in violence, hate, and despair; values clarification; relativism; and death education—parents have good reason to be concerned about what their children are being taught. This is by no means an all-inclusive list of moral concerns. Many parents are completely unaware of what their child is being taught today in the public school. Do you really want your child to stay in a government-controlled school that lives and breathes debauchery and moral insanity?

F in Socialization

The socialization going at public schools comes primarily from peer group association. Most of this kind of socialization is negative in nature. Studies have shown that a child placed into an institutional setting before he has an understanding of his own values will lock into the value systems of his age-mates. Because he spends more time with his peers than with his family, he becomes peer-dependent, adopting the habits, mannerisms, and language of those around him.[75] Research funded by Cornell University found that children who spend more time with their peers than with their parents become peer-dependent. Peer dependency undermines creativity and diminishes optimism and respect of parents.[76] But worst of all, the peer group holds the trump card in making final evaluations of self-worth. When was the last time you had friends over to talk dirty, use the F word, and tell filthy jokes, just so you could feel properly "socialized?" Never, I hope. Why then should you subject your children repeatedly to the negative social contagion of public school?

Children in a secular society tend to judge another's worth or value on three factors:1) beauty, 2) intelligence, and 3) wealth. All it takes to be the target of criticism and ridicule at school is to have one perceived physical flaw, a seemingly slower learning ability, or to be poor. Imagine the emotional impact on a young child who has any one of these factors drawn to his attention. For example, one who is tall and slender is called "Lamp-post"; one who is short "Runt"; one who is redheaded "Carrot-top"; one who is heavyset "Porky", "Fatso", "Lard-bucket", or "Tubby"; one who has protruding teeth "Bucktooth"or "Beaver"; and a hundred other names that go along with having freckles, large ears, heavy eyebrows, big noses, hairy arms, glasses, clumsiness, etc. And we all know that these remarks are mild compared to what is often hurled. Oftentimes criticism results not from actual but perceived flaws. Some names and comments are created out of sheer cruelty and meanness.

The same ridicule accompanies those who are slightly behind in intellectual development, for they are earmarked "idiot," "stupid," or "moron." If one comes from a family in a lower economic bracket, they ridicule their car, clothes, father's job, etc. Each remark, along with its accompanying body language and social stigma, has the crushing capacity to erode self-respect. It can alter the way children feel about themselves for years, perhaps for the rest of their life.

Two experts in the field of adolescent self-esteem write: "The way his peers perceive him strongly influences the adolescent's conception of himself, which generally remains unchanged throughout his life. Peer influences are at their zenith during preadolescence and adolescence when youngsters are most inclined to feel socially, emotionally, and even intellectually inept."[77] Child psychologist Dorothy C. Briggs points out that "no child can see himself directly, he only sees himself from the reflection of others. Their 'mirrors' literally mold his self image . . . what goes on between your youngster and those around him, consequently, is of central importance."[78]

The presence of peers in one's environment for seven hours a day, five days a week, creates peer dependency. Dr. Bronfenbrenner has found that a child who is peer dependent loses a crucial sense of self-worth.[79] This is because he begins to trust the values and judgments of his peers more than his own or his family's. It is at this point that parents find it hard communicating and relating to their child, the so-called "generation gap." But since there are excellent educational alternatives, this need not be. For all these reasons, the public schools get an F in socialization.

F in Discipline and Controlling Violence

Many public school students suffer from senseless *discipline problems*. A survey by the National Association of Secondary School Principals found that middle school students listed the bullying and disruptive behavior of their classmates as their main concern.[80] How can a child learn under such appalling circumstances? There is no excuse for allowing such badgering and blatant personal violence. Schools should not be pens for undisciplined hoodlums, but hallowed halls of learning commanding respect for those in authority. Why then is it tolerated? Why are those who cannot appreciate the value of education not expelled or placed on work farms so that children who want to learn have that opportunity? Why has discipline in our public schools been allowed to get so far out of hand?

That is a very good question. Note, for example, the dramatic change in top offenses that have taken place between the 1940s and the 1980s in the public schools. In 1940 they were:

1) Talking
2) Chewing gum
3) Running in the halls
4) Wearing improper clothes
5) Making noise
6) Not putting paper in wastebaskets
7) Getting out of turn in line

As compared to the 1990s:

1) Rape
2) Robbery
3) Assault
4) Personal theft
5) Burglary
6) Drug abuse
7) Arson
8) Bombings
9) Alcoholic abuse
10) Carrying of weapons
11) Absenteeism
12) Vandalism
13) Murder
14) Extortion
15) Gang warfare
16) Pregnancies
17) Abortions
18) Suicide
19) General disease
20) Lying and cheating[81]

It seems evident that our public schools have lost that essential quality of schoolroom discipline that is needed to have a wholesome and effective educational environment. If you are like most parents, proper school discipline is very important to you too. Some of you are probably frightened by what you see, but you do not know what you can do about it. Do not let anyone suggest that you must simply accept things as they are. That is an unnecessary compromise of principle. If discipline is important to you, ask yourself, is leaving my child with those who are unruly and undisciplined a hindrance or a help to my child's future?

Have you noticed the upsurge in *student violence* in our public schools? Poll after poll show that a high percent of parents in America fear for the safety of their child in schools. And rightly so, for there is a great deal of violence perpetrated against students. The National

Crime Survey found that 1.9 million teenagers are victims of violent crime annually, including rape, robbery, assault, and murder. Out of these, approximately 485,000 occurred at school or on school property. Experts also estimate that a third of all violent crimes go unreported, which means these figures are probably much higher.[82]

There is also crime and violence committed against teachers. A survey taken by Metropolitan Life found that 95 percent of all teachers believe it would be a positive step to give much higher priority to school discipline and safety. Further, a poll by the National Education Association revealed that 28 percent of teachers had been victims of theft or vandalism and 4.2 percent had been attacked by students. Such misbehavior has had deleterious effects on teaching performance.[83] According to a National Education Association survey:

> Some 110,000 teachers—one out of every twenty— were physically attacked by students on school property during the school year. Another 10,000 were attacked by students off school property. The 110,000 victims represent an increase of 57 percent over the estimated 70,000 teachers who were attacked the previous year. Of the teachers who were attacked, an estimated 11,500 required medical attention for physical injuries and an estimated 9,000 required medical attention for emotional trauma.[84]

Another survey shows the problem continues unabated. Some 640,000 teachers either had personal property stolen or intentionally damaged by a student within the twelve months previous to the survey, while approximately eighty thousand teachers were physically attacked by a student.[85] Perhaps this, in addition to low pay, explains why a Louis Harris poll reveals that 55 percent of classroom teachers have seriously considered leaving the profession.[86] For all these reasons, the public schools receive an F grade in discipline.

F in Manners and Etiquette

Good manners are the perfect complement to a student's social development and success in life. Whatever happened to the treasured qualities of common courtesy, social etiquette, and personal grooming? Instead of being encouraged, they are neglected in our public schools. Exhibit A for parental consideration is the growing number of youngsters today who have the social grace of a drunken sailor, the manners of a wild animal, the courtesy of a pompous fool, and the grooming habits of swine. It is true that these are areas of self-discipline, but they are disciplines that are taught and nurtured. How important is it to you that your children develop these quality of self-discipline?

Someone once asked Emily Post, an authority on etiquette, if manners are still important and relevant. She replied:

> They are just as important to us now as they were to previous generations . . . all good manners are based on thoughtfulness for others, and if everyone lived by the golden rule—"Do unto others as you would have others do unto you"—there would be no bad manners in the world . . . . A knowledge of etiquette—and good manners—carries many advantages. It imparts a comfortable feeling of security, self-confidence, and self-respect.[87]

How many public schools work with parents to reinforce this vital area of personal development? How many care? I challenge you to visit your local public school for one whole day, and you will quickly find out. I'm confident you, too, will give them a grade of F.

F in the Promotion of Democratic Ideals

This is the final area in our imaginary report card. A mother and chairwoman for parent representatives in the Pittsburgh public schools testified before a United States Department of Education hearing in Pittsburgh, Pennsylvania. In a portion of her testimony, she said:

> Plays presented to students with actors dancing on the United States flag are not uncommon and were a big problem here in Pittsburgh. Kids are definitely being programmed to accept a new global perspective.[88]

The America of our forefathers is not beautiful anymore. But the United Nations and global New World Order are. School textbooks often remark that government subsidies and foreign aid are considered more effective than private enterprise, even though studies show the opposite more often is true. The grandiose schemes of socialist third world governments are touted and their failures hardly mentioned; governments allowing extensive freedom for free enterprise, if not given demerits, are ignored. Does this not bring distress to your freedom-loving heart? For those parents who want to investigate further, I encourage you to read your child's history textbook. Look up figures like Stalin, Gorbachev, Castro, and Ho Chi Minh.

Fourteen hundred public schools in the United States have accepted the children's global flag which is to fly beside the national and state flags in school classrooms. Schools which fly the flag have signed an agreement to teach the children a moral code of ethics which includes world government and a pagan form of worship which teaches that "Mother Gaia (or Mother Earth) is the fountainhead of life." The program is designed to teach children an internationalist mentality, and that they are children of a universal pagan deity.[89] Is patriotism important to you? Do you want your child to grow to be a loyal American, faithful to his country? Are you tired of the perpetual attacks on American sovereignty while the United Nations is glorified?

University professor Gene Veith argues that American schools have actually become fascist indoctrination centers. Veith, author of the book *Modern Fascism*, writes that modern public schools "work from assumptions that are literally and demonstrably fascist." He points out some interesting parallels. For example, the concept that all reality is culturally constructed and can be imposed by power is shared by Nazis and the politically correct movement which has seized American schools and campuses. Establishment education theorists try to silence their critics. Lawsuits, state legislation, economic pressure, and political assassination are brought to bear in an attempt to crush educational reformers. Teachers' unions block new ideas by political clout. These, Veith identifies, are the marks of fascism.[90]

This brings up the subject of America's largest teacher's union—the National Education Association. The NEA was founded in Philadelphia in 1857. From the very beginning their goal was to create a national educational system, something our wise forefathers clearly left in the hands of state and local governments. At their very first organizational meeting, a call was made for a federal department of education. That goal was realized when President Jimmy Carter formed the Department of Education and gave the Education Secretary cabinet-level status. The NEA has always been committed to the idea of government-owned and government-controlled schools.

Many believe the NEA, through a carefully orchestrated and largely stealth agenda, has deliberately steered the public schools down the tragic road to socialism, humanism, subjectivism, radicalism, planned failure in literacy skills, suppression of Christianity, and the disposing of traditional values and beliefs. One thing is for certain—they are a tremendously potent political force, both locally and nationally, and their continual drive for more and greater power is both frightening and mind-boggling. Decades ago the executive secretary of the NEA predicted:

> NEA will become a political power second to no other special interest group . . . . NEA will organize this profession from top to bottom into logical operation units that can move swiftly and effectively and with power unmatched by any other organized group in the nation.[91]

This has since become true. Today the NEA is the largest and most powerful union in the country. They have over two million members—bigger than the AFL-CIO, bigger even than the union of government workers. They have a massive three-quarter-billion-dollar budget. And because of their far-reaching, left-wing activities and political clout, they might be more appropriately dubbed the "National Extortion Association" or the "Educational Mafia."

Since the NEA is a tool of the radical left, their goals and purposes have often been radically different than the teachers they represent. A poll of over a thousand randomly selected teachers found a wide disparity between the NEA and the rank-and-file members. Sally Reed of the National Council for Better Education gives this description of the NEA:

> It has initiated policies which, in the end, have demoralized teachers, made their jobs more difficult, and compromised the legitimate needs of all educators.
>
> It has helped to undermine parental authority, and thus the family unit; it has portrayed itself as representative of teacher views when such is not the case.
>
> In short, the NEA has betrayed the public trust, and in the process created a negative attitude toward public school teachers and public education."[92]

The question is, why has the Goliath-like NEA been allowed to operate with impunity, considering its goals and excessive political activity? Why is this powerful teachers union, which is secretly controlled by an elite board, even needed? Since their members are firmly entrenched politically in all 435 congressional districts, and every school district in the country, how can concerned parents ever hope to win the war of what they teach your children? The resolve of the ungodly is strong and their purpose is clear. *The Humanist* magazine carried this battle cry to their constituency:

> I am convinced that the battle for humankind's future must be waged and won in the public school classroom by teachers who correctly perceive their role as the proselytizers of a new faith: a religion of humanity that recognizes and respects the spark of what theologians call divinity in every human being. These teachers must embody the same selfless dedication as the most rabid fundamentalist preachers, for they will be ministers of another sort, utilizing a classroom instead of a pulpit to convey humanist values in whatever subject they teach, regardless of the educational level—preschool, day care or large state university. The classroom must and will become an arena of conflict between the old and the new— the rotting corpse of Christianity, together with all its adjacent evils and misery, and the new faith of humanism . . . .[93]

There is no question about where they stand or what their goals are. To them it is all-out war, and your children are the booty. It is not a matter of "what" or "where"; to them it is a matter of "how quickly?" This being the case, three all-important questions rise to be answered: One, how strong are your convictions about raising a godly, profamily, pro-American child? Two, are you willing to counter this radical anti-God movement with an equally radical commitment to your child's education? And three, are you ready to seriously explore your educational alternatives?

Conclusion

Are you tired of the assault on educational excellence? Are you sick of the retarding of America and the imprisoning of potential? I believe that you are, or you wouldn't be reading this book. That is why it is essential to remove the blinders and see public education today as it really is. Secular schools no longer make learning their primary objective. Instead, our public schools have become conduits to the minds of our youth, training them to be uneducated, undisciplined, anti-God, anti-moral, anti-family, anti-free enterprise, and, in my opinion, anti-American.

As a parent, you must decide if these are the things you want for your child, or if you want something better. The resolve of Christian parents all over this land is being tested and their convictions questioned and undermined. There are many educrats who want parents and their values out of the education picture altogether. Their position is that the schools should be able to teach whatever they want to the schoolchildren—and that the schools should not be accountable to the parents for anything.

Every August and September across America approximately four to five million innocent five-year-olds enter kindergarten. Their beautiful eyes are bright with the excited expectation that they will get an education that will help them all through life. But too often that is not what happens. Based on national statistics at this writing, this is what does happen:

1. One million girls, almost 50 percent, will become pregnant out of wedlock before graduation day. By age eighteen, 72 percent of boys, and 69 percent of girls have become sexually active.[94]

2. Most will be taught to read using "whole language" methodology instead of phonics. That's why one-third of them will be functionally illiterate by 12th grade. Those who do learn to read might be subjected to homosexual propaganda readers such as *Heather Has Two Mommies*, *Daddy's Roommate*, or *Gloria Goes to Gay Pride*.

3. All these children will be taught evolution as a fact of science. Few will learn that there is more scientific evidence to support the belief that man was really created by God. Consequently, they will be led to believe they are animals—therefore they can do anything their animal appetites desire.

4. Most of these children will not learn to write well, and some will not learn to write at all. Most will do poorly at math, and many will fail to learn to add, multiply, or divide.[95]

5. Many of these children will be exposed to 180 hours of very explicit sex education courses, held in mixed company without the benefit of moral values.

6. Many will be exposed to New Age teachings, yoga, transcendental meditation, witchcraft demonstrations, and Eastern religions—while forbidding any mention of God, Jesus Christ, Christianity and prayer.[96]

Public education, if it were to receive a report card from parents, would get an F in Academics, F in Morality, F in Socialization, F in Discipline, F in Manners and Etiquette, and an F in the Promotion of Democratic Ideals. Evaluate for yourself. Look at each function or activity of the public schools below and pencil in your own grade.

☐ Acknowledges America's strong religious and moral heritage in text books.

☐ Acknowledges rights of taxpaying parents as "owners" of the public school system.

☐ Carefully avoids contradicting parents' religious values.

☐ Decides as many issues as possible at the local level rather than taking orders from Washington

☐ Encourages parental involvement in deciding curriculum issues.

☐ Keeps spending to a minimum and insists on high value for each dollar spent.

☐ Lets parents remain the primary moral influence in their children's lives.

☐ Makes academic achievement of students its top priority.

☐ Observes traditional, objective view of right and wrong.

☐ Produces good return for dollars invested.

☐ Promotes sexual abstinence among students.

☐ Promotes free enterprise rather than socialism.

☐ Respects individual teacher's right not to join the union.

☐ Supports pay for teachers on basis of merit and achievement.

☐ Teaches traditional phonics rather than "guessing" approach to reading.

☐ Treats children as human beings, not animal subjects for experimentation.

☐ Focuses energy on academics and avoids political maneuvering.

☐ Focuses on core skills such as reading, writing, and mathematics.

☐ Helps students achieve increasingly higher scores on standardized tests.

☐ Holds its members to the highest possible standards via competency testing.

☐ Includes biblical creation in science curriculum.

☐ Keeps as many decisions as possible about the teaching of morality in the hands of parents.

How did the public schools fare according to your own grades? If your children are in public school, and if you are fed up with the metamorphosis of American schools into some kind of an educational Frankenstein, then ask yourself: Is this what I want for my child? Or do I want something better? If so, read on.

FOUR

Why Home Schooling Is the Best Alternative

RADICAL INNOVATION #307:
A NEW STANDARD IN
PUBLIC SCHOOL CLASSROOM DESIGN

© Matt Arnold, 1991

Having examined the failures of the public school system, we now want to consider why home education is an excellent alternative. In light of the current performance of public education, responsible parents could hardly do any worse than the public school. But research shows most home educators are doing a superior job compared to the public schools.

Responsible Parents Qualify

One of the first thoughts of potential home schoolers is, frequently, *I am not qualified*. That is exactly what the educational bureaucrats want you to think. They do not want parents to entertain the idea of teaching their own children. Though school officials masquerade themselves as "deeply concerned" over your child's welfare and socialization, they actually are guarding their own interests. First, parents who effectively home school expose the miserable failures and inadequacies of public education. Second, home schoolers are a growing threat to their educational monopoly. Third, home schoolers are seen as robbers of their vast enrollment coffers, since public schools receive funds according to their per capita attendance.

The truth is that responsible and literate moms and dads are qualified by virtue of their God-given responsibility and divine charge as parents (Deut. 4:9, 6:6-9; Prov. 22:6). God has not just made parents responsible, He has equipped them for the task. Many parents feel very unsure about themselves due to constant criticism of their abilities. Parents are capable of doing a great deal more than what they are given credit for. Despite what certain humanistic government officials say about them, parents are not just vehicles of procreation for the state. They are divine instruments of progeny whose parental purpose includes the overall development and oversight of their children.

At this point, it is essential that we define the word "qualified." It would be difficult to agree on who is or is not a good musician if we do not agree on what is or is not good music. Yet much educational propaganda tries to absolve teachers on similar grounds. How many educators agree on what makes a good teacher? Apparently not many, based on the dismal records of the school system. Further, when charged in court with negligence, educators defend themselves by saying that they cannot be judged guilty of not having done what should have been done because no one knows what should have been done. If this argument is accepted, then how can these same people who don't know what should have been done judge who is or is not competent to do it? Educators define "qualified" to mean teachers trained in education, holding teaching certificates, and certified by the state as qualified. Yet look at their results! They assume that to teach children involves a host of mysterious skills that can be learned only in schools of education; that people who have this training teach much better than those who do not; and that people who have not had this training are not competent to teach at all. In fact, none of these assumptions are true. In one state it was found that fully half of the teacher applicants scored lower in math than the average highschool junior, and a third scored lower in English.[97] Personality ratings were deplorable. The truth of the matter is that a teaching certificate does not guarantee good teaching.

To be qualified as a Christian home educator parents must meet three general requirements. First, *you must be literate*, that is, able to read and write yourself. Second, *you must discipline your home life and commit yourself to the process of teaching and learning.* Prior to making the decision to home school, parents should sit down and seriously count the costs involved (Luke 14:28,29). A deep interest and commitment to the home schooling process must be evident. You must be willing to make the time demands that home education will require. This may mean sacrificing some unessential and superfluous activities that are often scheduled on life's agenda. It may mean forgoing some personal free time that you might have otherwise. Home schooling takes time! It is not acceptable to leave a child at home to do school while both parents go to work. That is not home schooling. Third, *parents need to develop, nurture, and exhibit a godly example.* This means education begins with the parents and not with the children. If you meet these three basic requirements, you are indeed qualified to teach your own children. The requirements for being a good home school teacher are not unduly complex and do not require years of special training. Parents need only be responsible, loving, literate, responsive, and reasonably consistent, and salt these qualities with a little imagination, common sense, and willingness to follow a few simple suggestions.

Without a doubt, the tutorial method of instruction is an excellent method of educational instruction. Home educators can emphasize total personality development in harmony (i.e., academic, moral, self-respect, social, physical, spiritual). A child will become lopsided if one area is stressed to the detriment of another or when one or several areas are left out altogether. All humans were meant to have their body, mind, and spirit molded on a united front. This is known as educating the whole man. In the atmosphere of a warm, loving home, much can be accomplished toward this end.

What I intend to demonstrate in this chapter is that home schooling, with the parental motivation of divine responsibility, love, and concern, can help children develop excellence in virtually every area of education, making it the best educational alternative.

Do Parents Need to Be Certified?

As for the idea that certified teachers teach better than uncertified, or that uncertified teachers cannot teach at all, there is not a single reputable study in education research that supports a need for teacher certification—and a great deal against it. Two studies indicate that certification is actually a negative influence.[98] For millennia parents have been passing along information and skills to their children. It is interesting that highly sophisticated societies have come from such "teaching methods." Throughout these many years there have been very few vocational teachers as we know them today. It has only been with relative recency that special training for teachers has arisen. People always knew that before you could teach something you had to know it yourself. But contemporary thinking espouses that before you can teach you must spend years being taught how to teach. This is not to say one should look pejoratively at teacher certification and educational degrees but neither should parents be criticized and depreciated by haughty educrats who erroneously insist that only they can do the job right and in a superior fashion.

Character Development Advantage

Home educators have the opportunity to focus on building Christian character. When parents identify an area of character weakness in their child such as lack of patience, trust, joy, or forgiveness, they can immediately begin to stress the character trait that fills the child's need.

Most parochial schools would find it very difficult to individualize character training, and public schools, by-and-large, don't care. As a result, what may start out as a minor character flaw can mushroom into a major character problem in later life. But home schoolers can stay right on top of the character development process. They can daily and consistently help to mold and shape their child's character into the desired form.

Spiritual Advantages of Home Schooling

Inseparably connected with character development is the passing on of Christian precepts. Spiritual teaching gives home schoolers their power and effectiveness. Most parents who home school do so for religious reasons. That's why approximately 80 percent of the home school community is comprised of Christian parents.

Home schoolers have a unique advantage in building spiritual depth and appreciation. First, you know what your child is being taught spiritually. Outside of your home you can never be sure what is being taught. But home educators know and can tailor their spiritual instruction to conform to their beliefs and convictions. Growth in spirituality is viewed as a family experience.

Children learn primarily by example, emulating the spiritual model of those around them. If they are with their peers, they emulate them; if with parents, they will emulate their parents. When a child reads the Bible with Mom and Dad, prays with them, shares joys, and deals with problems together, this creates a unique spiritual bonding that is dynamic and inexplicable. There is truth to the maxim, "The family that prays together, stays together." Home schooling affords the opportunity to create spiritual depth and appreciation second to none.

Spiritual training is the most important area of education that parents are charged with giving their children. This is the number one priority. Everything else should take second seat. How does a child become wise? The Bible clearly acknowledges that "the fear of the Lord is the beginning of wisdom" (Proverbs 9:10). And this "fear of the Lord" only comes when priority is placed on the teaching of the Word of God. Back in the sixteenth century the great reformer Martin Luther made this astute prediction:

> I am much afraid that schools will prove to be the great gates of Hell unless they diligently labor in explaining the holy scriptures, engraving them in the hearts of youth.
>
> I advise no one to place his child where the scriptures do not reign paramount. Every institution in which men are

not increasingly occupied with the Word of God must become corrupt[99]

Timothy Dwight, an early president of Yale University, said this about our children's education:

> To commit our children to the care of irreligious persons is to commit lambs to the superintendency of wolves.[100]

Martin Luther and Timothy Dwight wisely foresaw the danger of losing a Christian influence in educational circles. Taking prayer and the Bible out of our public schools has only planted the seeds of godlessness, rebellion, and immorality. If parents are to take seriously Luther's and Dwight's advice, their primary educational concern should be: Is my child diligently being taught the Word of God? Are Scriptural seeds being planted in his heart, being fed and watered, nurtured and helped to grow? The Bible says, "See to it that no one carries you off as spoil or makes you yourselves captive by his so-called philosophy and intellectualism, and vain deceit (idle fancies and plain nonsense), following human tradition—men's ideas of the material [rather than the spiritual] world—just crude notions following the rudimentary and elemental teachings of the universe, and disregarding [the teachings of] Christ, the Messiah . . . let the word [spoken by] the Christ, the Messiah, have its home (in your hearts and minds) and dwell in [all its] richness (Col. 2:8; 3:16, *Amplified Bible*). The Bible is clear on the fact that parental responsibility includes the spiritual training of our children.

Numerous scriptures exhort on the purpose, power, and needed preeminence of the Word of God in the lives of people. Here are some of them:

> *Matthew 7:24-27*—"Therefore everyone who hears these words of mine and puts them into practice is like a wise man who built his house upon the rock. The rain came down, the streams rose, and the winds blew and beat against that house; yet it did not fall, because it had its foundation on the rock. But everyone who hears these words of mine and does not put them into practice is like a foolish man who built his house on the sand. The rain came down, the streams rose, and the winds blew, and beat against that house, and it fell with a great crash."
>
> *2 Timothy 3:16-17*—"All Scripture is God-breathed and is useful for teaching, rebuking, correcting, and training in righteousness, so that the man of God may be thoroughly equipped for every good work."

> *1 Peter 1:24-25*—"All men are like grass, and all their glory is like the flowers of the field; the grass withers and the flowers fall, but the word of the Lord stands forever . . . ."

Parents are negligent in teaching their children the Word of God when they delegate the crucial task to others without proper parental participation, oversight, and accountability. This is one job that is far too important to just leave to others! In God's eyes, parents are ultimately held accountable for the job and how well it is administered. This is one reason home schooling is so valuable. You know exactly what your children are learning and how well.

Academic Superiority

Research studies in the United States and Canada have consistently confirmed the effectiveness, and in most cases, the superiority of home education to traditional classroom instruction.[101] Yet accusations are still made. Spokesmen for the National Education Association have charged that home schools don't measure up to accepted standards, but the NEA has yet to produce one shred of evidence in support of this claim. Let's consider some of the evidence.

Statistical analysis of more than eighty studies demonstrates that a student taught individually achieves on the average thirty percentile points higher on norm-referenced standard achievements tests.[102] The Hewitt Research Foundation, an internationally recognized education research organization, studied several thousand home-schooled children across the United States and found that home-educated children rate consistently higher, usually scoring between the 75th and 95th percentile on both the Stanford and Iowa achievement tests. Frequently these children are taught by high school-educated parents.[103] The Imperial Tutoring and Educational Services conducted research on over 2,000 home-educated pupils from a variety of socioeconomic and ethnic backgrounds and discovered that the majority experienced significant scholastic progress and improvement in both attitude and motivation. The greatest progress was in the areas of language ares and reading.[104] A nationwide test using the Basic Battery of the Iowa Tests of Basic Skills, was given to 16,000 home-schooled children for grades K-12 in all fifty states. The results provided by Riverside Publishing Company and analyzed by researcher Dr. Brian Ray, revealed that home schooled students averaged at the 79th percentile. The nationwide grand mean in reading was at the 77th percentile, a ranking which means that home school students perform better in reading than 79 percent of the sample population on whom the test was normed. The 73rd grand mean percentile ranking in language and mathematics indicates that the typical homeschooler does better than 73 percent of the norming population in those subjects. Of particular significance is the fact that 54.7 percent of these home-schooled students are achieving individual scores in the top quarter of the population. This figure is more than double the number of conventional school students who score in the top quarter.[105]

A study by the National Education Research Institute of 2,163 home schoolers produced a report entitled, "A Nationwide Study of Home Education: Family Characteristics, Legal Matters, and Student Achievement." This study found the average scores of home school students were at or above the 80th percentile in every category. In other words, home schoolers scored, on the average, higher than 80 percent of the students in the country. Their national mean averages was 84 for reading, 80 for language, 81 for math, 84 for science, and 83 for social studies. Of further interest in this study is the fact that only 13.9 percent of the mothers (who are the primary teachers) were, or had ever been, certified teachers.[106]

Another nationwide study was performed cooperatively between the Psychological Corporation (publisher of the SAT test) and the Home School Legal Defense Association. It involved 5,124 home schooling students from kindergarten through twelfth grades representing all fifty states. The testing was performed under strict guidelines using the Stanford Achievement Test. The machine-scored results showed the home schoolers' composite score on reading, math, and language arts ranked 18 to 28 percentile points above their public school peers.[107]

Academic Achievement In Various States
In *Washington* state, 3,634 home-schooled students averaged in the top third of all students tested nationwide and better than students in public schools in the state.[108]

The National Center for Home Education performed an analysis of the achievement test scores obtained by home schooling students in *South Carolina*. Their findings: The average home schooler scores are 30 percentile points higher than the national public school average. What is more, the scores are being achieved in a state where public school SAT scores are next-to-last in national rankings. The most widely recognized achievement indicator among laymen is the "grade level" indicator. By definition those scoring at the 50th percentile or higher are "at or above" grade level. Also by definition, in the public school nationally, 50 percent of the students are at or above grade level, while 50 percent are below grade level. The South

Carolina results show that in math, 91.7 percent of the home-schooled students are at or above grade level. In reading, 93.4 percent of the home schooled students are at or above grade level.[109]

Both the *Oregon* Department of Education and the *Tennessee* Department of Education reported that the home-educated students (for whom they have scores) in their states, are scoring well above average on standardized achievement test. An *Alabama* study showed home schoolers scored at or above grade level in almost all subject areas on the SAT. Second-grade students scored significantly better than the Alabama public school students in reading and listening. In *Alaska*, students in a state-managed form of home education scored significantly higher than conventional school students nationwide on the California Achievement Test in math, reading, language, and science. The Centralized Correspondence Study home school students in Alaska also scored higher on achievement tests than conventional school Alaskans.[110]

Consider a few specific instances where home schoolers have excelled in academics. The first involves five western New York state couples who taught their children at home and were challenged for truancy. Each family agreed to submit their children to the Stanford Achievement Test. While the national average on this test is 50 percent, all seven children scored between 90 and 99 percent.[111]

Another instance took place in Wallace, Nebraska. A mother with only a high school degree began home schooling her daughter, who had been failing the sixth grade. Mrs. Rice began to teach her daughter about one to two hours a day, and then they worked side by side the remainder of the day in their family hotel. In nine months, her daughter's academic standing had risen almost three grade levels.[112]

Then there is the irony of a Pennsylvania girl whose parents had been denied permission to home school her because the public schools had identified her as learning-disabled. Her parents, the Smelzers, fought and won permission to proceed. Three years later, after she took the state's mandatory assessment test, the girl was told she couldn't be home schooled anymore because she was gifted and wouldn't get the special attention she needed at home.[113]

Studies also show that academic performance tends to accelerate in a home school environment. The longer children are home schooled, the better they tend to do (percentile-wise) on standard achievement tests. Test results of home schooled students at Cornerstone Christian Academy in San Antonio showed that children home schooled for six months or more scored on the average in the 79th percentile on the Wide Range Achievement Test. On the other hand, those home schooled for five years or more scored in the ninety-first percentile.[114]

These remarkable academic achievements come at the hands of parents who, for the most part, are not state-certified. In fact, only about one to two percent are certified to be teachers.[115] This shoots a hole in the bucket of the certification-means-successful-teaching theory. Research also shows that the educational accomplishments of the parents (beyond high school) do not appreciably affect the students' academic performance. Students taught by parents with a high school diploma score almost exactly the same on standardized achievement tests as those taught by a parent with a college degree.[116] The major factor for a home-schooled student's academic success is the commitment of teaching parents to make sure the student learns the required subject.

Home Schoolers Are Accepted into College

Home schoolers who desire to go to college upon graduation are having little trouble getting in. In fact, home-schooled students have no more trouble getting into college than those who have gone to conventional schools.[117] At least ten home schoolers a year are getting into Harvard.[118] Below is a partial list of over 200 colleges and universities that have accepted home schoolers at this writing. There are many others.

Adrian College, MI	Biola University, CA
Allegheny College, PA	Blackburn College, IL
Amasis Bible College, IA	Bob Jones University, SC
American River Comm. Jr. College, CA	Boston University, MA
Amherst College, MA	Brigham Young University, UT
Antelope Valley College, CA	Broome Community College, NY
Antioch College, OH	Brown University, RI
Appalachian Bible College, WV	Bryan College, TN
Arkansas State University, AR	Buffalo State, NY
Asbury College, KY	Calvin College, TN
Austin College, TX	Carleton College, MN
Baptist Bible College, PA	Casper College, WY
Barber College, OH	Cedarville College, OH
Baylor University, TX	Central Piedmont Comm. College, NC
Belhaven College, MS	Christendom College, VA
Belmont College, TN	Christian Brothers University, TN
Bethany College of Missions, MN	Christian Heritage College, CA
Bethany Lutheran College, MN	Christian Liberty College, VA
Bethel College, IN	Chowan College, NC

Cincinnati Bible College, OH
Circleville Bible College, OH
The Citadel, SC
Clearwater Christian College, FL
College of Lake County, IL
College of Southern Idaho, ID
College of William and Mary, VA
Colorado Christian University, CO
Columbus College, GA
Concordia College, MN
Cooke County College, TX
Corning Community College, NY
Covenant College, TN
Crichton College, TN
Criswell College, TX
Cumberland County College, NJ
Dallas Christian College, TX
Dartmouth College, NH
David Lipscomb University, TN
DeKalb Community College, GA
Delta College, MI
Diablo Valley College, CA
Dordt College, IA
Drake University, IA
East Central College, MO
Eastern Hillsdale College, MI
East Texas Baptist Univ. TX
Evergreen Valley Comm. College, CA
Faith Baptist Bible College, LA
Freed-Hardeman University, TN
Fresno Pacific College, CA
Garden City College, KS
Geneva College, PA
George Fox College, OR
George Mason University, VA
G.M.I. School of Engineering, MI
Gonzaga University, WA
Gordon College, MA
Grace College
Grand Rapids Baptist College, MI
Grand Valley State University, MI
Grove City College, MI
Harding University, AR
Harvard University, MA
Heritage Baptist University, IN
Hillsdale College, MI
Hope College, MI

Houghton College, NY
Houston Baptist University, TX
Indiana University of Pennsylvania, PA
Joliet Junior College, IL
John Brown University, TX
Kalamazoo Valley Comm. College, MI
Kenyon College, OH
Keystone Community College, PA
King College, TN
Kings College, NY
Lancaster Bible College, PA
Lansing Community College, MI
Lawrence Technological University, MI
Lee College, TN
LeTourneau College, TX
Liberty University, VA
Louisiana State University, LA
Loyola College, MD
Lutheran Bible Institute, WA
Magdalen College, NH
Maranatha Baptist Bible Colege, WI
Maryland Bible College & Seminary
MIT, MA
The Master's College, CA
Memphis State University, TN
Messiah College, PA
Michigan Institute of Technology, MI
Middlebury College, VT
Mid-Plains Comm. College, NE
Mississippi State University, MS
Mississippi College, MS
Modesto Junior College, CA
Montana Wilderness School, MT
Montreat Anderson, NC
Moody Bible Institute, IL
Morrisville College, NY
Mt. Vernon Nazarene College, OH
Nazareth College, NY
Nebraska School of Tech. Agri., NE
New Mexico State University, NM
Niagra University, NY
Northampton Comm College, PA
Northern Michigan University, MI
Northland Baptist Bible, WI
Northwest Christian College, OR
Oakland University, MI
Oberlin College, OH

Ohio State Uni. Ag. Tech., OH
Oklahoma Baptist Univ., OK
Okalhoma City Comm. College, OK
Oklahoma State University, OK
Oklahoma University of Science & Arts
Onondago Community College, NY
Oral Roberts University,OK
Owens Technical College, OH
Oxford Univesity, England
Penn State University, McKeesport
Pennsylvania State-York, PA
Pensacola Christian College, FL
Pepperdine University, CA
Piedmont Bible College
Prince Georges Comm College, MD
Princeton University, NH
Redwoods Junior College, CA
Rensselaer Polytechnic Inst.
Rice University, TX
Ricks College, ID
Roberts Wesleyan College, NY
St. Johns College, MD
St. Joseph's School of Nursing
St. Louis Christian College, MO
St. Phillips College, TX
St. Vincent College, PA
Salem College, WV
Samford College, AL
Sam Houston State, TX
Shimer College, IL
Simpson College, CA
Southern Arkansas Univ., AR
Southern Illinois Univ.-Carbondale
Southwest Baptist University, MO
Southwest Texas State University
Stanislaus State University, CA
Stockton State University, NJ
Taylor University, IN
Tennessee Temple University, TN
Texas A & M University, TX
Texas Christian University
Texas Tech University, TX
Texas Woman's University, TX
Thomas Aquinas College, CA
Thomas More Institute, NH
Towson State University, MD
Tyler Junior College, TX

Union University, TN
U.S. Air Force Academy, CO
U.S. Naval Academy, Annapolis
University of Akron, OH
University of Alabama-Huntsville
University of Alaska-Fairbank
University of Arizona, AR
University of Arts, PA
University of California-Berkley
UCLA
University of California-Santa Cruz
University of Colorado, Colo. Sprgs.
University of Dallas, TX
University of Delaware, DE
University of Evansville, IN
University of Houston, TX
University of Mary Hardin Baylor
University of Michigan, MI
University of Minnesota, MN
University of Mississippi
University of Missouri-Rolla
University of Nebraska-Lincoln
University of New York, NY
University of No Carolina-Chapel Hill
University of St. Thomas-Houston, TX
University of South Carolina
University of So. Indiana
University of Steubenville
University of the South, TN
University of Tennessee
University of Texas-Austin
University of Texas-Arlington, TX
University of Texas-El Paso
University of Virginia, Charlottesville
University of Washington, WA
University of Wisconsin-Madison, WI
Vanderbilt College, TX
Victoria College, TX
Virginia Polytech Institute
Washington University Medical Centr, MO
Western Baptist College, OR
Western Texas College, TX
Western Washington University, WA
Wharton County Jr. College, TX
Wheaton College, IL
Whitman College, WA
Whitworth College, WA

Wisconsin Lutheran College, WI   Yale University, CT
Word of Life Institute, NY   York College of Pennsylvania[119]

Clearly, home schoolers are performing well academically and above average on standardized testing instruments. Most Christian parents do not home school only for academic reasons, but they could make a good case for it. Responsible parents do not want illiterate, ill-informed children who demonstrate poor scholastic achievement. They want children who can read, write, do arithmetic, reason, and make value judgments in a highly skilled manner. That is why so many have taken the satisfying step towards high academic performance by home educating their children.

Moral Excellence

Most parents who home school do so for a mixture of reasons, but high on their list is the desire for moral excellence in their children. Gunnar Gustavsen of Andrews University in Michigan surveyed 221 home school families. The most prevalent reasons given by these parents for withdrawing their children from public school were "concern for the moral health and character development of their children, rivalry and ridicule and violence in conventional schools, and the poor quality of public education."[120] Concerned parents do not want their child's heart and mind filled with immoral sewage. The unescapable fact is that parents are ultimately responsible for their children's moral values, no matter where they may be going to school.

Christian home educators aim for moral excellence. They know that morality is *taught* by word and deed. Morality is transmitted to children by instructing and reinforcing what is true, honorable, right, pure, honest, respectable, and good. Parents, not the state, have the responsibility for the moral instruction of their children. This view is supported by God's Word (cf. Eph. 6:1). Morality is taught when traditional attitudes, beliefs, and values are instilled with great care and determination. Home educators can successfully accomplish moral excellence in their children by instilling in them the laws of God (summarized in the Ten Commandments), by using Scripture memory, and by demonstrating it through personal example. Home schooling parents can daily intertwine moral values and biblical life principles.

Morality is *corrupted* when teachers lead students to believe that morality has no absolutes. Public teachers portray themselves as morally neutral and often teach that life's decisions are relative. However, morality is not gray or borderline. It is either right or wrong, black or white, God-pleasing or not God-pleasing. When teachers attempt to instruct a class void of principles and values upon which students can make judgments, what are they really doing? They are undermining biblical morality and creating a vacuum. And children left in a moral vacuum will absorb whatever prevailing values are at hand.

Webster's Dictionary defines morality as "conformity to ideals of right human conduct."[121] But what is "right?" Rightness must be based on some set of values or principles. Scripture clearly states (cf. Romans 1) that moral absolutes exist. Traditional Christian morality is based upon Scripture. When children are so taught, they will become morally sound and develop values which are solidly placed on the bedrock of God's abiding Word. This is the parent's job. The Bible, talking to parents, says, "Train a child in the way he should go, and when he is old he will not turn from it" (Prov. 22:6).

Home educators know the importance of instilling morality when children are young and their spirit and character are developing. They can be taught how to resist the temptation to do evil. Home schoolers learn early the significance of the word "no," and to stand by it. Likewise, they can be taught to say "yes" to those things which are pleasing in God's sight. With a strong set of values in their hearts, their armor will be solid and their fortification sound against immoral attacks. Isn't this the kind of morality you want for your child?

Positive Socialization Is Successful Socialization
Another bright spot for home schoolers is their sociability. Socialization is an area where home educators are often unjustly criticized. Those who do the criticizing have bought into a common but false notion. In reality, home schoolers are some of the best socially-adjusted people around.

There are two types of socialization: positive and negative. Positive socialization helps a child to grow and develop to his full potential in life. When a child's personality develops in a warm atmosphere of love and acceptance, he will usually socialize well. The socialization of home schoolers is not regimented by age groups the way public schools do, which is unnatural. Negative socialization, on the other hand, separates a child from his parents and restricts a child's socializing primarily to his age-mates. This has detrimental and long-term effects on a child's sociability and his ability to mix among a wide age dispersement.

Home schoolers actually prefer their kind of social life, without all the cliques and snobbery you get in schools. They have a broader range of friends of all ages and types. This gives them the ability to engage in a variety of social situations with a high degree of success.

Home Schoolers Don't Live in Isolation

Home-educated children to a large extent adopt the values and sociability of their parents. But while they spend much of their time around their parents, home schoolers also spend time with other people at church activities, support group functions, field trips, Awana, music and art classes, community activities, 4-H clubs, Little League teams, choirs, scouts, YMCA, neighborhood children, and apprenticeships to name a few. So home schoolers are by no means antisocial, they just practice *selective socialization*.

Spending time with the local support group encompasses a large portion of selective socialization. There is a network of an estimated three to four thousand local home schooling support groups nationwide. These support groups offer everything from field trips to skating, competitive sports to chess clubs; some even offer foreign languages and upper-level math and science classes. All of it is voluntary.

A study by Seattle University researcher Linda Montgomery found that home schoolers between the age of ten and twenty-one were just as involved in social events like music, dance lessons, scouting, and 4-H as those conventionally schooled. Further, she found that home schoolers show leadership skills equal to or better than their public school peers.[122]

A Washington state home school research project surveyed homeschoolers and found that more than half spent twenty to thirty hours a month in community or volunteer activities. About 40 percent spent more than thirty hours a month with friends outside their families.[123] Home schoolers are not usually isolated from society, and they learn how to effectively live and work in it.

Research Confirms Home School Sociability Success

A study by Dr. Larry Shyers, Chairman of the Florida Board of Clinical Social Work, Marriage and Family Therapy, and Mental Health Counseling, compared home schooled and conventionally-schooled children ages eight to ten in behavior and social development. These children were either solely home educated all their lives or had been solely schooled in the conventional classroom. Three correlates of social adjustment were identified through a review of the findings: self-concept, behavior, and assertiveness. His study found that home schoolers were not behind their conventionally-schooled peers in social development. More significant, using the Direct

Observation Form of the Child Behavior Checklist instrument, Dr. Shyers found that home-schooled children had consistently fewer behavioral problems. Traditionally-schooled children tended to be considerably more aggressive, loud, and competitive. Shyers attributes this to the fact that home schoolers tend to imitate their parent's behavior. Conversely, conventionally-schooled children tend to imitate the attitudes and behavior of their peers.[124] In his abstract, Dr. Shyers concludes that "appropriate social skills can develop apart from formal contact with children other than siblings. This supports the belief held by home school proponents."[125]

Thomas Smedley of Radford University of Virginia submitted a master's thesis entitled "The Socialization of Home School Children." Using the Vineland Adaptive Behavior Scales to evaluate social maturity, Smedley measured the communication, socialization, and daily living skills of demographically matched home-schooled and public-schooled children. The scores were combined into one composite which reflected the general maturity of each subject. Scores on the Adoptive Behavior Composite were at the 84th percentile for home schoolers and 27th percentile for public schoolers. The results indicate that home-schooled children are significantly better socialized and more mature than those in public school.[126]

Research results performed by Dr. John Wesley Taylor of Andrews University found that home schooled children rate superior in socialization. Based on one of the best-validated self-concept assessment instruments available, the Piers-Harris Children's Self-Concept Scale, a random sampling of 45,000 home school children found that half of these children scored "at or above the ninety-first percentile"— 41 percent higher than the average, conventionally schooled child. Only 10.3 percent score below the national average. Since self-concept is considered to be a basic dynamic of positive sociability, this answers the often-heard skepticism suggesting that home schoolers are inferior in socialization.[127]

The effects of positive socialization appear to be long-term. A study of adults who had been home schooled found that not one of them was unemployed or on welfare. Ninety-four percent said home schooling prepared them to be independent persons and seventy-nine percent said home schooling had helped them interact with individuals from different levels of society.[128]

Putting the "Real World" Argument to Rest
Some accuse home school parents of protecting their children from the "real world." They contend that children need exposure to dirty

language, rebelliousness, and a degenerate environment, because after all, this is a part of reality. But this is an unsatisfactory argument that home educators simply aren't buying. How would you define the real world? Is the real world that lifestyle embellished on television and videos with their sordid wickedness and vile filth? Is the real world primarily made up of violence, rebellion, foul language, selfishness, and fornication found in the public school environment? Absolutely not! The real world is learning to be a success at work and at home. It's learning how to be productive in society, how to be a good father or mother, and how to get along with people, which is the biggest challenge in life. By this standard or measure of success, home schoolers are indeed ready to meet the challenge. In fact, they are better prepared than public school graduates. It is true that there is wickedness in the world due to the fall of man. But putting your children in the midst of it when their values are being formed is not going to solve the problem. Nor will it improve their character or the condition of our society.

There is a measure of sheltering that exists among home schoolers. But is this not the place and function of the home? Responsible, godly parents should stand as a buffer between their tender, young child and the evil harshness of his world. Parents should not allow their children exposure to the raw onslaughts of worldliness and demonic activity all in the name of socialization. Nurseries grow seedlings in greenhouses because that is where they grow best. The new plants can flourish because they are protected from subfreezing temperatures and strong, winter winds. When spring arrives, the plants are stronger and more mature and ready to be transplanted. Soon they will to become productive, but the early sheltering was a necessary part of the growth process. Children too need time to grow and be trained before they are ready for the stark realities of the world.

Suppose you were in a theater with your young child and someone cried from the back, "Fire!" Would you put him down amidst the trampling of feet and say "Run, kid, I hope you can make it outside." No, you wouldn't take the risk. You would pick him up in your arms and carry him safely outside. Protection and godly training in the early years make a child stronger and better prepared for the world—not weak and unprepared, as some suggest. As a result of a certain amount of sheltering, they can become productive citizens, bearing the fruits of the godly life in Christ Jesus.

Parents should not feel obligated in the least to subject their children to a hedonistic and debauched philosophy of life for the sake of exposure. That line of reasoning is totally without merit. It naturally leads into the idea that if a little exposure is good, then more exposure is better. The implications from here are obvious. When a child is young, not even a little exposure to evil is proper. Who wants a little exposure to the AIDS virus just to know what it is like? No one! Exposure for the sake of exposure is a bankrupt argument. Those who buy it will pay a high price.

The pages of Scripture are replete with examples of this. Righteous Lot tried living among the evil men in the city of Sodom. Though he loved God, the city's powerful influence overwhelmed his family's convictions, leading to his wife's death and corrupting the morals of his daughters (Gen. 18:22-19:38). Because he was peer dependent, young King Rehoboam ignored the counsel of his elders, and instead tragically followed the advice of the boys he grew up with (cf. 1 Kings 12:1-6). We may think our child is strong enough to ignore or stand up against negative socialization, but the Bible clearly states that "bad company corrupts good character" (1 Cor. 15:33). Like Joseph, sometimes the best thing we can do for our child is to help him flee that environment that so easily sways him from God (cf. Gen. 39:7-12). This refutes the argument that Christian children need to stay in public school to be a witness. Biblical history makes clear who is most likely to be influenced, especially at that age. Only when evil is seen in the light of God's displeasure and His just retribution does it benefit a child.

Once we clear away the semantic underbrush, we can decide intelligently what kind of socialization we want for our children, positive or negative. As has been pointed out, home-schooled children engage in the former. The results demonstrate that home-educated children are indeed socially well-adjusted, often in a superior way to those who are conventionally schooled.

A friend of mine planted a peach sapling in his backyard. One day while visiting I remarked that the small tree was growing crooked. He said he planned to stake it up so it would grow straight. Several years went by. I noticed that the tree was much larger and still growing crooked. Inquiring about it, my friend said he never got around to staking it until this year. However, he said all his efforts to get it to grow straight so far had been futile. He confessed, "I waited too late to start the correction." Don't wait until it is too late and the negative socialization damage is done on your precious children.

Healthy Self-Respect

Another area home schooled children can excel in is self-respect. A healthy self-respect is a significant need among children everywhere.

Self-respect is the capacity to see yourself as a child of God. As a result, a child knows he or she is valuable, important, having certain unique talents and worthwhile insights to share in relationships with others. It is definitely not conceited or self-centered, but demonstrates a realistic awareness of who you are in Christ. In a sentence, it means to honor your uniqueness and, spiritually, to accept your life as a gift from God. In a time when so many people lack this essential ingredient which builds strong character and good leaders, the home schooling movement is stimulating its revival. Home-schooled children tend to radiate a higher degree of self-respect and confidence.

In a conventional school setting, peer criticism and ridicule can play havoc with a young child's self-image. Children are often brutal in what they say, and tend to taunt and ridicule one another. A well-behaved child is often dubbed a "sissy." A child with genuine respect for his teacher is labeled "teacher's pet." The studious are pegged "egghead." Social rejection by a sensitive or intelligent child can be sheer torture. Contrary to the juvenile saying, "Sticks and stones may break my bones, but words will never hurt me," words can do extensive damage to a young child's self-esteem. When placed in a setting where peer value assessments rule supreme, your child becomes subject to the societal judgments of worth.

Wherever there are peers, there will be an inheritance of peer pressure. The younger the child, the more harmful its effects. As has already been discussed, a regrettable and time-revealing flaw of mass education is peer dependency. Peer-dependent children have a negative view of themselves. They also show much greater concern for what their peers think and say than what their parents think and say. Extensive child development research has found that peer-dependent children "are pessimistic about the future, rate lower in responsibility and leadership and are more likely to engage in such antisocial behavior as lying, teasing other children, playing hooky or doing something illegal . . . . More serious manifestations are reflected in the rising of youthful runaways, school dropouts, drug abuse, suicide, delinquency, vandalism and violence."[129]

Beginning with a child's first year away in public school, a distancing often develops between a parent and child, and it can increase every year a child remains in the government educational system. It may be unnoticeable at first, but the seed has been planted, and as the years go by, a rebellious, anti-parent philosophical indoctrination will often reveal its indelible mark.

A distinctive advantage of home schooling is the near absence of destructive peer ridicule and criticism. In a warm home environment a young child is free to be creative instead of faddish, initiating instead of peer-reliant, and individualistic instead of an age-mate clone. At home school, peer criticism can be kept to a minimum. Children can be taught by the parents the importance of a "no-knock" policy. They can be taught that constant self-criticism can become a bad habit and accomplishes nothing.

Home-schooled children evidence self-respect in part due to parental nearness and bonding. A child who grows up and is educated around a loving mom and dad will usually develop a good self-image. Maslow and Felker point out that a person with self-respect has a sense of "belonging."[130] Otto Weininger's studies confirm that children who remain home longer are more likely to demonstrate emotional "well-being."[131] John Bowlby says that numerous direct studies make it obvious that when deprived of maternal care, a child's development is almost always impaired physically, intellectually, and socially. Some children are gravely damaged for life. He further points out that "all" children under seven are vulnerable and "many" who are much older than that.[132] Children place a high value on parental nearness. The catalyst that develops and builds a child's self-respect is just knowing the proximity and affection of Mom and Dad.

This closeness also helps develop bonding. Home schooling helps to build an emotional integrity and a precious rapport between a child and parent like few things can. All across this nation, public school parents have told me they feel like their child is no longer theirs, and, like sand falling between their fingers, their children are slipping away from them. Many feel as though they are losing control over their children, that their personalities are changing, yet they feel so helpless. However, many parents who pull their children out of public school and start home schooling them can barely believe the kind of emotional intimacy they are able to build in a short period of time. After six months to a year of home schooling, the child has an entirely different attitude of respect for parental authority. This is because the togetherness, shared values, and experiences build a love and an understanding between them.

Furthermore, parent-child bonding produces deeper interrelationships, love, trust, and family dependency. This, in turn, produces more meaningful communication, emotional intimacy, and a closer family life. In a day when teenage/parent communications are often shallow and inadequate, home schooling offers you time with your child—time to talk, time to build relationships, time to interact, time to share frustrations and joys, and time to mold Christian attributes.

One home schooling mother who took her two daughters out of a conventional school commented on how they are redeveloping love and affection for each other. She said, "They used to get along so well until they started school. Before long they began to fight and bicker with one another. Since we started home schooling, they are once again learning to love and get along with each other. There is less rivalry and strife."

Home schoolers feel good about themselves because self-respect is carefully monitored and encouraged. When a child receives a stinging remark from a neighborhood playmate, Mom and Dad can help them counteract it and deal with the pain. When they can't grasp an area of schoolwork and feel incompetent, Mom or Dad can give them immediate comfort and reassurance of their abilities. Parents are not to eliminate every challenge for their children but serve as a confident ally in their behalf, encourage them when they are distressed, intervene when the threats are overwhelming, and above all, give them the tools to overcome the obstacles.

Regarding your child's self-respect, no one has summed it up more distinctly than developmental psychologist Dr. James Dobson. He says:

> The building of self-esteem in your child is one responsibility which cannot be delegated to others. The task is too difficult and too personal to be handled in group situations. Without your commitment and support, Junior is on his own against formidable foes. With few exceptions, our materialistic society is not going to reinforce healthy self-concepts in your children, and if these desirable attitudes are to be constructed—only you can do it. No one else will care enough to make the necessary investment.[133]

How important is self-respect? It is apparently the foundation of every sound quality desirable in human beings. George Gallup Jr. conducted a poll on the self-respect of the American public. The poll conclusively showed that people with a strong self-image demonstrated the following qualities:

1. They have a high moral and ethical sensitivity.
2. They have a strong sense of family.
3. They are far more successful in interpersonal relationships.
4. Their perspective of success is viewed in terms of interpersonal relationships, not in crass materialistic terms.

5. They're far more productive on the job.
6. They are far lower in incidents of chemical addictions.
7. They are more likely to get involved in social and political activities in their communities.
8. They are far more generous to charitable institutions and give far more generously to relief causes.[134]

Are these not the qualities that you want your child to have? If so, then the building of self-respect in a culture where so few have it becomes paramount. By lovingly and responsibly home educating your child, you can help your child build and develop a healthy and positive self-respect.

Physical Stamina

There is no magic here. Home schoolers have more physical stamina because parents can easily monitor their diet. I have talked with many public school teachers who say it is not uncommon for students to have a Coke and potato chips for lunch. What kind of nutrition is that? Why is it that "13 of every 100 elementary school children are obese. And as many as 40 percent of all youngsters suffer obesity."[135] It is conceded that some obesity problems are due to metabolism and chemical imbalance, but the vast majority are due to diet. Most nutritionists agree that colas, chips, candy, sweets, and carbohydrates consumed in large quantities can adversely affect a child both physically and mentally.

Home-schooled children can be monitored carefully to ensure ingestion of wholesome, nutritious, vitamin-packed meals. Tests have been performed that show a definite correlation between diet and mental acuity. These same tests show diet also can affect one's personality.[136] It naturally follows that responsible parents will want to control their children's diet and maximize their learning ability. Home educators can do this better than anyone else.

In addition, they can encourage and oversee a systematic exercise program. A national conference on youth fitness discovered that less than 50 percent of children in the six to seventeen age bracket meet desirable fitness levels.[137] Home educators can offer their children a wide variety of physical exercise through community recreation centers, local sports, and family-centered activities. Physical education is often more pleasurable to home-schooled students because they are not confined to the track, field, or gym and because they do not have to endure the competitive atmosphere of a school locker room. Public showers combined with peer ridicule have probably done more to damage an adolescent's body image than anything else. Home schoolers avoid such emotionally dangerous situations which can effect a child's enjoyment of physical education.

Home-schooled children usually do not have to sit behind a desk as long as their conventionally-schooled peers; therefore, they can enjoy a greater amount of recreation throughout the day.

Finally, think of all the viruses and germs children are exposed to in the public schools through coughing, dry hacking, water fountains, and tightly-packed, germ-filled hallways. Talk about germ warfare! When a child picks something up, they usually bring it home. And then who picks it up? Think of all the lost days at work and school caused by viral contamination in public school day after day. Home-schooled children have a limited exposure to this kind of environment.

The physical argument is small in the scheme of things, but it is one which when combined with other factors, makes home schooling a distinct advantage.

When all is said, home schooling that is lovingly and responsibly carried out has a superior report card. In the areas of academics, morality, self-image, social adjustment, and physical care, home schooling has a terrific track record. Home schooling is an excellent educational alternative and may very well be the best for you.

Advantages of Home Education as a Tutorial Method

Tutorial (one-on-one) education offers many special teaching advantages. Perhaps this explains why the children of royalty have always been educated by this method. Responsible Christian parents can make excellent tutors. There are six teaching advantages afforded to those who home tutor over against all other educational alternatives.

1)*Home educators do not have to contend with the disadvantage of large classes.* Home schools are far more efficient than institutional schools because of their low teacher to-student-ratio. In most conventional schools, teachers have to contend with twenty, thirty, or more students under varying circumstances, leaving little time for one-on-one personal encounters. Despite a good teacher's best efforts, this can often impede the learning process. Home educators, on the other hand, are able to engage in relatively large amounts of one-on-one instruction. This enables them to provide a quality education and with far less time and expense. It also allows for instant feed-back, so Mom knows if her son or daughter have grasped the material just explained.

2)*Home educators, as the sole or primary teacher, can enjoy their children more.* It follows quite naturally that when you are around the ones you love the most, you get great enjoyment out of it. I can think of no greater pleasure for a parent than to watch his child grow, develop, and share his life's experiences. If there is any tragedy of modern family life today, it is the fact that parents don't enjoy their children as much as they could. One of the most common parental regrets I have heard over the years in the counseling room is that they didn't spend enough quality time with their children while they were growing up. They wish they could turn back the hands of Father Time. But as we all know, that's impossible. Conventional schooling restricts your potential time with your child to the evenings and on weekends. I say "potential" because by the time you subtract personal time, eating and hygienic necessities, playing, recreation, homework, extracurricular school activities, social events, etc., how much time is left? Home schooling will not solve every time obstacle, but it will give you more time to enjoy your child.

3) *One-on-one education has fewer distractions.* Those of us who have had public education experience know the sorts of things that go on in a typical classroom—note passing, giggling, spitballs, wiggling, surly remarks, cheating, and disruptive behavior, to name a few. This makes learning a great deal more difficult. Add to that a child with a short attention span, and you can see why Johnny has trouble learning. The home environment is much quieter and much easier to control.

4) *A tutor can monitor closely the pulse of their child's development and can, with great effectiveness, concentrate on their child's needs and interests. Curriculum can be customized to meet the individual needs.* No one is as concerned and observant of a child's interests and talents as a loving mother or father. Hence, who better could help and encourage them to excel in their natural gifts and aptitudes? Who better to motivate them? Parental tutors can individualize their curriculum to maximize their child's education. In public school children are just part of the classroom mix, with little attention given to their individual needs.

Also, no one is as sensitive to a child's emotional hurts and needs as a concerned parent-tutor. Every child has his own individual personality needs and special concerns. Parents have the unique ability to become specialists on their child's overall growth and development like virtually no one else on the face of the earth.

5) *Home tutoring avoids the "spillover" exposure that can permeate private schools due to societal contamination.* Many children are placed in private schools for improper reasons: they need discipline; they need a change of friends; they need to counteract bad home life; etc. But the net effect is that many private schools are getting some malcontents of public education, along with their values, language,

and lack of discipline. While moral instruction admittedly receives higher priority in private schools, they have not been left untainted with confused societal mores. Young children in particular are susceptible to moral confusion.

In addition, many private school teachers hold the same views as their public counterparts. I have talked with Christian teachers who ardently hold to the teaching of evolution. Tainted by secular humanism and liberal continuing education courses, some teachers have slowly dismissed doctrines, values, and beliefs they at one time cherished so highly. Others have begun using faulty and ineffective methodologies used in the public school system.

Curriculum is also a concern. Some parochial schools use the same humanistic texts you would find in the state-funded elementary school down the road.

6) *Home schoolers enjoy a unique freedom that allows them to take advantage of practical education methods and experiences.* Conventional schools follow a rigid time structure that does not allow for a wide variety of family learning experiences in the daytime. For home educators, every hour of every day is a learning opportunity. Home educators do not have to maintain carefully defined fifty-minute class periods in the home. This is unnatural in the real world. How many employers give you an hour to work, ring a bell, give you another hour, ring a bell again, etc.? Instead, home schools have greater freedom and a more natural environment. This allows youngsters to be involved in first-hand learning experiences instead of confining learning primarily to books. They can also investigate a variety of occupations, apprenticeships, skills, and crafts. Teens might take on a part-time job working for Dad or a trusted community employer that will help them build responsibility and learn money-management skills.

7) *Home-schooled children can avoid the unhealthy atmosphere of early, formal, institutionalized education.* Many development psychologists have attested to the inherent dangers of early education. Here is how Dr. Moore puts it:

> For most children, reasonable maturity for formal learning seems to bring together or integrate all their senses and organs between the ages of eight and ten or eleven. We call this chronological age period the *integrated maturity level* or the optimum time for most normal children to start school, entering at the level of their age-mates at grade three, four, or five. They will quickly catch up and usually pass the children who started earlier. Parents can judge the maturity of their children within the eight-to-ten age range to deter-

mine their readiness for school. If there is any doubt, it is usually better to wait . . . .

There is no systematic body of research that indicates that young children who can be provided a good home will do as well or better if they go to preschool! The child who goes to school later, entering with his age-mates, nearly always comes out better academically, behaviorally, and socially.[138]

Other leading psychologists freely underscore the teaching quality of the home. David Elkind of the University of Rochester, Meredith Robinson of the Stanford Research Institute and William Rohwer of California-Berkeley join in suggesting that the home, provided it is good, is the best learning nest until near adolescence.[139]

8) *Tutoring offers more flexibility.* When a student is not straitjacketed to a conventional school schedule, the flexibility allows him to actually learn more. For example, home schoolers can make more field trips to a wider variety of places. Some businesses and manufacturing plants will not let a crowd of thirty or forty children tour their operations. But they might let a family group in. Many home educators combine vacations with extended learning opportunities. Flexibility allows children to travel with their parents during off-peak seasons when the roads are less congested and the expenses are lower.

Conclusion

No conventional school can hold a candle to a home school where the parental ingredients of love, responsibility and commitment are found. Are parents qualified? Many parents have the impression that the best teaching is done in the conventional classroom. The bloated educational bureaucracy is desperately trying to extol the virtues of teacher certification because it is the one credential that gives teachers standing and protects their jobs. So they continue to perpetrate this myth. In fact, any literate parent with discipline, patience, and some curricular help can start their child on a path which few classroom teachers could ever match. It might require the realignment of some priorities, but the benefits, in the long run, are tremendous.

Properly run, home schools are superior in academics, moral development, building spiritual growth, sociability, and physical nurturing. No conventional schoolroom can match the simplicity and power of the home in providing a three-dimensional, first-hand, Christian education. One-on-one tutoring has always been considered the preferred method of instruction. Finally, remember that the school, not the home, is the substitute.

FIVE

The "How" of Home Schooling

Though home schooling requires no special education or expertise, there are some practical considerations that make it easier to carry out. In this chapter, we want to take a look at the "how" of home schooling. Parents who follow a few simple guidelines outlined here will find that home schooling is not only within their ability to carry out but immensely rewarding as well.

The home schooling support structure gets better and better with each year that passes. It's better organized on the local, state, and national level than ever before. Every year new and better Christian curricula and teaching aids are becoming available. As the market continues to grow, more publishers and manufacturers are catering to it. New computer and video-based educational tools are being introduced like never before. Home schooling is much more resource-friendly than it was just a few years ago.

Religious Conviction vs. Preference

All potential home schoolers should understand the difference between a religious conviction and a preference. It is paramount that Christian parents home educate for the right reasons. Home schooling should be entered upon with the heartiest of Christian conviction. What is Christian conviction? *A Christian conviction is a strongly held personal belief rooted in Christian values and biblical principles that guides every aspect of your thinking and decision-making. Christian convictions compel you unto a distinctive lifestyle. You must do it! You have no other choice but to follow your conviction.* A preference to home school is a simple desire or want. It is a belief subject to change. But a conviction rests on an unshakable truth which you believe is ordained by God. A conviction is part of the fabric of your belief system. It is an unalterable truth you firmly believe is of divine origin. It is a fundamental, compelling interest based on God's Word.

There must be a conviction about parental responsibility under God! That is, that God has given you, not the government, the responsibility and the authority to educate your children. The United States Supreme Court, in the *Yoder v. Wisconsin* case, mandated that the free exercise of religious convictions may not be abridged by any law or state. In that 1972 case, a compulsory education statute was challenged by the Amish because they chose vocational home education in the years after grade eight through age sixteen. The Court ruled in favor of the Amish, stating that they were "protected by the free exercise clause of the First Amendment, and the traditional *interest of parents with respect to the religious upbringing of their children* . . . ."[140] (emphasis mine). Hence, home schooling out of religious conviction is the most legally defensible.

Home educators represent a wide variety of socio-economic, educational and religious backgrounds, but over 75 percent are Christians.[141] One thing most Christian home schoolers have in common is a conviction to make the necessary personal sacrifices to provide a solid Christ-centered education for their children. They home school not just because they want to, but because they are convicted that it is the right thing to do. Conviction sets committed home schoolers apart from the uncommitted. Those with conviction find home schooling has more meaning and purpose, and they are more likely to stay the course and not fall through the cracks of attrition a year or two down the road.

Since home schooling is not the choice for everyone, it is not something to be undertaken lightly or impulsively. The Bible says,

> "Suppose one of you, wants to build a tower. Will he not first sit down and estimate the cost to see if he has enough money to complete it? For if he lays the foundation and is not able to finish it, everyone who sees it will ridicule him saying, 'This fellow began to build and was not able to finish'" (Luke 14:28-29).

Count the costs and know what is involved. Understand that home schooling is a serious decision that requires a serious commitment. Your commitment will not only involve your time but also your money, emotions, abilities, and biblical resolve.

Home schoolers, as traditional families, will be challenged in various ways. To be sure, the mettle of their commitment will be tested. That is why it must be solid. A few things home schoolers face are: 1) continuing to pay local school taxes and financing public schools even though you chose an alternative education; 2) dealing with friends and relatives who may criticize or ridicule what they don't understand; and 3) a daily time commitment to your children's education that may force other activities out. Is it worth it? You bet it is! But a strong commitment must be there!

Understand the Goal of Christian Education

It is important for those considering home schooling to think on what the ultimate goal of Christian education is. The goal will determine the direction and presuppositions for the whole educational process. Historically, education has been provided with many purposes in mind. A summary of the educational goals of various individuals spanning the centuries follows:

1) Character, morality: Plutarch (Spartans), Herbart.
2) Perfect development: Plato, Rabelais, Montaigne, Comenius, Locke, Parker.
3) Happiness: Aristotle, James Mill.
4) Truth: Socrates.
5) Citizenship: Luther, Milton.
6) Mastery of nature: Bacon, Huxley.
7) Religion: Comenius.
8) Mental power, discipline: Locke, Van Dyke, Rendign.
9) Preparation for the future: Kant.
10) Habits: Rousseau, William James.
11) Unfolding: Froebel, Hegel.
12) Holy life: Froebel.
13) Interests: Herbart.
14) Knowledge: L. F. Ward.
15) Complete living: Spencer.
16) Culture, liberal education: Dewey.
17) Skill: Nathaniel Butler, E. C. Moore.
18) Inheritance of culture: N. M. Butler.
19) Socialization: W T. Harris, Dewey.
20) Social efficiency: Dewey, Bagley.
21) Adjustment: Dewey, Rendign, Chapman, Counts.
22) Growth: Dewey.
23) Organization of experience: Dewey.
24) Self-realization: Dewey, Tufts.
25) Satisfying wants: Thorndike, Gates.
26) Insight: Gentile.[142]

As you can see, there are many different views on the goal of education. The question is, what is the Christian view? Let us first state what it should not be. The ultimate goal of education should not be the knowledge of facts in a particular subject matter, nor mental discipline and the ability to think, nor the creative and/or spontaneous expression of problem-solving, nor social adjustment and efficiency. Each of these things have their place, but for the Christian, they should not be the ultimate goal of education. These are the goals of the secularist.

For the Christian, rather, the goal of education is spiritual restoration. The true aim of education is redemptive. The purpose of education is to restore the image of God in man through Christ, which leads to Christlike character and conduct. Parent educators are challenged to integrate all knowledge with a Christian worldview. Parents who find all things centered in God, coming from God, existing for God, and evaluated by God will view subject matter only as a means to a Christ-serving end. A child so taught will enter society as a witness and work effectively to bring society to the ideal of the kingdom of God.

The best way to begin Christian home schooling is with a proper understanding of the goal of education. The goal of education is to bring our children to God to be forgiven, renewed, and given purpose by Him. It is the transformation and growth of the child's body, mind, and spirit that they might serve God and live for Him. It is to so excite and direct the self-activities of the pupil that he will volitionally strive for the best possible integration of personality on the human level but directed toward the ultimate objective of the "perfect man in Christ." This is the true goal of education!

Practice Good Principles of Time Management

A frequent cry of many potential home schoolers is "I don't think I have enough time to home school. I can't even take care of the responsibilities I have now!" While home schooling does indeed take time, we must recognize that the above statement is really an admission of time mismanagement. Everybody at one time or another feels "Where has all my time gone? If I only had more time!" But in reality *each of us has enough time to do what God placed us here to do*. That must be our central focus—to work earnestly in what we have been placed here to do. God in His wisdom rations out the same amount of time each day to every human being: twenty-four hours. The question is, how are you spending yours? Are you investing diligently in the most important things God has placed in your life and under your stewardship? Or have you become a slave to busyness? If God has given you a family and children, they are your number one responsibility in life!

God in His love, goodness, and infinite wisdom will never overload you with more than you are able to do. Whenever you feel over-whelmed with time demands; details to take care of; frenzied with schedules to keep; exhausted by the demands of meetings, social engagements, shopping, household chores, etc., you are probably following the agenda of the world. God will never give you more to do than you can handle. We are the inconsiderate culprits who lay inordinate burdens upon our fragile shoulders. It is not God who squeezes out time for communion with Himself and fellowship with the family. No, these priorities are self-imposed.

Here are four principles for getting the most out of your time if you decide to home school. *First, get your priorities aligned with the Word of God.* As you walk in the will of God and His plan for your life, you will have all the time you need. That's the key to time management. Practice living according to God's plan and His priorities instead of your own. The following incident is recorded in Scripture to show the need for realignment of our priorities:

> As Jesus and his disciples were on their way, he came to a village where a woman named Martha opened her home to him. She had a sister called Mary, who sat at the Lord's feet listening to what he said. But Martha was distracted by all the preparations that had to be made. She came to him and asked, "Lord, don't you care that my sister has left me to do the work by myself? Tell her to help me!"
>
> "Martha, Martha," the Lord answered, "you are worried and upset about many things, but only one thing is needed. Mary has chosen what is better, and it will not be taken away from her" (Luke 10:38-42).

American life has become so complex. There is this form to fill out, that bill to be paid, children who need to be taken to ball practice; there are purchases to be made, household and automotive maintenance to perform, a lawn to be mowed, a house to be painted, meals to be prepared, schoolwork to do, investments to manage, deadlines to meet, and on and on. We get exhaustingly busy doing so many things that we forget the one thing that is the most important. What is that one thing that is really necessary? It is ordering your life with the Christian simplicity of God's Word. It is taking care of your spiritual life and raising and nurturing your family according to the plan of God. Home education can play a big part in God's plan for your family life.

Aligning your priorities with God's Word means to know the difference between what is *urgent* and what is *important*. There is a continual tension between all the things that press us into involvement and then there are those things that are important. The urgent rarely needs to be done today, or even in the immediate future. The important, however, should be placed at the top of our priority list where it belongs. General Eisenhower once insightfully remarked, "The urgent is seldom important, and the important is seldom urgent." The Christian family must constantly seek Holy Spirit-delineation between those things that are urgent and those that are truly important. Your children and family fall in the category of the important.

Second, *home schoolers must learn to say "No."* Over-busyness is not the sign of a wise man. Rather, it is a sign of someone who cannot properly manage his time. If you plan to home school you need to ask God to help you be a good time manager. It is a human tendency to imprudently stack our calendars with appointments and over-obligate ourselves. But that is not a characteristic of a well-ordered, Spirit-guided life.

The life of Jesus gives us insight into our own needs. In Luke 5:15-16 we read, "Yet the news about him spread all the more, so that crowds of people came to hear him and to be healed of their sicknesses. But Jesus often withdrew to lonely places and prayer." Even Jesus, the most gracious and compassionate man who ever lived felt it necessary to say "No," even when many other people were in need of healing. And note how He spent this time of social withdrawal— in spiritual communion with the Father. Jesus always remembered the "one thing" that was necessary.

Third, *home schoolers must learn to be flexible.* At one time or another everyone has their plans or routine interrupted. How you handle those interruptions is a sign of your Christian character and maturity. Do you deal with them with a quiet flexibility or some other way? Perhaps you just settled down for a rest and the phone rings. Or you're ready to leave on vacation when your child becomes ill. There are a thousand and one interruptions: an attention-seeking child who feels neglected, sickness, loss of employment, a surprise pregnancy, an unexpected bill, a spouse with a pressing need, or a death in the family. These are a few of the all-of-a-suddens that unexpectantly jump out in front of us at times.

It is important to realize that "interruptibility" is a mark of a good home schooler. Instead of falling apart at an unexpected circumstance, the mature parent displays the positive quality of accommodating resiliency. Human interruptions are often divine opportunities. What we may at first think of as an interruption may really be divine appointment to shape us and mold us.

Home school families should plan a built-in expansion factor in their daily schedule that allows for interruptions. Instead of getting bent out of shape when disruptions occur, the home schooling parent looks for an opportunity to serve God in and through the occasion. Granted, not every interruption is a move of God to get our attention or else we would get little schoolwork done. But there needs to be a sensitivity to the Spirit of God which examines the unexpected to see if His purposes might be served through a timely and Christ-honoring response.[143]

Fourth, *learn to make the most of every moment.* Home educators should have as their goal to do the most productive thing possible at every given moment. Time is too precious to waste. Along with the Psalmist, we should pray, "Teach us to number our days, that we may present to Thee a heart of wisdom" (Ps. 90:12 NAS). Your most valuable resource in life is time. Every day you have twenty-four hours to use and invest for the glory of God. Guard it jealously, for the hours you squander vanish forever. You have 86,400 seconds a day. Make everyone of them count. Getting the most out of time is what good Christian stewardship and successful home schooling is all about.

Scheduling

Sometimes it takes a while to set up a schedule that works for your family school, but once done it will only require infrequent and minor alterations. At first it may seem a bit rigid, but with time you will learn where your flexibility lies. You can pattern your own schedule following the sample below or even design your own. The main thing is that it works for you and helps you accomplish your goals and objectives.

Suggested Weekly Schedule For A Lower Elementary Student

TIME	MON.	TUES.	WED.	THURS.	FRI.
7:00-8:00	Rise, morning prayers, breakfast, make bed, get dressed, brush teeth (and any other morning routines)				
8:00-8:15	*Opening:* Prayers, Pledge of Allegiance, songs of praise, discuss day's schedule _____				
8:15-8:45	Bible instruction _____				
8:45-9:30	Math _____				
9:30-9:45	Break _____				
9:45-10:15	Reading _____				
10:15-10:45	Language Skills _____				
10:45-11:00	Handwriting _____				
11:00-12:00	Arts and Crafts _____				
12:00-1:00	Lunch/Recess _____				
1:00-1:30	Quiet Time _____				
1:30-3:15	Living skills (domestic work, apprenticeships, gardening, etc.), field trips				
3:15-4:00	Gymnastics or physical education				
4:00	Piano				

Evening Instruction by Dad

TIME	MON.	TUES.	WED.	THURS.	FRI.
7:00 7:45	Character Lesson	Science Lesson	Character Lesson	History Lesson	Character Lesson
7:45-8:15	Storytime Devotions	Storytime Devotions	Storytime Devotions	Storytime Devotions	Storytime Devotions

Every task is easier when you are organized. Home schooling is no exception. Good organization will make teaching easier for you and help your child maintain a strong learning interest. Further, it will eliminate many unnecessary behavioral problems. There are two logical areas where home educators need organization.

First, decide on how much time you plan to devote to sit-down, academic learning and how much time for life-experience learning. Both kinds are educationally important since learning occurs through both mediums. Though the time period for academic learning will vary with grade level and individual ability, a good average is approximately four hours a day for fourth grade up. Life learning should take place continually, with every remark, activity, and duty becoming a form of learning. Adjust sit-down academic time requirements according to your child's needs and age.

Never compromise regular teaching time on important subjects. Some subjects allow for more flexibility than others, such as science. Other subjects do not (i.e., character development, learning to read and write, Scripture memory). On crucial subjects, never allow yourself to get in the habit of saying, "I'll teach it if I have time left over." You will discover that leftover time will never come.

It is critical to avoid or minimize "time leaches." That is, those activities which quickly consume precious minutes and hours. Here are a few time leaches: unnecessary phone conversations, television viewing, overcommitments outside the home (recreational, civic, church, etc.), and excessive extracurricular activities. There are many other time-wasters that disguise themselves in a multitude of ways. Beware of them or frustration will soon be knocking on your door. Let me also be straightforward on a related point: except in extreme emergencies or justifiable financial necessity, mothers who home school should not work outside the home. It is unfair to the children who depend on your daily attention and guidance.

Early morning, right after breakfast, is a preferable time for many families to get most of the sit-down school work done. My home schooling experience has taught me the value of having a routine. Routines help both you and your child to know what is expected and when. However, don't be so rigid that the value of home school flexibility is destroyed.

Keep Character Development in the Forefront

The most important area of education is not the three R's, science, government, or even Bible history. No, the most important area of instruction is the development of godly character. It is the precious foundation-stone on which all other learning is built. If a person has great intellectual knowledge but little godly character, his life will not have much positive impact upon the world in which he lives. His life will become nothing more than a sandcastle, here today and gone tomorrow. It is true that a child must grow physically, mentally, emotionally, and socially, but the most important growth of all is spiritual.

Character is comprised of those qualities and virtues that emanate from the heart of Almighty God and make this world a better place to live. They comprise, but are not limited to, love, joy, peace, patience, kindness, goodness, gentleness, faithfullness, self-control (the nine fruits of the spirit), honesty, industry, initiative, obedience, attentiveness, thankfulness, meekness, diligence, friendliness, perseverance, a forgiving nature, etc. These are the traits that make a person complete and ready for life.

Corporations and businesses all across our country are concerned about the disturbing character of their youngest employees and new hires. There is a predominant self-centeredness and lack of devotion to the company. The most common attitude is, "What's in it for me?" instead of "How can I make this company better and more productive?" It has reached a critical point. Personnel offices everywhere are actively looking for young men and women whose character they can trust.

Sometimes the difference they look for is nothing more than a good attitude. Once a man was walking near a construction site in the city. He noticed several men digging with shovels in the earth. He walked up to one and said, "What are you doing?" He responded, "Are you blind? I'm digging a blasted ditch." The observer walked on around to the other side where he saw another man engaged in the same work. He inquired, "What are you doing?" The man turned and greeted him with a big smile and said, "Mister, I'm building a cathedral to God." The work was the same, but there was a big difference in the attitude.

Character-building requires a fear (godly respect) and love for God. Wise Solomon said, "The fear of the Lord is the beginning of knowledge, but fools despise wisdom and discipline" (Proverbs 1:7):

It must be sought diligently as for a treasure. Again Solomon says, "If you look for it as for silver, and search for it as for hidden treasure, then you will understand the fear of the Lord and find the knowledge of God" (Proverbs 2:4, 5). Home schoolers should learn the value of a daily, family wisdom search or Bible time.

When a child receives Jesus as his personal Savior, he is born again spiritually into the kingdom of God. At this point, he starts on a lifelong spiritual growth process. Hence, development of godly character is the most important fruit to nurture in your child's life. It also happens to be the most difficult and demanding to instill. Why? Because the world, the flesh, and the Devil all fight and rebel ferociously against the inculcation of godly character. Paul said, "For our struggle is not against flesh and blood, but against the rulers, against the authorities, against the powers of this dark world and against the spiritual forces of evil in the heavenly realms" (Ephesians 6:12). These demonic forces are continually vying for control of your child's heart and soul. They want nothing more than to rob him of his love for God and the character that His Spirit gives.

Since godly character springs from a deep relationship with Jesus Christ, you must teach your child to pray, and to read and commit to memory the Scriptures, and model for him as a Christian witness, teach him the importance of obedience to God's Word, and seek out fellowship with like-minded Christians. Your child needs to be taught to love God and to daily seek after Him with all his heart. As your child develops a deep and abiding relationship with Jesus Christ, he will be enabled to grow in divine character. A brief biblical explanation of the teaching process might be helpful here. The Bible uses several key words for teaching and training. One of these words is the Hebrew *chanak*, which means "to train, dedicate, or make narrow." This word occurs five times in the Bible: Deuteronomy 20:5 (two times), 1 Kings 8:63, 2 Chronicles 7:5, Proverbs 22:6. The ancient root of this word means "to make narrow" or "to strangle." Applied to the teaching process, it implies that parents are to restrict the path their children may take. The Bible teaches that parents are responsible for getting their child started in the right direction. A child must not be allowed to go whatever course or direction he so chooses. Contrary to the leading of his old nature, parents are to set him on the right course and help him remain there. His path must be restricted or narrowed, for ". . . narrow the road that leads to life, and only a few find it" (Matt. 7:14) .[144]

Proverbs 22:6 says, "Train (*chanak*) a child in the way he should go, and when he is old he will not turn from it." The common usage of the word *chanak* implies dedication of a building or child (cf. references above). The Old Testament rite of dedicating the Temple is analogous to the dedication of a child, especially in the fact that both are done when they are new or young. The only comparative difference is that for a child, dedicating and training is not a one-time initiation but a continual process.[145]

Another biblical word for the teaching process is *shanan*, which means "to sharpen, to inculcate, to teach by repetition." Godly values and standards are taught best when children are inculcated with the Word of God repetitiously throughout the day. Deuteronomy 6:6-7 clearly gives this responsibility to parents: "These commandments that I give you today are to be upon your hearts. Impress them on your children. Talk about them when you sit at home and when you walk along the road, when you lie down and when you get up." The holy writer clearly intends for godly teaching and training to take place daily, utilizing every opportunity. Obviously, Christian truths are to be repeated continually until the child begins to walk in the way of God on his own.[146]

Yet another biblical word for the teaching process is the word *lamad*, which means "to teach by intensive drill" (cf. Deut. 4:10 and 11:9). *Lamad* is used to describe the goading of cattle (Hosea 10:11), and the training of military recruits (1 Chron. 5:18). A goad is a sharp stick used to penetrate animal hide to prod and thus direct cattle. Children sometimes need to be figuratively prodded to keep them moving in a godly direction. Soldiers are trained intensively that they might be prepared for the potential threat of warfare. We know that every Christian is subject to intense spiritual warfare from demonic origin. Hence a child must be taught intensively how to deal with it, like a soldier preparing for battle.[147]

Implicit in biblical thought is the idea that teaching authority has been divinely given to the parents. That is where it properly belongs. Like the charge given to the apostles to ". . . present everyone perfect in Christ" (Col. 1:28), parents are charged with a similar training responsibility for their children and are held accountable for the end result. No one can adequately fill the shoes of this great responsibility quite like parents. To reach maximum effectiveness, proper teaching of character requires 1) daily inculcation, 2) life application, 3) parental modeling, and 4) merging with all other disciplines. Who better than parents can fulfill these qualifications?

This is not to say that parents are an educational island unto themselves, teaching and imparting knowledge apart from any social context whatsoever. Parents must also view their teaching and training responsibilities as citizens in their local community and, more importantly, as part of the body of Christ. It is to be remembered that home schooling is an educational endeavor centered around the home but extends outside of it as well.

The important thing for parents to know is that true education should begin with, be centered around, and end with their child's love for God and the development of Christian character. This is both the origin and apex of all knowledge. Home educators have the rewarding advantage of giving it the priority it is due.

Teach by Example

There is an aphorism that goes like this: "What you do speaks so loudly that I can't hear what you say." There is truth evident herein. Children learn more by what they see than by what they hear. Well-intentioned parents often talk about the importance of solid values and Christian character but have a lifestyle that is inconsistent with what they teach. Parents must learn that how they live is far more important than what they say. For example, if a father tells his son that personal devotions are important, and yet he himself is never seen praying or reading his Bible, which carries the greater weight? If a mother tells her daughter that internal beauty is more important than external, yet spends excessive time and money on cosmetic enhancements, what has she really taught? If parents tell their children that TV viewing is a waste of time, and yet themselves spend hours in front of it, what do the children really learn? "Monkey see, monkey do," so to speak. While children aren't monkeys, they do emulate what they see. Guard yourself against empty words by practicing what you teach. The best and most lasting form of childhood education comes by the observation of parental example.

Children can grow cognitively or intellectually without growing spiritually. That is why children can easily parrot beliefs and values their parents want to hear without believing it in their own heart. For example, a child can recite John 3:16 and yet not know personally the God of love described therein. He can recite Ephesians 4:32 and still be mean and unforgiving to his brothers, sisters, and playmates. Satan's work is very subtle here. Like adults, children can mimic Christian behavior but still be spiritually lukewarm. Do not look merely for intellectual recitation of values and beliefs. Rather, look for complete transformation of character and lifestyle which conforms to the will of God.

It all comes down to what your educational goals and priorities are. Do you want a child who is very intelligent but who lacks beauty of character? Or do you want a child who not only knows the three R's but loves and honors God with his heart? Both lifestyles are learned. One reason we have many problems with public school children these days is because of the so-called "wall of separation between church and state," a phrase found nowhere in the Constitution. It was never the intention of the founding fathers to expel Christianity from the schoolhouse. However, many parents have been propagandized into thinking their children should get head-knowledge in school and heart-knowledge in church. But in reality the two go hand in hand. When they are separated, peer pressure and influence throughout the week will teach significantly more values than parents can deprogram on evenings and weekends or that the pastor can unteach on Sunday mornings. This creates irrreconcilable value contamination. The big advantage of home education is the ability to teach Christian values by example and through interdisciplinary coordination with the Word of God. This is how godly education takes place.

Learning is a continual process where a child absorbs information from many sources. All five senses are employed in the process. But there are many things Christian parents do not want their child to emulate. Because of this, a child's environment should be well-regulated. Below are some key areas where children can be negatively affected by their environment. An element of control and/or restraint must be placed in each of these six areas:

1) television and video viewing.
2) the friends they keep.
3) the books they read and music they listen to.
4) the forms of entertainment they engage in.
5) the places they are allowed to go.
6) the toys and possessions they are allowed to collect.

There is one thing that is essential to effectively educate your child unto godliness. You must live what you teach. You must be what you ask your child to become. David said, "I will walk in my house with blameless heart" (Ps. 101:2). You must set the godly example yourself while orally teaching him to do it. In addition to your own example, you must also pray for him. Every Christian parent should spend time on their knees seeking divine guidance and protection for their child. How else can they fulfill the command of Ephesians 6:4, where parents are commanded to bring up their children in the nurture and admonition of the Lord? Many hours of behind-the-scenes prayer is a crucial part of the educational process. Diligently ask God to give you the wisdom to present knowledge in an effective way.

Organize for Effectiveness

Planning and coordination is the home educator's best friend. Parents who organize will find that home schooling is not a difficult endeavor. It may be challenging at times, but it is always worthy of your best effort. Sure, you will make mistakes, but you will learn by them as well. Part of home schooling, like parenting, involves some trial and error. When you make an error in judgment, you will find your child is quite understanding and accommodating. Perfection is not required of home educators, but a measure of organization is. And with it, you will find remarkable success.

Organize your supplies. Have a specific place for commonly used items like textbooks, ruler, scissors, pens and pencils, paper, computer disks, crayolas, water paints, glue, etc. Your child will enjoy knowing where to find these items and helping you keep them neat and orderly. Many parents have plastic trays or tackle boxes to hold supplies for the younger students of the family.

Determine the Place for School

Anything that helps your children learn is an educational asset. Having a specific place or location will help your children make the learning identification they need in a home environment. Many home educators establish a certain room for instruction, and then purchase instructional furniture like school desks, a marker board, globe, maps, alphabet charts, and even an American flag. All these are helpful, but none are absolutely necessary. Others have had great success use nothing more than their kitchen table. Whatever place you choose, make sure that it has good lighting and is relatively free from bothersome and unnecessary distractions.

Choose a Curriculum

Before you consider curriculum, it is helpful to assess your child's learning style and temperament. Is he visually, auditorially, or kinesthetically oriented? "Come again?," you say. This simply means some children learn best by seeing, some by hearing, and some by doing. A simple test for identifying a child's strengths and weaknesses is to use a list of numbers (about eight or nine will do). First say them to your child, in order, and ask your child to repeat as many back to you in order as he can. Then write a list of numbers, show it to your child, and ask him to again repeat them out loud back to you. You might notice a significant difference in how many numbers your child is able to recall in each situation. A child who recalls more of the spoken numbers is stronger auditorially (hearing), while a child who recalls more written numbers is a stronger visual-spatial learner.[148] For more information on learning styles get a copy of *One of a Kind* by LaVonne Neff, published by Multnomah.

Keep in mind that a child's modality can change or he could have a combination of several modalities. Categories are seldom as clear-cut as they are made to sound. But it is helpful to know.

Choosing curricula is one of the important decisions you make in the area of home schooling. Look carefully at the curriculum of veteran home schoolers before you buy. Talk with them and ask about its strengths and weaknesses. Learn all you can before ordering. Many larger communities sponsor home school book fairs which expose you to a multitude of publishers and their educational wares. But in the final analysis, remember that there is no "perfect" curriculum, and you will not ruin your children by selecting the wrong curriculum.

Curriculum usually falls into four categories:

- *Traditional*—These are textbooks and accompanying workbooks designed for use in conventional schools. The advantage of traditional curriculum is that the books can be reused by younger children again and again, since the material is not consumed. The disadvantage is this material is designed and structured with a typical classroom setting in mind. Some parents feel it's too rigid for use in the home environment, because it demands too much teacher instruction and involvement. Samples: Bob Jones University Press, A Beka Books.
- *Self-Paced*—This kind of curriculum is less teacher-intensive than traditional texts. It is primarily comprised of consumable workbooks offered in a variety of subjects. The advantage of self-paced curriculum is the user-friendly teacher aids that make it easy to get started. Also, the workbooks can be easily structured for completion by weeks or by the month, allowing the student to see small but encouraging accomplishments along the way. The disadvantage is that the workbooks cannot be reused, and parents must fight the temptation to let the child teach himself apart from daily student/teacher interaction. Samples: Accelerated Christian Education, Alpha Omega Publishing.
- *Unit Study*—This is a lesson plan which merges or integrates several academic disciplines under the study of a single theme or topic. The advantage of unit studies is that when they are properly prepared, they require less teaching time than separate lessons on a variety of school subjects. Students enjoy seeing the application of various subjects to a certain topic or field of study. The disadvan-

tage is that unit studies require more work in planning than pre-structured curriculum. Samples: Konos, The Weaver, Alta Vista.

• *Home-designed by parents*—Parents may use a mixture of all the above curricula simultaneously or at different times. The advantage of home designed is the customizing that can occur for the student. For example, one publisher may be strong in math or history, while another's forte may be language arts or science. Parents select their choice for each subject and then integrate the curriculum for the child. This is the method we prefer in my home. The disadvantage is that it requires trial and error experimentation to find out what works best for your children.

Below are some of the things you should consider no matter which curriculum you choose.

1) Is it Christian in nature?
2) Is it well-organized for both the teacher and the child?
3) Was it designed for individual or group instruction?
4) Are teacher manuals and lesson plans available?
5) If all your subjects are chosen from the same publishing house, does the publisher offer a master plan which coordinates the teaching of all subjects?
6) Does the reading curriculum teach true phonics?
7) Does it undergird solid morality and godly character?
8) Does it have a proven track record among other home educators?
9) How are children testing who use this curriculum?
10) Can the same educational objectives be accomplished less expensively? Inexpensive material which teaches the same information is often available.
11) Does it overly emphasizes worksheets/busywork?
12) Is it lean on teaching hints and suggestions?

Begin with the curriculum that seems easiest for you to use. I recommend new home schoolers with children second grade and up,start with a self-paced curriculum. Remember, your first choice doesn't have to last forever. After your first year or two, you will likely reevaluate anyway. If you're like most, you will end up using a combination of different publishers.

Cost of material varies widely, but figure on average about $350 a child per year. Conventional curriculum usually costs less than self-paced curriculum, especially when it's used through several children, but the latter requires less teacher preparation. Let the kind of curriculum you need be the deciding factor, not the initial monetary outlay, otherwise you might be disappointed down the road. Oftentimes you can save money if you buy your curriculum at a state convention or book fair. When ordering by mail, allow time for delivery, remembering that suppliers periodically back-order due to heavy demand, especially right before school starts. So order as early as possible.

Learn the Secret of Teamwork

Teamwork is making the maximum use of available human resources in your home. Any project can become burdensome if it is left in the hands of only one person.

Moms are an essential part of the team. In most homes she usually takes on the bulk of day-to-day teaching responsibilities. In fact, mothers provide about eighty-eight percent of home schooling instruction.[149] Moms can find help and encouragement at local support groups and from other home schooling moms. Without a doubt, home schooling takes time and a deep commitment, but the fruits are worth the effort. Energy limitations mandate that priorities be set, as you will not have time for everything. This is especially true for moms with younger children. Often it means the temporary acceptance of less-than-perfect housekeeping conditions. Dads need to give special empathy in this area and help out as much as possible. It is all part of teamwork.

Older children also serve as members of the team. Since younger children naturally imitate the behavior and attitudes of their older siblings, the latter become very valuable as teaching assistants. Hence, home educators will want to utilize them as much as possible. Older brothers and sisters convey surprising amounts of basic knowledge and skills. They can help answer questions; explain directions or teaching concepts; and model independent study habits, attitudes, and character traits they themselves have mastered. But older children should never become an educational substitute for the parents, as that would cheat the younger ones out of essential time they need with Mom and Dad and hinder their learning. In addition, every child should be expected to learn and assume domestic responsibilities such as washing dishes, sorting clothes, meal preparation, sewing, etc. Sometimes we feel that it's easier and faster to carry out home tasks ourselves. But in the long run, the time investment you make to spread out these responsibilities will make your home more domestically efficient, while serving to instruct in important practical skills as well.

Dad, as head of the household, carries the ultimate responsibility for the proper training of his children. Since most Dads work full-time to supply the family's needs, they usually delegate the primary day-to-day teaching responsibilities to Mom. She brings the consistency that is needed in order to maintain a place of learning. But Mom can't do it all alone, so she calls on the assistance of Professor Dad. Dad's involvement is covered in detail in the next chapter.

Bottom line, the whole family gains by utilizing the team teaching concept. Both Mom and Dad's work is made much easier, younger children are given extra guidance and attention, and the older children have their own learning and awareness of others reinforced. Teamwork builds mutual cooperation and respect in the educational process as well as family camaraderie, unity, and love.

Multilevel Teaching

Home educators with two or more children will want to learn the value of multilevel teaching. Teaching children of various ages or grade levels requires a little extra planning, but it is by no means an impossible task. After all, this was the method of the old one-room schoolhouse that helped launch early American education. Since all children need time and attention, you may, at times, wish you had six arms and could be three places at once. However, organization will allow you to make educational progress while keeping everyone happy most of the time. Though challenges will still arise, you can make multilevel teaching much easier by following two basic rules.

Rule number one is to teach jointly as many subjects as possible. Science, physical education, history, and character development are all examples of subjects that will frequently allow this. Science projects and experiments can easily become a family endeavor with great enjoyment and satisfaction. Think how much fun the family could have on the subject of weather. For example, while younger children are learning to distinguish between the basic weather conditions of hot and cold, dry and wet, windy and still, the older children can be making instruments that scientifically measure wind speed and direction (i.e., wind sock, weather vane). Physical education classes can be a joint venture that builds both a spirit of competition and cooperation. Exercise and learning good health practices are more enjoyable in a warm, family environment and can be easily taught on a multiage basis. There are subjects where a younger child cannot really understand what is going on but still enjoys working side by side with big brother or sister. For example, a kindergartner may not understand second-grade math but may still enjoy writing random numbers on a sheet of paper while the older student works. The key to combined-grade teaching is cognizance of the different attention spans and levels of comprehension in your children, while adjusting your expectations accordingly.

Rule number two is simply this: at times where joint teaching is not an option, learn to productively divide your time and attention. For example, an older child should be assigned lessons conducive to independent work, while a younger child needs one-on-one tutoring. You can expect a first or second-grader to occupy more time and attention since you are laying for them the groundwork for all future educational advancement. By occasionally checking in on the more mature scholars, time will be kept available to those minds which presently demand more personal attention. By emulating your example, older children will learn how to manage and efficiently occupy their own time when you are temporarily inaccessible. This in itself will greatly help them towards autonomous evaluation of the varying circumstances of life and give them a healthy dose of personal discipline to boot. Naturally, you will want to be continually sensitive to the older child's feelings and needs.

Record Keeping and Testing

Remember the eleventh commandment, "Thou shalt keep good records." While rare, it's possible you may be asked by a state child-welfare officer or local school district official to respond to request of reasonable inquiry. Keeping annual standardized achievement tests, grades, attendance records, and written work (insofar as storage is feasible) will arm you with the credible documentation you need. They will be invaluable in defending your home school validity in court or for preparing a transcript for college entrance. Several curriculum supply houses offer good record-keeping tools to assist you.

Annual norm-referenced achievement testing is another important area in the home school. Testing will assist you in reviewing your child's academic progress, point out where he needs to go, what his strengths and weaknesses are, and tell how he is scoring against his peers. Testing promotes learning by stimulating study and helps students with recall, which enhances the memory process. Testing, therefore, is just another tool in the educational process. It also manifests the extent to which parental academic goals are being reached. Hence, home educators are strongly encouraged to test their children once a year with a standardized test, maintaining a file of the test results. Parents do not need to submit the results to anyone, except where required for legal or academic purposes (i.e., a court of law, entering a school or university).

I realize there are differing opinions on whether or not home school students need standardized testing. However, if test results are kept in perspective and the indicators of progress are properly understood, then in my opinion, the positives of testing outweigh the negatives. Home schoolers who plan to go to college will be required to take the SAT, ACT, or a similar exam. Those who have tested all along will be familiar with that type of testing and will be less likely to choke on an entrance exam. Some states require home schoolers to be tested.

Standardized testing can be carried out in several ways. Parents can obtain and administer the test themselves. You will usually have to mail in the answer sheet and wait for the results from a scoring service. However, authorities may consider the results of parentally-given tests skewed or compromised. To avoid this perception, home schooling parents often band together and have a neutral, third-party proctor administer the test (a co-op). Or you can have your child tested at a local Christian school or an umbrella school for home schoolers. If the test results are for your own personal use and you are not concerned how outsiders view the credibility factor, Bob Jones University Press has a testing and evaluation service that allows you to administer the test at home. Parents may need to meet certain qualification requirements. For information call BJU at 1-800-845-5731.

I recommend regular testing with well-recognized instruments like the Iowa Basic Skills Test, Stanford Achievement Test, or the California Achievement Test. While acknowledging there are differing opinions on whether home-schooled children should be tested or not, in the final analysis the parents must be the final judge.

There are two cautions regarding testing. First, testing should not be used primarily for peer comparison. A hidden danger lurks therein which can cause parents to unfairly judge their success and effectiveness solely on test results. A child's self-worth can also be negatively affected by an overemphasis on test results. Wise parents judge their success in light of the educational goals they have for their children. They realize that test results do not give the whole picture. Some very bright children test poorly. Testing at best only measures academic acuity. It cannot measure the heart or the soul. It is better to view test results as just one piece in the whole evaluative pie. Parental standards of success should be based on many factors, including comparison with your own educational goals, general observations of a child's daily/weekly academic performance, and growth of his overall character and self-esteem. All these factors, along with test results, give a more accurate picture of what is going on in your child.

A second caution is to remember that the most important kind of evaluation comes from within the child himself. A child should learn to look within his own mind, heart, and soul and make an evaluation of his progress. He should also learn to assess his priorities. Show your child the importance of making evaluative determinations based on God's Word. Guide him to ask questions like these: "Who am I in God's eyes? What is my purpose and role in the world? Am I moving steadily toward that purpose? Am I making spiritual progress, growing in my love for God? Am I giving my best in everything I do, including my schoolwork?" When a child is able to answer these kinds of questions, then he is able to more readily evaluate his pursuit of academic objectives and take the appropriate action.

Watch for two extremes: avoiding achievement tests altogether and overemphasizing them. Evaluation is a necessary part of the education process. So learn to make testing an enjoyable and pleasant experience for both you and your child. You will find it has several benefits.

Discipline and Manners
Home educators have the opportunity to reinstate the qualities of discipline, manners, and respect that are personally and culturally valuable. Like every other form of knowledge, they are a learned behavior and must be taught.

When children are small, their world must be structured and ordered for them. But as they grow, they should be taught the importance of self-discipline. Discipline is required in the spiritual, physical, mental, and social realms. A child needs to learn the spiritual value of daily personal devotions and the danger of its neglect. Physically, he should be taught the right kinds of foods to eat, how to exercise properly, and good hygienic procedures. He should learn the consequences of eating junk food and physical inactivity. Mentally, he must be taught that knowledge requires a price. He must take time to read, learn, and ask questions beyond what is absolutely necessary. Socially, he must learn to discern those places and friends that are good and those that are not. He needs to learn when he has socialized enough.

There is a thread, however, that ties all four of these areas together. A child needs to become master of his time. Time is a very precious commodity, and we have all been dealt the same daily amount. Yet it is so fleeting, so easy to waste. Scripture says we should be "making the most of every opportunity, because the days are evil" (Eph. 5:16). Some will accomplish great things in their life with the amount they are allotted. Others will achieve little or nothing. Learning to be the master of time requires learning how to set priorities. To gain discipline in this area will place a child in the top one percent of Americans. But here again, he learns by example.

Manners are an all-but-forgotten growth area in modern life.

How refreshing it is to be around children who have been taught graceful table manners, politeness, respect for elders, and proper social etiquette. Jesus always exhibited the best of manners regardless of where He went or what He did. Teach your child to emulate His example. No one likes to be around a rude, spoiled, insensitive brat. The Bible says, "A child left to itself disgraces his mother" (Prov. 29: 15b). Bad manners are not something a child grows out of, but something he grows up with. Dads, do you openly complement Mom's appearance and cooking? Simple courtesies like this show your children that you respect their mother. Do your child a great service by teaching him thoughtfulness, graciousness, amiability, and excellence of behavior. It will help him go a long way in life. Remember, your children and their manners are a reflection of you.

Field Trips and Extracurricular Activities

Field trips are an important and exciting part of education. Whether it be the library, ballet, bakery, museum, historical site, or a manufacturing plant, children will always be elated with these memorable experiences. Make sure you count field trips as a part of your overall school program. Mom and Dad may be the tour guides, or the children may travel with a group of area home schoolers. Either way, these educational excursions help make the learning process more meaningful. The trips need not be exotic and can be merged with your daily family activities. Even a routine trip to your local bank vault, shoe repair shop, or veterinarian can become a learning experience. Encourage your children to record these trips to help reinforce learning. Photographs, written reports, and crayon picture booklets are several ways this can be accomplished.

Extracurricular activities are also important but should not be overemphasized. You may want your children to take voice or instrument lessons through a local music instructor. Or you may take advantage of gymnastics, swimming, ballet, art, or ceramics offered at a nearby YMCA or city recreation center. There are many extracurricular possibilities. Like field trips, remember to count them as a part of your overall school program. Not only will your child learn through these activities, but they will provide a good opportunity to round out their educational process.

Grading

Regular letter grading is optional in a home school setting. The best advice here is simply this: use routine letter grading in school work if it helps stimulate educational growth, and dispense with it if it causes a negative learning environment. In the end, grades become a record keeping necessity in order to maintain a transcript. Grades, like testing procedures, should be viewed as an educational tool. If regular grading causes your child anxiety, it is suggested that you make comments on the top of their school papers that give praise or positive reinforcement for work well done. Children respond favorably to this.

Length of School Year

The emphasis on home schooling should be on full-life education, therefore, don't allow yourself to be hemmed in by the public school cycle. One of the unique strengths of educating at home is being able to maximize on year-round learning. Summer is a good time to do outdoor experiments or to learn the principles of gardening. Vacations are also a terrific opportunity to learn. We should not think of education as a nine-month-a-year activity. Instead, plan for it to be a continual learning experience on the child's road to maturity and preparation for life.

Some parents choose to parallel their academic and holiday scheduling to that of the local school system, believing this helps the child to avoid feelings of oddity while giving his mind a rest. This is fine as long as you encourage the educational process to continue. Other parents feel that teaching year-round takes a great deal of pressure off them since they have a longer time to complete course requirements. Whichever way you choose, remember that children are learning even in the summer months. Certain areas like character education and Scripture memory should never cease.

Managing with Preschoolers

Parents with preschoolers will be delighted to know that many families are successful home educating with preschoolers around . . . without going nuts. Why? Because most home schoolers consider children a joy and a blessing. Sure, preschoolers will at times challenge you and tax your patience. However, the key is to learn to work with and around their needs.

For example, let the small ones play quietly nearby while you are teaching. Preferably, encourage them to play with toys that build creativity and motor development, such as Lincoln Logs and Legos. Discourage profitless computer games like Nintendo. Sometimes they will make a mess that they can't clean up without adult supervision. Simply take a short break or have your child momentarily practice Scripture memory or math facts. You might even have him read aloud to you. When small children go down for a nap, that is a time period that needs to be exploited to the fullest. Home schooling with preschoolers is a challenge but definitely not an impossible task.

Home Schooling High Schoolers

Don't be frightened by the concept of teaching your teen through high school. The first thing many parents do is try to imagine themselves teaching molecular biology, physics, chemistry, or Latin. But then, how many high schoolers actually take these subjects? The reality is they involve fewer than two percent of high school students. Indeed, your children may not go that far. If they do, and the subject matter becomes too difficult for you, you can always join a home school co-op (discussed later in this chapter.) My children have used co-ops for advanced math courses and foreign language. However, most parents can effectively teach the bulk of high school courses just by making use of the teacher's manual.

High schoolers have the unique advantage of independent study and critical thinking. Learn to use this to your advantage. Home schooling teens requires more accountability for planning and evaluation by parents. But think of the tremendous impact you have on their lives as their sole curriculum selector and guidance counselor.

It is important to train your teen to abide by a schedule and keep a daily journal detailing his work. Otherwise, independent study can easily be sabotaged by time bandits. Lay out clearly what you expect of them each week, where you expect them to be at the end of the month, middle of the year, and by year's end. Then monitor their progress by reviewing their work and their daily journal.

All the reasons you chose to home school your child before high school still exist during high school years, plus a few more. A later chapter reviews sixteen reasons to home school through high school.

Apprenticeships

Too many students today are enrolled in college and do not really know why. Most are convinced it's a necessity in order to get a good job. Others go because it is the family tradition. However, since colleges are inordinately expensive, have shifted dramatically to the extreme liberal left, and since so many graduates can't find jobs, many home school parents are reconsidering the alternatives to college. Some parents encourage their children to do both—learn a trade and experience college.

The *Encyclopedia Americana* defines an apprenticeship as "the procedure by which young persons acquire the skills necessary to become proficient in a trade, craft, art, or profession under the tutelage of a master practitioner." Apprenticeships comprise four areas of learning: novice, journeyman, craftsman, and master. Since apprenticeships usually entail a balance between book learning and hands-on experience, parents should keep in mind that they are not automatically exempt from any cost in higher education. There will still be some expenses for transportation, books, and tools of the trade. However, it will be much less than the cost of a college education.

Apprenticeships help teens with a unique opportunity to develop career and life goals. It is not uncommon for students to desire a certain vocation, only to change their minds once they have actually experienced it. For example, your teen may think he wants to be a dental technician but, after working alongside one for a month, decides he would rather be a dentist. It is much better to find this out before time and money is spent than to discover it the hard way.

Apprenticeships also serve as an opportunity to receive practical experience in a pre-determined field. Home school teens often finish their schoolwork in fewer hours, having time left for obtaining hands-on experience in learning a preferred skill or trade such as carpentry, electrical, photography, midwifery, auto mechanics, etc. In addition, apprenticing teens can earn and save money to establish their own business at the right time.

There's a superb Christian resource by Ronald and Inge Cannon entitled *Apprenticeship Plus: Preparing Lives Unto Service* that gives home schoolers extensive information about preparing for apprenticeships. For information write:

Education Plus
P.O. Box 1029
Mauldin, SC 29662

Larry Burkett has an excellent evaluation program to help parents assess their teen's gifts, talents, and interests. It is entitled *Career Pathways*, and can be ordered by calling Christian Financial Concepts at (800) 822-1943 or (800) 722-1976.

To get his feet wet, your teen might look into internships that offer exploratory training opportunities without the commitment of an apprenticeship. A good information handbook for this is *Internships* by Peterson's Guides, which lists over 50,000 on-the-job training opportunities available through internships. The Home School Legal Defense Association has an internship program for 18- to 21-year-olds who were home schooled through their high school years. The internships run on a six-month rotation schedule—from January through June, and from July through December—and enable young adults to learn writing, researching, and lobbying skills on home school issues. Research abilities, proficiency in WordPerfect, experience in political and public relations activities, and HSLDA membership are a plus. Housing will be provided as well as a modest salary to cover living expenses. For more information, call or write:

Intern Supervisor
HSLDA
P.O. Box 159
Paeonian Springs, Virginia 22129
(703) 338-5600

The Distance Education and Training Counsel offers many home study or correspondence courses that provide complete vocational training. Some lead to academic degrees. For information, a list of subjects and accredited institutions, write:

Distance Education and Training Council
1601 18th Street, N.W.
Washington, D.C. 20009-2529

The Bureau of Apprenticeship and Training recognizes over 800 occupations as apprenticeable. You can obtain a list of these occupations by writing:

U.S. Department of Labor
Employment and Training Administration
Washington, D.C. 20210

Graduating Home Schoolers

If you plan to graduate your high schooler from home school, the process is not difficult. First, make sure your son or daughter completes the equivalent of regular high school level courses and the number of credits recognized for graduation in your state. If certain subjects are required, like state history, keep a record of that as well. Second, determine a school name and prepare a detailed transcript. Blank transcripts are available through several Christian curriculum suppliers. Type the transcript up in a professional-looking manner, as it will be required by all colleges and universities your student applies to. Also, issue a diploma with the date of graduation. You can obtain a diploma made especially with home schoolers in mind from the Home School Legal Defense Association. Some home schoolers use the GED to show completion of high school, but a regular graduation is usually more meaningful. If a college requires your teen to take a GED for enrollment purposes, view it as entrance requirement instead of the mode of graduation. Third, though optional, formally recognize your teen's accomplishments through a public graduation. Many home school co-ops and support groups now offer group commencement services to their affiliates. This helps validate the completion of their efforts and makes them feel good about their accomplishment.

College Opportunities at Home

There are some 14 million students in college today. Nearly all will be strongly influenced by one or more of the approximately 600,000 American professors. Considering the current state of American colleges and universities, parents should seriously evaluate whether they want their teen to enroll as a resident, on-campus student. A better route that avoids the sea of degeneracy at secular universities is becoming a day student and commuting to classes. Or consider taking college courses at home by correspondence. Several accredited universities now offer Associate of Arts and Bachelor of Arts degrees solely by correspondence. Most will require your teen to take the SAT or ACT and submit their scores to the admissions office. There are preparation courses and computerized tutorials that will help them improve their score.

Below is a listing of resources where you can obtain information about nontraditional college credit at home:

- *The Independent Study Catalog: A Guide to Continuing Education Through Correspondence Courses* (Peterson's Guides, Dept. CS93, P.O. Box 2123, Princeton, NJ 08543-2123). Both high school and college level courses are listed.
- *The Electronic University: New Educational Alternatives for Student and Adults* (Peterson's Guides). Profile of colleges that offer degrees through innovative means.
- *Bear's Guide to Earning College Degrees Non-Traditionally*, by John Bear (C & B Publishing, P.O. Box 826, Benicia, CA 94510).
- *Walston and Bear's Guide to Earning Religious Degrees Non-Traditionally*, by Rick L. Josh Walston and John B. Bear. (C & B Publishing).

Joining the Military

Home-educated students have entered the military and the various armed forces academies. Though there has been some discrimination in the past because home schoolers lack a traditionally-issued diploma, the situation is improving. The military uses a three-tier educational policy which favors graduates of traditional high schools. However, this policy is subject to change since home schoolers have the second lowest attrition rate of all groups inducted into the military. Military enlistment by home schoolers can be aided with good ASVAB (Armed Services Vocational Aptitude Battery) test results and assistance from the Home School Legal Defense Association. A home schooler from

Mississippi received the highest ASVAB scored ever obtained in that state. Another option is to successfully complete one year of college before applying for enlistment. Those desiring to apply for a military academy appointment are encouraged to contact HSLDA early for suggestions.

By the way, military parents are allowed to home school their children. This right has not gone without occasional challenges by some overly zealous commanders and uninformed social workers. As the movement grows and the caliber of home school students becomes well-documented and recognized in defense circles, this too will decline. I encourage all home schooling military families to belong to HSLDA and subscribe to a home school information newsletter for families in the armed services (see Appendix).

Local Support Groups

Teaching parents depend on local support groups, home school magazines, seminars, and other home schoolers for their encouragement and guidance. Most communities of size now have a home school support group. Support groups offer help to mothers and fathers in the form of field trips, parental support meetings, monthly newsletters, joint graduation services, group HSLDA membership (explained below). Contact a veteran home schooler in your area to find out what is available. If you don't know any home schoolers, all fifty states have organizations that help facilitate the flow of information to the local support groups within their state. To contact them, see Appendix for the addresses of state organizations.

Umbrella and Correspondence Schooling

There are some practical advantages for home educators, especially new ones, who go through an umbrella school. One of the most important benefits is *accountability*. Umbrella and correspondence schools help parents plan a program and then encourage them to follow through with it. They also offer teaching tips, supervise formal testing, and guide you in selecting curricula. Correspondence schools will even grade lessons and return them by mail. Umbrella schools usually maintain enrollment records and transcripts which are available if transferring to another school.

Many home educators receive teaching experience under the auspices of an umbrella or correspondence school until they feel competent enough to go it alone. Others start independent from the word go. Independent teaching requires more organization, planning, and discipline but leaves parents in complete control. The important thing to remember is that parents are ultimately responsible for their children no matter which option they take.

There are several good umbrella schools, but here are a few of the larger ones:

Christian Liberty Academy
502 W. Euclid Ave., Dept. G,
Arlington Heights, IL 60004
(800-832-2741)

Calvert School
Tuscany Road
Baltimore, MD, 21210
(301-243-6030)

Advanced Training Institute International
Box One
Oak Brook, IL. 60522-3001
(708-323-7073)

School of Tomorrow
2600 ACE Lane, P.O. Box 1438
Lewisville, TX 75067-1438
(800-925-7777)

Home Schooling Co-ops and Cottage Education

Another option in home schooling is involvement with a co-op or cottage education. They are actually two names for the same thing. For our purposes, we will refer to them as co-ops. Co-ops use the cooperative teaching efforts of two or more families. You might call it the halfway point between conventional Christian schooling and home tutoring. For some who feel uneasy about "going it alone," this may be an ideal solution.

Co-operatives essentially consist of several families banding together to form a loose-knit educational assistance organization. Properly initiated and convened, co-ops can provide a warm and educationally stimulating environment. Some parents feel more comfortable when they are not the sole teacher. Teaching duties for some subjects are shared, co-oped, or group-tutored. It is especially helpful with some of the upper level courses such as foreign language, algebra, chemistry, and physics, but can be used with any area of need.

Parents usually share the teaching responsibility, concentrating where possible on their subject strengths. Therefore, one couple may teach math, another history, another science, etc. These are also known as subject co-ops and are growing in popularity. Or they may choose to teach all subjects and separate the children by general age groupings; one couple taking ages 7-10, another ages 11-13, etc. Still another possibility is for the cottage parents to hire a teacher from its own parents. Often, it's fathers or mothers with previous teaching experience. Should a teacher be hired from the outside, it is very important for the parents to screen the teacher very carefully and maintain a high level of involvement. A parent hired from within is best because it allows optimal control to remain in the hands of the parents. Though some groups grow to a dozen or more students, co-ops work best when they remain small.

Regarding location, co-ops are sometimes taught in a home environment. In a home setting, adequate space for each child must be given due consideration. Though several homes could be used for different subject matter, shifting locations should be kept to a minimum to avoid disruption and confusion. Co-ops may meet with regularity at the largest home, while changing only the parental teacher. If the instructional group is kept to a reasonable size, each student will benefit from the warm home environment and the opportunity to learn alongside other home schoolers.

Some co-ops use a room at a local church. Unless the premises are currently committed during the week, many churches will cooperate with co-ops for a minimal amount of rent. Most Sunday school rooms are adequately supplied with chairs, proper lighting and ventilation, a chalk or marker board, and nearby restroom facilities. In addition, a neutral location in a more spacious setting is a conducive learning environment when larger class numbers are involved. When parents work in unison, they can also afford to buy certain equipment (i.e., lab equipment, teaching videos, microscopes) that may be expensive to purchase on their own.

Pre-Paid Legal Protection

Though home schooling is legal in some form in all fifty states, there are still serious challenges and allegations that pop up against individual home schoolers. The primary reason is because state education officials are notorious for overstepping their legal authority and boundaries. Hence, no home schooler should go without legal protection and ongoing legal updates.

Membership can be obtained cost effectively in the Home School Legal Defense Association, also known as HSLDA. Their success rate in protecting member families from harassment or worse is more than phenomenal, it's miraculous. I believe God's hand of blessing is upon them. In addition to legal protection when you need it, they keep you informed about current or proposed legislation in your state via the *Home School Court Report*. You will also learn about court and legislative victories that sustain your freedoms. Thirty-four states have enacted specific home schooling statutes or regulations, many of which protect home schooling rights-thanks to HSLDA. At this writing, HSLDA has 40,000 plus members and is growing at a rate of twenty-five percent per year.

Founded by Michael Farris, a Christian home schooling father and constitutional attorney, HSLDA offers legal support to parents of all religious beliefs. To obtain membership, parents fill out an application for approval and pay an annual fee of $100. That's a bargain considering what you get. If you belong to a group that has twenty-five or more HSLDA members, you can get a $15/year discount. Once a family is approved, the yearly fee usually covers the parents and all the home schooled children, no matter how large the family. HSLDA reserves the right to reject an application they feel does not meet their criteria. One thing you must keep in mind. You must be accepted before they will defend you or provide legal assistance. Don't wait until trouble comes and then expect HSLDA to rush to your aid. Like auto or homeowners insurance, you must be covered to be protected. On your own, legal bills can mount quickly. For a membership application or for more information, contact HSLDA at:

Home School Legal Defense Association
Paeonian Springs, VA 22129
Phone: 703-338-5600

Goals and Objectives

Having no goals and objectives is like trying to sail a ship without a rudder or like taking a trip without a destination. God's Word says, "We should make plans counting on God to direct us" (Proverbs 16:9, TLB). The simple fact is, your child can only go where you take him. If you do not know where you are taking your child educationally, how will you know when or even if you have arrived? A goal is an end toward which your effort is directed, while an objective is a short-range step you take to ensure the meeting of your longer-range goal.

Setting goals should include three things. First, your goals should be clearly defined. Foggy or unclear goals only lead to frustration and confusion. In fact, they are really not goals at all—they are only ideas or wishes. Be specific with your educational goals. For example, what basic knowledge, skills, attitudes, and godly character traits would you like your children to develop? What Biblical doctrines and concepts would you like them to learn? What are your academic goals for each subject? I'm not talking about daily/weekly lesson plans or objectives here but the identifying of knowledge, concepts, abilities, and character traits you would like for your child to grasp by year's end. You may want to start with only one-year goals at first, and later add five-, ten-, and beyond.

Academic goals can be easily assessed through the use of annual standardized testing. Other goals like the development of character traits and the child's love for God cannot be tested and hence must be appraised in the parent's heart. Goal-setting is not as hard as it sounds, and with time you will grow to master it. Most Christian curriculum publishers provide academic goals for you. This is of tremendous help to the new home educator. Further, if you're interested in comparing your goals with public school goals, every state educational agency publishes the essential elements for each subject for grades K-12. These can often be obtained discreetly through a public or private school and may help you in your academic planning. Do not let planning and goal-setting overwhelm you. It should be a tool, not an albatross around your neck.

Very important! List your goals in order of importance. Spend most of your teaching time on the character traits, attitudes, and subjects of highest priority. When all is said and done, what is it exactly that you want your child to learn? What knowledge and attitudes do you want your child to carry with him throughout life? Your priorities should be determined by God's Word, and God's Word places its greatest emphasis on the development of love towards God and man. There are some goals that will require an indefinite time to fulfill. For example, character traits or attitudes may take several years to sprout and a lifetime to properly develop. Though they are crucial in the goal-planning process, they must remain flexible and in accordance with the child's age and spiritual maturity. Teaching should not be confined to the classroom. Remember, learning is a life experience.

Secondly, goals and objectives are best when they are *put into writing*. A fact of human nature is this: unless you write your goals out, your chances of achieving them are very slim. Putting them in writing will do five things: 1) it solidifies them in your own mind and makes them more real; 2) it shows your seriousness; 3) it helps you to get organized; 4) it makes you feel better about yourself; and 5) it makes your teaching much easier. You only need to write your goals out once a year, making occasional minor revisions if they are needed. Your goals need not become so detailed that they become a drudgery, but they should road map your desired educational destination for your child. Most teacher's guides will supply daily/weekly academic objectives to help you meet your goals, saving you from detailed scope and sequence work and complex lesson planning. Some publishers will even provide a coordinated master plan which integrates all of your subjects for you. Get all the help and advice you can from publishers and friends, but ultimately let your broad goals be from your own pen. The reason is simple: personally written goals keep you involved in the process, they help you sort out your individual priorities, and help you make adaptations to fit your child's subjective needs. This is one of the unique advantages of home schooling. Below is a sample of some written annual goals for a typical first-grader. Notice how they give direction and steer a course for the year.

Goals

Character

- Learn the names of the different types of godly character.
- Concentrate on the character development of love, attentiveness, and patience.
- Learn how the different character traits were demonstrated in the life of Jesus.
- Encourage the importance of character-building over all other types of knowledge and skills.

Bible

- Learn the key characters of both Old and New Testament.
- Learn the books of the Bible.
- Learn to differentiate between key Old and New Testament stories.
- Lay out a basic Scripture memory plan.

Reading

- Learn the letters of the alphabet in their proper order.
- Learn consonant sounds in initial, medial, and final positions.
- Learn long and short vowel sounds.
- Learn "r," controlled vowel sounds.
- Learn vowel digraphs.
- Learn initial and final consonantal blends.
- Learn basic sight words.
- Learn elemental reading practices.
- Learn to answer basic questions about stories they have read.

Math

- Learn to count to 100 (also by multiples of 2, 5, and 20).
- Gain sight recognition of numerals 0-100.
- Learn to distinguish numerical order.

- Know how to distinguish numerals being greater than, less than, or equal to.
- Learn basic addition and subtraction facts of numerals 1-10.
- Learn place value in a three-digit number.
- Learn to tell time by the hour and half hour.
- Be able to solve simple story problems of addition and subtraction.
- Learn the value of a penny, nickel, dime, quarter, and half-dollar.
- Learn numerical word symbols (1-100).

Writing
- Learn how to write manuscript in both upper- and lower-case.
- Learn how to hold a pencil/pen in the proper way.
- Learn to judge size and form of letters.
- Learn to write simple sentences neatly and legibly.

Science
- Learn what science is: finding things out.
- Learn that God's Word is the ultimate source of all truth.
- Learn what the five senses are and how we use them.
- Learn about weather and seasons.
- Learn about basic scientific classification.
- Learn good health habits.

History
- Learn what history is and what it teaches us.
- Learn that God's Word is the source of historical fact on the original creation of the world and the condition of man.
- Learn basic facts about home, church, community, and country.
- Learn the importance of Thanksgiving, Christmas, and Easter.
- Learn about patriotism.
- Learn the importance of the flag and the Pledge of Allegiance.
- Learn that individuals and families are the building-blocks of society.

Objectives
Short-range objectives should work toward the achievement of your long-range goals and are usually integrated in the teaching manuals of the various curricula. Below are sample objectives you might have during the course of a one-week period for the subject of Bible.

This week we will:
- Memorize John 3:16.
- Read/tell the story of Saul's conversion.
- Have them explain what salvation is.
- Complete Bible worksheets on pages 23-29.
- Complete Bible craft on Paul.

Or these weekly objectives for the subject of Math:

- Count out loud by tens to 100.
- Go through sample addition problem on board.
- Complete workbook exercises on pages 8-15.
- Work on hour-identification on clock face.

Goal-setting and objective-setting will bring overall organization to the teaching process and direction to your school year. Without this essential phase of planning, home education will be more difficult to carry out.

Thirdly, goals and objectives should *be achievable.* If you set goals for yourself or your child that are unrealistic or unachievable, both of you will become frustrated with home schooling. If you sense one of your goals is too broad or too difficult, don't be afraid to change or amend it. Goals are not meant to bind you; they are meant to free you by giving you purpose, direction, and guidance.

Television in the Home

Television and cable network programming has grown so crude and objectionable, the value of owning a TV set has lost its appeal. This is especially true for home schoolers. Tragically, most American children spend more time watching television than they do in school. Between the ages of 6 and 18, the average American child views 15 to 16,000 hours of television compared to 13,000 hours spent in school. According to a *Neilson Report of Television*, children watch thirty to thirty-one hours of television weekly, more time than any other activity except sleeping.[150] The argument about learning deprivation for children who are without a TV set are highly overstated and pretentious. However, a California study of a half million public school students in the 6th through 12th grades did find a strong correlation between television viewing and poor academic performance. In fact, they found that the more TV they watch, the worse they do scholastically.[151]

In America, television helps to formulate the images that mold and shape our culture. Who decides the content of the shows that America is held captive by? Producers and writers do. What kind of people are they? A revealing poll by the American Enterprise Institute for Public Policy Research in Washington shows what kind they are. Among television writers they found that:

- 45 percent profess no religion at all
- 7 percent attend a religious service once a month
- 80 percent do not regard homosexual relations as wrong

- 97 percent favor abortion on demand
- 75 percent call themselves political liberals
- And only 17 percent condemn adultery[152]

Are these the kinds of people you want to give thought control to? Doesn't your family deserve to be shielded from their deceptions and lies, and instead "take captive every thought to make it obedient to Christ?" (II Cor. 10:5). When all the defensiveness and ballyhoo about the merits of TV are laid to rest, we can objectively see that there is very little there worthy of our time and attention.

Arguments about television's net worth for news, sports, nature, and religious shows, etc. lose their potency in light of the unrealism of strict confinement to that kind of programming. The truly honest will admit that very few have that kind of rigid monitoring. The actual statistics indicate what most people are watching. Even if you are determined to only watch reruns of *Little House on the Prairie*, or *The Waltons*, or old Walt Disney movies, there are still three overwhelming arguments against watching.

First, *you cannot control the advertisements* that market everything from underclothing to tight blue jeans, contraceptives to douches. Children between the ages of six and eighteen are exposed on average to 350,000 commercials. Television stations advertise for the evening movie by highlighting the most steamy scenes, trying to entice viewers to tune in later. They'll show a glimpse of a man and woman in a passionate love scene commenting "You won't want to miss this exciting romance film tonight at 8." Furthermore, the liquor industry bombards viewers with very effective advertisements that glamorizes alcohol consumption. Your children notice these commercials. Some flippantly try to dismiss them saying, "We just tune the commercials out of our minds." Really? Sponsors don't pay hundreds of millions of dollars to advertising firms that don't produce results. It is hard to guard your heart and mind when advertisers use it for a graphic garbage dump.

Second, TV ratings are determined by the number of people who view a particular program. The more who watch, the more revenue that program produces. Hence, *TV viewers subsidize the program they watch and the network that produces it.* It puts money in network hands. The opposite is also true. By abstaining from viewing television, you are exercising the power of the purse, which the sponsors understand all too well.

Third, *time spent staring at the TV is valuable time that could have been spent with the family.* Not only does it rob family interaction time, but experts worry about the values being passed on. The average

American home watches six hours and forty-eight minutes of television each day. That's about fifty to seventy-five thousand hours of television in a lifetime.[153] In those hours the average person, per year, views approximately 9,230 sex acts or implied sex acts on TV. Eighty-one percent of that sexual activity is outside the commitment of marriage. The average sixteen-year-old has watched 18,000 murders on television.[154] That's an awful lot of violence, murder, sex, and foul language.

The heart can be no cleaner than what is stored in it. "Above all else, guard your heart, for it is the wellspring of life" (Prov. 4:23). Jesus said, "For from within, out of men's hearts, come evil thoughts, sexual immorality, theft, murder, adultery, greed, malice, deceit, lewdness, envy, slander, arrogance and folly. All these evils come from inside and make a man unclean" (Mark 7: 21-23).

Where the home is school, the television is of special concern. Generally speaking, television viewing is a poor use of time. A better way to spend your time is reading to your children, playing games with the family in the evening, spending time in the Word of God and in prayer, physical fitness, and catching up with household chores. I personally believe that all home schools would be far better off without a TV set in the house. It makes more time available for family communication and interaction, and avoids being a perpetual temptation and distraction to the children. At the very least, TV-viewing should be limited to a fixed number of hours with programming strictly censored. This would teach your children both discipline and restraint. Most of all, remember that children learn by example.

TV Addiction

If the truth be told, we must admit that we live in a society of TV addicts—including many Christians. As with any addiction, few are willing to own up to it. Since TV addiction will negatively effect the home school, the symptoms of a TV junkie are listed below for your self-evaluation.

1) Denial of the addiction. Making statements like, "I can cut it off any time I want to."
2) An overwhelming compulsion to flip the TV on throughout the day.
3) A daily need to relax by television viewing.
4) The inability to cut the TV off. Chain viewing for hours on end.
5) The inability to go without TV viewing for a few weeks at a time without withdrawal symptoms like boredom, complaining, inactivity, etc.
6) Sense of remorse over inability to control personal viewing.

A good test is for the whole family to go cold turkey off the TV for a month. If during that month you identify symptom number five in your home, chances are you have one or more addicts in the family. In this case, you need more than a TV diet, you may need to remove the temptation altogether.

Conclusion

There is as much to say on the "how" of home schooling as there are parents who home school. Myriads of home-spun techniques, ideas, and practical applications are being created as you read. No book could include them all. Nor should it. What works well for one family might not work well for another. Much of the "how" of home schooling comes by: 1) praying for God's guidance and wisdom in all that you do, 2) modeling personally the behavior and lifestyle you want your child to learn, 3) employing a certain degree of trial and error while keeping your eyes fixed on predetermined goals, 4) designing a workable schedule which serves both your child's and family's needs, and 5) interacting with other home schooling parents on a regular basis. Remember that home schooling should be a continual learning process incorporating all of life's experiences. A great deal of learning takes place outside the classroom. Hence, supermarket shopping becomes a mathematical challenge for youngsters learning addition, subtraction, and percentages. The kitchen becomes a science lab. The workbench becomes a carpentry shop. A camping trip becomes a scientific encounter with nature. If you diligently apply the suggestions outlined in this chapter, and add creativity and love, you will be surprised at your abilities, talents, and educational effectiveness. But most important of all, teach your child to delight himself in the Lord and to acknowledge Him in all his ways. For that is a parent's highest achievement in life.

SIX

Why Fathers Should Be Involved in the Home School

In traveling across the country speaking at home school conventions, I've found a common complaint that moms seem to have above all others— they wish dad would do more in the home school beyond giving his passive consent. Dads, here are reasons why you should be involved in the home school.

First, *it's your responsibility as the spiritual head of the house.* Scripture says, "For the husband is the head of the wife as Christ is the head of the church, his body, of which he is the Savior" (Ephesians 5:23). If a Martian landed in your backyard and said to your child, "Take me to your leader?" Who would he go to? Dad or Mom? Headship is a deep burden and responsibility, like a fifty pound sack on your head. Many men in our culture run from it.

No matter where your children go to school—public, private, parochial, or home—you are accountable to God for what they learn. Realizing this, growing numbers of godly dads are finding the job much easier when they have daily oversight over their children at home.

Your position as head of the house does not mean you will not make mistakes. If anything, they are amplified before the eyes of the family. But don't let that frighten you from the execution of your responsibilities. Like all dads, home school fathers make mistakes, but that doesn't mean you have a bad home or you are not right for home schooling. Thomas Edison had 10,000 failures before he invented the light bulb.

Dad's leadership make his wife's role a little easier and a lot more pleasant. This is a part of spiritual headship. A dad who won't lead makes a good roadblock. Leadership involves knowing where you are going and taking your family with you. Fathers, be the leaders of your home. If a ship captain doesn't know where he is going, no one on board knows either. Chart your course. It has well been said, "No wind serves him who has no destined port." Pilots don't land planes in the fog by the seat of their pants; they have a flight plan. Contractors don't build houses without blueprints. Dad, it's your job to provide your family with the blueprints.

As God holds fathers accountable for headship of the household, so fathers must hold family members accountable for their learning and growing up in the Lord. Challenge your family to spiritual maturity. Check up on and assist them in their devotional life, Scripture memory, and their witness for Christ.

Second, *you should be involved because your life is to be a model of God's truth.* God calls on dads to reflect the truth of His Word. What a man is determines what he says and does. A man's character is shaped by his relationship with God or the lack thereof. You can mask it for a brief period, but sooner or later what you are will come out in the way you live your life at work and at home. How you live your life is largely determined by the contact you have with God and His Word. If you want your children to have a hunger for God's Word, you must have a hunger for God's Word. When you come home from work you're hungry. You don't put two or three peas on your plate, a spoonful of mashed potatoes, and one or two kernels of corn. No, you take a man-sized portion of each. In a similar way, if you are interested in modeling truth, you will show a hunger for God's Word. Some dads have a personal habit of not eating breakfast until they've spent twenty to thirty minutes alone with God in the morning. What a model! In Psalm 78:72a we read, "He shepherded them according to the integrity of his heart." Home schooling is an opportunity to model God's truth and shepherd your family according to the integrity in your heart. Remember, the primary method of teaching in the home school is by example.

Third, *your involvement will help shape and mold godly character.* As has been mentioned, this is the most important part of education. It is far better to fail in the three R's and succeed in character. It is very easy to take a well-constructed arrow and hit the target. But if you pull a crooked branch off a tree and try to shoot it out of your bow, it probably won't get very far. Why? Because the arrow is not properly shaped. It is a dad's job to help shape his children's character so they will arrive at the target God has for them. Dads play a big role in shaping character, for better or for worse.

Fourth, *you must transfer truth to your children through mentoring.* It is not enough that you know the truth. You must pass it on. Psalm 78 says, "He decreed statutes for Jacob and established the law in Israel, which he commanded our forefathers to teach their children, so the next generation would know them, even the children yet to be born, and they in turn would tell their children." The most critical point in a relay race is the hand-off. Dad, how is the hand-off of God's truth going with your family? Joshua's generation did not pass on God's truth. As a result, the next generation turned their hearts away from God. You must use daily opportunities to equip your children. A home school is the perfect complement to this.

Fathers, it is your responsibility to teach your children how to effectively pray, read the Bible, witness, and fellowship with other Christians. Even the wee ones can learn these simple faith-building steps. As they get older, grow with them to more complex subjects and issues. You don't need a seminary education to instruct in the rudimentary teachings of biblical apologetics and biblical law. Josh McDowell's *A Ready Defense* and Rousas John Rushdoony's *The Institutes of Biblical Law,* make excellent primers on these subjects. And there are many others as well. Remember, Hebrews 6:1-2 says, "Let us leave the elementary teachings about Christ and go on to maturity, not laying again the foundation of repentance from acts that lead to death, and of faith in God, instruction about baptisms, the laying on of hands, the resurrection of the dead, and eternal judgment."

What we are talking about here is the concept of mentoring. Fathers, be eager to restore the lost art of mentoring. In years gone by, mentoring was the chief method of learning and a rather commonplace occurrence. Agrarian fathers mentored their sons while mothers mentored their daughters. They taught masculinity and femininity in their proper form, what work was and how to carry it out, the essence of character, the formation of values, and their duties and responsibilities in society.

By contrast, mentoring today is near extinction. It has been lost in the home, where most children are separated from their parents for the better part of the day and garner an average of only eight to eleven minutes of parent-child communication. It is lost in educational circles where faculty and students scarcely meet outside the classroom. It is lost in industry where craftsmen have given way to the technician. It is lost in the church, where one-on-one, holistic discipleship has been overshadowed by dealing with the masses, sundry programs, television ministries, and pulpit evangelism. The art of discipling another to spiritual maturity through regular, individual encounters is all but gone.

Mentoring must be rediscovered if we are to redevelop maturity and character depth in our families, churches, and society. Virtually all training of Bible personalities was accomplished in the mentoring context. Moses mentored Joshua, Naomi mentored Ruth, Elijah mentored Elisha, Elizabeth mentored Mary, Jesus mentored the twelve, Barnabas mentored Paul, Paul mentored Timothy, and Priscilla and Aquila mentored Apollos. Today we desperately need godly men and women who are willing to mentor others, starting with their own family, and then gradually widening the circle from there.

A mentor teaches primarily by example and close supervision. He offers much-needed individualized assistance in areas such as discipline, encouragement, correction, confrontation, and a calling to accountability. The goal of mentoring is to develop a mentoree's maximum potential for Jesus Christ in every aspect of life, with special emphasis on discipleship. A mentoring father not only teaches his child how to read the Bible, pray, witness, worship God, and live in obedience, but also models for him until he becomes an effective discipler himself—which is the ultimate goal.

Jesus, our model, intensely discipled the twelve. Though He did what He could to help the multitudes, He devoted Himself primarily to the twelve, rather than to the masses, in order that the masses could at last be saved. His evangelism strategy called for training dedicated men who could carry on His work when He was gone. He literally poured His life into these men. As the ministry of Christ lengthened into the second and third years, He gave increasingly more time to the disciples, not less. When He departed this world He had actually spent more time with His disciples than with everybody else in the world put together.[155] Hence, discipleship was not only personally practiced by Jesus, it remains His sole plan for bringing a lost world back to Him.

Part of the problem with our society today is that we have too much individualism and not enough accountability. A large percentage of pastors have themselves never been discipled. Some see no reason to maintain an ongoing mentor-student relationship with someone more spiritually mature than themselves. Church leaders have fallen into sin because they have no one to whom they are accountable. Whatever the reason—pride, ignorance, shortage of mentors—this practice of being a spiritual lone wolf has filtered down to the pew. But home schooling fathers have a unique opportunity to recapture the all-but-lost art. Enough of spiritual independence! God desires His people to be interactive and mutually accountable. He wants mentoring and discipleship to take place. (See Prov. 13:10,14,18,20; 15:31; 20:5; 24:26; 27:17; Romans 12:10-11; I Thess. 2:18.) We are to follow His own example. Only in this way can we ever hope to alleviate the pitfalls of self-accountability.

Mentoring is one of the best and most proven methods for building a strong family, church, and society. James Dobson, Charles Swindoll, Bruce Larson, Charles Colson, and Ted Engstrom are just a few successful Christian men who have been mentored. Dads, have you been discipled? If not, seek out a mature Christian who will serve as your mentor. Then experience the joy and privilege of passing on to your children what you yourself have learned. Learn to be a mentor to your sons and daughters.

Fifth, *fathers are to help reinforce the mom's authority.* Once I was in a home where a young, upstart child called his mom a dummy. The dad overheard the comment and went over to the young boy to *immediately* put the child in his place. Even when an event happens while Dad is gone, Dad can augment Mom's authority when he comes home. It goes a long way in the home school.

Sixth, *Dad need to be involved because Mom needs his help.* Mom only has so much time to teach, do housework, prepare meals, settle childish disputes, and care for little children. Therefore, she needs all the help she can get. I'm reminded of a man who went to his doctor and told him he was unable to do all the things around the house he used to. When the examination was complete, he said, "Doc, I can take it. Tell me in plain English, what is wrong with me." "Well, in plain English," the doctor replied, "you're just plain lazy." "Okay," said the man, "Now give me the medical term so I can tell my wife."

I hope none of the dads reading this book falls into that category but instead does all he can to support his wife as teacher. She needs your help and involvement in the home school, not just your passive consent in the beginning.

For example, it is very important for Dad to choose a subject or subjects he can be involved in, including a Bible, character-development, or history course. These courses can easily be adapted around Dad's work schedule and can be taught in the evenings and on weekends. Plus, they tie in with the spiritual responsibility of being the family priest. Dads are specifically charged, "Fathers . . . bring them (your children) up in the training and instruction of the Lord" (Ephesians 6:4). Other subjects which you could teach that require only two or three classes a week are science and physical education. Dad's participation in some measure in the teaching process will not only ease the burden of Mom "doing it all," but it will show his support of and family government over the home schooling process.

Seventh, *your involvement builds intimacy—both with your wife and with your children*. Your involvement helps you get closer to your wife. Home schooling is one of the most unselfish things I know of. While many women are out pursuing careers, home school moms are working diligently to maintain the integrity of the traditional home. Dads should appreciate the willingness of a wife who stays at home, often in the exclusive company of jelly-faced toddlers and strong-willed adolescents, to love and teach them. While your wife is at home all day trying to communicate on a two-year-old level with impatient and all-too-often tired, crying children, you spend your best hours with reasoning adults. So when you come home, talk to her, support her, encourage her, and love her for her commitment to your children. Show a genuine interest in the home school. Your involvement will strengthen the bonds of your marital relationship and keep the fires of intimacy kindled. Your involvement will also help you build and maintain emotional intimacy with your children, which is one of the secrets of a happy home.

Eighth, *dads need to be involved to build a spirit of moral chastity*. Dads are placed on earth in part to be a hedge or barrier against immorality for their children. It is a dad's job to help explain the facts of life from a biblical perspective, to communicate warmth and acceptance so his children will not seek it outside the home, and to carefully explain the temptations of one-on-one association with the opposite sex. I personally do not hold with the Western custom of dating but rather prefer the biblical concept of courtship.

The world's approach of dating, engagement, and marriage is just the reverse of God's order. It begins with a fixation on outward appearances, then promotes physical and emotional involvement, and possibly considers the responsibilities of marriage down the road. God's order of friendship, courtship, and marriage is first to promote spiritual oneness in friendship, then oneness of soul in engagement, and finally physical consummation in the bonds of marriage.

Christian teenagers can have a terrific time socializing with godly friends without the moral temptations of dating. Socializing is spending time with other Christian peers in a group setting for the purpose of fellowship, companionship, and fun. Unlike dating, socializing has an underlying motive of reaffirming Christian convictions and strengthening one's faith in Jesus Christ.

It is the responsibility of dads to educate their children in the protocol of Christian socialization and in the inherent moral dangers of contemporary dating. The first rule of thumb is this: Don't permit a son or daughter to go out alone for hours at a time. This affords an opportunity for stumbling. Socializing should be carried out in groups. Your child may ask, "Dad, don't you trust me?" You can counter, "No. I don't even trust myself." We are all susceptible to the temptations of the flesh and must take protective steps to guard ourselves. Paul told Timothy to "flee the evil desires of youth."

Fathers should teach their youngsters to avoid situations that put them in physical contact with the opposite sex. Our culture is so permeated with sexual stimuli that it doesn't take much to get a teen's motor running. A young boy or girl's passion switch can be flipped by merely holding hands or kissing. The best way to handle temptation is to avoid the environment where it is strongest. Dads should teach their children to do no less.

Dads, teach your children early to socialize within the family context. If your seventeen-year-old daughter likes a young man, let her invite him over to the house for the afternoon. They can enjoy each other's company without separation or seclusion. The whole family can go bowling or picnicking. There is no need for "being alone," especially at the junior high and high school level. It is imperative to reestablish the process of respect for and interaction with the entire family. It's important to build activities around the family. This will provide built-in chaperoning that helps keep young emotion in their proper perspective.

Fathers, build and maintain a rapport with your children that encourages them to be accountable to you for their actions. They should be taught from little on up the importance of accountability to parents, pastors, and Christian peers. This is a moral philosophy that can easily be reinforced in the home school. If your son or daughter is professing to be a blood-bought follower of Jesus Christ, and someone comes up to ask them about their moral purity, they should answer honestly and forthrightly. They should always warmly receive and respond to a challenge from their parents or Christian friend. A Christian's life should be an open book and not a locked box. Explain to your children that if the question about their moral purity can't be asked, then that in itself presents a problem. This is what Christian accountability is all about, and it must be practiced by every member of the family.

Also realize that concocting ground rules is not enough to overcome the temptations and the lack of safeguards that typical dating entails. To lay down extrinsic guidelines that intrinsically encourages a behavior that can't be kept is a sham. To tell a youngster "stay morally pure," while letting him spend time alone with the opposite sex is begging for trouble. He can't help but be influenced by the environment he is in. Instead of worrying about your children's moral purity of a date, why allow them in that kind of situation? Dads, just teach your teenager a whole new way of thinking.

Teach them the basic rules for engaging the opposite sex and how to build moral safeguards. Should they confront situations that are not specifically mentioned in God's Word, here are four questions they can ask themselves that can help them know right from wrong:

- Is it helpful to me physically, spiritually, and mentally?
- Does it bring me in the company of unwholesome influence?
- Might it bring shame to the cross of Christ?
- Does it glorify God?

What about Courtship

Courtship is the Scriptural approach to preparing for marriage. Courting requires a more serious character evaluation and decision-making process than mere socializing, and thus mandates greater maturity. A young man or woman is prepared for courting when the following is understood:

1) When you have prayed seeking God's leading and guidance for the right person to be a lifetime partner.

2) When you understand that the courting process should incorporate the same safeguards as socializing. Try especially to avoid "alone time" and other opportunities for temptation. "Make no provision for the flesh."

3) When you understand that parents should be involved from start to finish. Parental approval of your suitor, especially by a godly father, demonstrates your maturity and submission to proper authority. Parents should even be included in the prayerful selection process.

4) When you develop a strict schedule or agenda prior to leaving for an event and are accountable to your parents (or some other godly authority figure) for compliance.

5) When, under God's guidance, you have worked out a set of scriptural standards and goals for yourself.

6) When you understand that the foremost purpose of courtship is to develop a oneness of spirit, which, when achieved, can be the basis of a lasting marriage. Center on relationship building that is spiritual, emotional, and social, instead of physical.

7) Above all else, when you remember to court **only** a born-again Christian with the same moral convictions as yourself. Scripture clearly states: "Do not be yoked together with unbelievers. For what do righteousness and wickedness have in common? Or what fellowship can light have with darkness? What harmony is there between Christ and Belial? What does a believer have in common with an unbeliever?" II Corinthians 6:14-15. The bottom line is this: Spiritual oneness in Christ is the basis for the deepest and most lasting of any relationship, especially a relationship whose goal is marriage.

Fathers have a serious charge and responsibility to protect their God-given offspring from moral and spiritual danger, to educate them in moral chastity, to teach them the inherent dangers of dating and the benefits of biblical courtship. Though this is only a brief summary of the subject, I hope it plants a seed and spurs you to prayerful research of the concept. I am confident that God will give you the wisdom to move in the right direction with your children.

Finally, *fathers should be involved in the home school to help preserve our heritage of liberty and teach responsible citizenry to his children.* Our children need to be reminded that the freedoms they have must be cherished and tirelessly defended. If we take a light view of our responsibility, we inadvertently hasten the loss of our precious freedoms. Dads must teach that the price of freedom is eternal vigilance and reinforce it with examples from Biblical and secular history. The Christian father has a special responsibility to be a faithful steward of the liberties God has entrusted to him, and to instill that sense of responsibility in the hearts of his children.

Your children must be taught the extreme importance of historical, freedom-promoting documents like The Mayflower Compact, The Federalist Papers, and the United States Constitution along with its various amendments. Further, they must be taught that the Constitution must be perpetually defended against those who will abuse it and misrepresent its intentions. Teach your children how our government works, how laws are passed, how to be politically active, how to lobby effectively, and how to pray for our leaders.

Furthermore, it is critical that fathers pass on unrevised and uncensored history, especially American history, to their sons and daughters. Our children are growing up with a public school generation who will have a completed slanted view of history. Some public school texts give more attention to movie stars than the first American president. Dads, you cannot correct the whole system, but you can be the family historian, training your family to understand a correct view of history. What were the strengths and flaws of Christopher Columbus? What drove the pilgrims to come to America? How was the Christian faith uniquely intertwined with the founding of America? In what ways did it influence our early leaders? Why do we have a system of checks and balances, and how can Christians make it work for them? These are just a few of many questions you can help them understand. Our children will need that knowledge to fight the corruption of democracy and collapse of American freedoms. Pick a good history text or a biography on one of the founding fathers and start reading it out loud. I encourage you to read the enlightening Peter Marshall historicals, *The Light And The Glory*, or *From Sea To Shining Sea*. They will give your family a whole different perspective of history and will spark questions for bright eyes and attentive ears. Another excellent historical series was produced by Steve Wilkins entitled *America: The First 350 Years*, and is available from The Paradigm Co. It is also available on audiotape (16 tapes) for $60. For information call (208) 322-4440.

Dads, train your children in the principles of American freedom. Make sure they understand what the Bible teaches about government. In Deuteronomy 17, beginning at verse 14, we have very explicit instructions on deciding who to vote for. There you will find eight principles on how to pick a political leader. You should train your children on what it says. God, in Hosea chapter 8, punished the nation Israel for choosing the wrong man. Some people think God controls an election in the sense that whoever wins is the one God wants to win. But that's not true! If it was, why would God punish Israel for picking the wrong guy? There is a right candidate and a wrong candidate, and sometimes the punishment is the political figure we elect.[156]

Part of the reason we have such weak choices in elections, is because not enough Christian people are working their way up the ranks over the course of time. We have too often deferred our freedom to the good civic-minded people who have stolen our freedom away. Make sure your children understand American history. A lot of children, for example, don't know that regiments of the Continental Army were made of men from local congregations who were led by their pastors. Further, don't just teach the facts about American history, but also

How a Bill Becomes Law

This graphic shows the most typical way in which proposed legislation is enacted into law. There are more complicated, as well as simpler, routes, and most bills never become law. The process is illustrated with two hypothetical bills, House bill No. 1 (HR 1) and Senate bill No. 2 (S 2). Bills must be passed by both houses in identical form before they can be sent to the president. The path of HR 1 is traced by a solid line, that of S 2 by a broken line. In practice most bills begins as similar proposals in both houses.

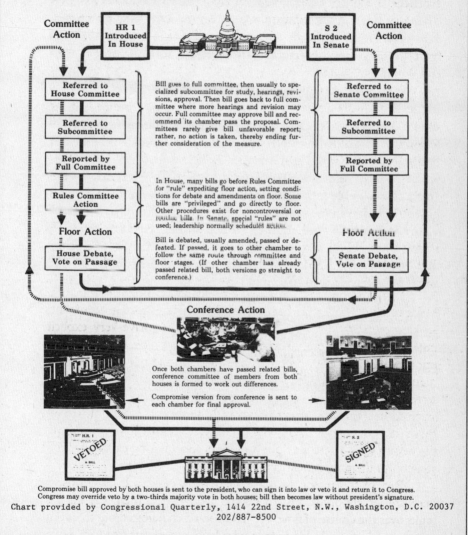

Committee Action

HR 1 Introduced In House

S 2 Introduced In Senate

Committee Action

Referred to House Committee

Referred to Subcommittee

Reported by Full Committee

Rules Committee Action

Floor Action

House Debate, Vote on Passage

Bill goes to full committee, then usually to specialized subcommittee for study, hearings, revisions, approval. Then bill goes back to full committee where more hearings and revision may occur. Full committee may approve bill and recommend its chamber pass the proposal. Committees rarely give bill unfavorable report; rather, no action is taken, thereby ending further consideration of the measure.

In House, many bills go before Rules Committee for "rule" expediting floor action, setting conditions for debate and amendments on floor. Some bills are "privileged" and go directly to floor. Other procedures exist for noncontroversial or routine bills. In Senate, special "rules" are not used; leadership normally schedules action.

Bill is debated, usually amended, passed or defeated. If passed, it goes to other chamber to follow the same route through committee and floor stages. (If other chamber has already passed related bill, both versions go straight to conference.)

Referred to Senate Committee

Referred to Subcommittee

Reported by Full Committee

Floor Action

Senate Debate, Vote on Passage

Conference Action

Once both chambers have passed related bills, conference committee of members from both houses is formed to work out differences.

Compromise version from conference is sent to each chamber for final approval.

H.R. 1 VETOED A BILL

S. 2 SIGNED A BILL

Compromise bill approved by both houses is sent to the president, who can sign it into law or veto it and return it to Congress. Congress may override veto by a two-thirds majority vote in both houses; bill then becomes law without president's signature.

Chart provided by Congressional Quarterly, 1414 22nd Street, N.W., Washington, D.C. 20037 202/887-8500 the political theories, the values, and the principles that have shaped our country. And don't stop with identifying those values only, like the public schools do, "those people believe this and these people believe that." Explain to them which ones are right and why.[157]

Home School Fathers Can Help Return America's Liberties

I believe home schooling holds a special place in America's future. There are a couple of things God can do through America's home schoolers. Home schoolers and their progeny can become the catalyst to return America to its foundation of freedom by fighting the liberal, humanist agenda.

Dads must train their children with the expectation of becoming leaders. A child who is told that he is not very bright will act dumb. A public school child who is told he is an animal through evolution will act like an animal. A home-educated child who is told that he can lead America will lead America. Dads, I urge you to train a corporate Moses, a generation that is going to lead America back to God and a true state of revived freedoms. There are more than enough potential leaders in the home schooling movement right now![158]

Second, train your children to believe that God can change a nation when people get right with Him. We must have a long-range outlook and attitude. Many Christians have been brought up on TV, and it perverts and warps the mind in so many ways. One of them is that every problem has got to be resolved in thirty minutes. We've got fax machines and we want our problems solved that quickly. We've got to have a long-range view of things.[159] We need to have a stepping stone mentality that recognizes that we may not be able to restore our freedoms as quickly as we lost them, but we can lay a foundation that our children can build on and perhaps finish. The Israelites from Egypt never saw the Promised Land, but their children did. There is an old proverb, "He who rides on another man's shoulders will see farther than the one who carries him." Don't dump society's problems on your young children rather, carry them on yours for awhile. As they grow and mature, they can be trained to pick up the vision for the future.

Dads have a special responsibility to be faithful stewards of the liberties God has entrusted to them, and to instill that sense of responsibility in the hearts of their children.

[For a more in-depth look at father involvement in the home school I recommend the book *The Homeschooling Father*, by Mike Farris.]

SEVEN

How to Begin

What we do in life is determined by our priorities. The Bible makes crystal-clear that the godly upbringing of children should be the top priority of parents. Many parents, unfortunately, have placed their priorities elsewhere: wealth accumulation, career development, material possessions, recreational pursuits, friendships, etc. But **the top priority of parents should be their children!**

Understand Your Parental Duties Before God

According to Scripture, parents have several main duties in fulfilling this priority. *First*, parents are to reflect God's love toward their children. They are charged with surrounding their children with love, warmth, and care that would be pleasing unto God. The core of all family life is to be composed of divine love, understanding, and self-giving.

Second, parents are required to provide for their children. This provision should incorporate the following: spiritual nurturing, meeting of material necessities, and mental and emotional development. By providing for your child in these areas, it will give him vitally-needed security, protection, companionship, and spiritual stamina.

The concern over material needs causes some potential home schoolers to wash out before starting. Why? Mostly because they are scared the family can't survive on a single income. More often than not this is not true. Interestingly, a study found that when a mother works outside the home, total "usable" family income is only marginally increased—by about $1,500 a year. Up to one-half of a working woman's income is consumed by work expenses (such as child care, transportation, clothes, meals) and taxes.[160] Mothers in two-parent households who work full-time not only forfeit the all-important bonding time with their children, but they also lose the opportunity to home school, at least legitimately and responsibly. Studies show that children have a higher interest in seeing more of Mom at home than the dubious consequences of having her away at work.

Third, parents are charged with their children's overall instruction (Prov. 22:6). This task is clearly and firmly placed upon the parents. It is implicit that even if others teach your child, you are still held accountable and must carry the prime responsibility for the results. Though this instruction should incorporate all critical subject matter, spiritual instruction should be the heart of all knowledge conveyed to the child. In light of the humanistic domination of the public schools, parents obviously need to spend a great deal of time in the company of their children to best accomplish this.

Fourth, parents are charged with loving discipline of their children. Biblical discipline calls for parents to give Scriptural guidance and correction, punishment for wrongdoing, praise for rightdoing, and to serve as obedient models for the child. In essence, it means to raise a child in such a way that he displays loving obedience to God and parental authority, self-control, and responsibility. The results bring a blessing to the parents. The Bible says, "Discipline your son, and he will give you peace; he will bring delight to your soul" (Prov. 29:17).

Home schooling finds its place and purpose in each of these parental duties. If, after reading this book, you're leaning towards home schooling your children rather than delegating that responsibility to others, here are steps to getting started.

Steps to Help You Begin Home Schooling

Number One: *Before you make any final decision, pray about it.* The Bible says, "They that seek the Lord understand all things" (Prov. 28:5, KJV). Seek out the wisdom of Almighty God to see if home schooling is for you. Home schooling is not for everyone. Many couples are concerned about their children's development and education. However, they may not be willing to give it the priority or make the sacrifice and commitment it often requires. In this case, home schooling would be an injustice to their children. Private Christian schooling then becomes their best alternative.

Number Two: *Read, research, and familiarize yourself with the topic of home schooling.* Reading will help you gain knowledge.

Knowledge helps confirm in your mind that you are making the right decision. You will also gain a multitude of insights and ideas about starting and improving your home school. By reading this book, you've made a good start. Books, magazines, home school videos, monthly newsletters, and book fairs all help provide an unending source of current information. (For a list of resources, see Appendix.). These sources will give you detailed information about available curricula, state laws, satellite schools, support groups, scheduling, spiritual training, home planners, plus many other topics. Please don't move on to step three until you have completed this step, or you might ask unnecessary questions that are easily answered by just reading. Invest in a few good home schooling reference manuals. Your local library probably has several on hand as well.

Also, attend a home schooling seminar or workshop when it comes to your area. There are numerous good ones going on all the time. Several helpful ones are:

Christian Life Workshops by Gregg Harris
(for workshop information in your area, call 1-800-225-5259)

Home School Legal Defense Association
(for HSLDA speaking engagements information, call 703-882-3838)

Institute in Basic Life Principles by Bill Gothard
(for seminar information in your area, call 708-323-7073)

Your state most likely has a convention each year to encourage and support home schoolers and potential home schoolers.

HSLDA produces a brief radio program in most states called, "Home School Heartbeat Radio Broadcast." The stations airing this informative program at the time of this writing are listed for your convenience in the Appendix. New stations are being added all the time.

Number Three: *Talk with veteran home schoolers.* Veteran home schoolers are parents who have home educated for two years or more. Besides being an information resource beyond books, they can provide you with the spiritual and emotional support necessary for getting started. They can share valuable knowledge that comes only with experience. Talk to as many home schoolers as possible. The Bible says, "Plans fail for lack of counsel, but with many advisors they succeed" (Prov. 15:22).

Number Four: *Structure and organize the home for learning.* Children learn best when there is a sense of order and household discipline. If this is not addressed from the outset, it will inevitably lead to frustration down the road. In short, make sure you establish your authority and that your children understand the Scriptural principles of submission and obedience. This needs to be your first lesson. A rebellious child is an unteachable child. Even toddlers can be taught simple boundaries, like not interrupting constantly during home school hours. Let your children know exactly what you expect and then hold them accountable.

Setting up household routines will also serve your household and your home school well. This way the children know exactly when to do chores, when it is time for school, and when it is leisure time. Routines can and should be flexible enough to allow for a last-minute change of plans. This is part of the value behind home schooling. But on the whole, let your routines provide enough structure to guide your family through the days and weeks.

Next, you can begin to organize your home for learning. Some people by nature are not very organized or self-disciplined, but the good news is you need not remain that way. With sincere prayer, a little planning, fellowship and mutual accountability with other home schoolers, you can increase your ability to be organized and self-disciplined for home school.

Teaching tools and organizational aids will also help. Let's consider a few of them. Obviously, you will need a good place for the children to study. Some purchase desks, chairs, and set up a little school room in the home. Others work around the kitchen table. The place really doesn't matter as much as the consistency of a genuine learning time.

More importantly, don't hesitate to purchase good teaching tools that help you as teacher. Here are a few: 1) the *teacher's manual* for the curriculum you choose; 2) *wall charts and posters* (such as alphabet demonstrators—print and cursive—parts of speech, breakdown of the books of the Bible) 3) good *Bible study aids* (concordance, Bible dictionary, Bible encyclopedia, atlas) 4) build a good *home library*, which may include an encyclopedia set (used encyclopedia sets are often available at Goodwill, the Salvation Army, and used-book stores); 5) a *monthly planning calendar* of family and home school events; 6) a *family bulletin board* to display information, school papers, awards, and school projects; and 7) a *personal computer*. Children need to be taught how to type, how to use a computer, and the basics of using a word processing program. This is a skill they will use all through life and certainly in college if they choose to go.

Number Five: *Become a member of the Home School Legal Defense Association.* In my opinion, every home schooler should have the pre-paid legal services of the Home School Legal Defense Association. With HSLDA, you have a team of smart, Christian lawyers in your corner, ready to defend your rights at a moment's notice. If your local school district begins to harass you, HSLDA will protect you—all the way to the Supreme Court if necessary. Beyond that, HSLDA is of immense value to the movement as a whole. They help protect the corporate rights of home schooling parents by their vigilance and legislative efforts at the state and national level. Through their subsidiary, the National Center for Home Education, they provide general information, leadership conferences, legislative updates, and other ancillary support services to home schoolers across the fruited plain. At an inexpensive $100/year, the extensive protection they provide is a bargain. Whatever you do, "don't leave stay home without them."

Number Six: *Consider your child's learning orientation and select your curriculum.* Attending a curriculum fair for the first time can be a little overwhelming because there are so many choices and options. Count it as a blessing, for it wasn't always this way. Fifteen years ago, when home schooling wasn't so popular, there were only a handful of publishers catering to the home educator. Now there are literally dozens and dozens of them. Too much choice, however, can give a new home schooler a well-justified feeling of information overload.

Make sure you have taken care of steps two and three above. Read a couple of good books on understanding and selecting curriculum. I recommend the *Christian Home Educator's Curriculum Manuals*, by Cathy Duffy (there are two: one for elementary grades and one for high school), and *The Big Book of Home Learning* by Mary Pride (there are four in the series pre-school, elementary, junior high, and high school). Both series are available at your local Christian bookstore. Also, talk with other experienced home schoolers to find out what they are using and why.

While selecting curriculum is one of the bigger decisions in starting your home school, it is certainly not a final one. Home schoolers change curriculum all the time. Don't become overly worried about making a mistake in judgment. There is no perfect curriculum, and you will not ruin your children by accidentally selecting the wrong one. Despite all your reading and question-asking, there still remains a measure of trial and error in selecting the right learning material for your family. Remember, you can always change curriculum. Nothing is embedded in stone. (You might want to review the subheading "Choosing a Curriculum" in chapter five, which discusses the four categories of curriculum: traditional, self-paced, unit study, and parentally designed.) Select the curriculum category that best fits your teaching orientation and preference, and one that you can adapt easily to your child's learning mode. The bottom line is, with a little adaptation, your child can learn well using any one of a variety of publishers or curriculum providers. The only question is, how much adapting do you want to do?

Having said that, let me share a few things to consider as you make you final selection. Ask these questions:

1) What is the publisher's philosophy of education? Traditional written work? Memorization? Experiential? Activity-oriented? Worksheet-oriented? What?
2) Will you be coordinating your teaching for more than one child? If so, will the curriculum your considering help you streamline the teaching process or complicate it?

3) How creative are you, given a few teaching concepts? Would it be better for you to have a more structured curriculum?

4) Is the curriculum teacher-intensive or is it more self-paced? Which would work best for our family?

Curriculum selection can seem overwhelming in the beginning, but this will pass. Soon you will grow to rely on divine guidance along with your own judgment and instincts.

If after considering all the above you are still confused, then start with a self-paced curriculum or affiliate with an umbrella school. Regarding the first, two popular, self-paced Christian curriculums that are user friendly are Alpha Omega (800-622-3070) and Accelerated Christian Education (800-925-7777). Both offer diagnostic testing to help you learn where your child is and where you need to begin. This is particularly helpful if your child is coming out of the public school.

Secondly, consider a satellite or correspondence school. These schools offer academic-level evaluation of the student, curriculum screening, support services, and accountability that are often helpful. Even many veterans prefer these same benefits.

Number Seven: *Join and become involved in a local support group.* As soon as you have settled on your decision to home school, join and become involved in a local support group. If you are not sure where one is, contact your state home schooling organization and find out. (The addresses and phone numbers for state organizations are in the Appendix.) What help will you find there? You will find like-minded parents (the biggest plus), support meetings, newsletters, and joint field trips. Many others offer a lot more, like cooperative classes, sports programs, choir, drama, art and music, testing assistance, corporate graduation services, Moms' night out, and HSLDA discounts, just to name a few. Every home schooler needs support and encouragement, and this is the best way to obtain it.

These seven steps will help you begin your home school right. Experience has shown they are of great value when followed sequentially and purposefully. The only thing to add before we go on is this: Do the best you can and don't worry about making a mistake. We all make them, even those of us who have been teaching at home for years. It is hoped that this book will help you eliminate many of the big, costly, and unnecessary mistakes. In your first year or two, you will learn a lot. You will discover teaching styles, methods, schedules, and curriculum that fit your family's personality and needs. Over time, you will inevitably jettison one curriculum for another, one class schedule for another, and one teaching approach for another. This is a natural process because we all learn as we go. You will find that what works for one family may not work for yours. Furthermore, since every child is different, you may discover that what worked for one child may not work for another. That's okay, because home schooling allows you to tailor your child's education to best meet his abilities and gifts.

How to Take Children Out of the Public School

For a smooth transition that doesn't draw unnecessary attention, it is always best to take your child out of a public school during the summer or at a semester break. If asked why you are taking your child out, don't be afraid to tell them you plan to home school. It is a legitimate right. If your school district and state allow parents to obtain your child's school records, which many do, be sure you receive *all of them* when you ask. Your state home school organization will know the law on this (see Appendix). Follow the normal withdrawal procedures for your school district so your child does not remain on their rolls. You don't need a truant officer unnecessarily showing up at your door a few months down the road.

Be sure you find out what your state laws are concerning home schooling. HSLDA offers a free one-page summary of your state's home-school law. Some states are very liberal, having few home school regulations, while others are more oversight-oriented.

Some Do's and Don'ts of Home Schooling
Some Do's

1) *Do* make sure both parents are in general agreement with the decision to home school.
2) *Do* explain to your child your reasons for home schooling. While it should not require his approval, he should have it explained to him in detail.
3) *Do* expect to have both parents involved in home schooling. Fathers should get involved in some way to show their support and headship. They should not just leave the whole thing to Mom. There must be a commitment to mutual involvement and support if you are to accomplish your best effectiveness. Fathers can help teach and give moral and physical support to Mom. Fathers must not expect the whole job to fall on Mom's shoulders. It is his responsibility to get involved and help in every way possible. This is part of "counting the cost."
4) *Do* expect to invest time. No matter what the product, quality craftsmanship is best produced when it is afforded full attention. Similarly, parents must give home schooling the time it needs in order to produce quality results. Specifically, mothers who want

to give home schooling their best and most serious effort should not work outside the home. Those couples who maintain that they need the extra money must reevaluate that decision in light of new priorities.

5) *Do* get organized. Organization is crucial to successful home schooling. Good organization will permit you to do many of the other things that are also important to you.

6) *Do* have a good attitude. Your child will detect immediately any frustration or disinterest, which in turn will be reflected in his desire to learn from you. Remember, your attitude is contagious.

7) *Do* be disciplined. Discipline is vital to your home schooling success. Set up a schedule for yourself and your child. Try to conform to certain times and places for study. Structure your day to give your child consistent tutoring, especially in the morning hours when it is easiest to learn.

8) *Do* be flexible. Though it sounds contradictory with the previous point, it is not. Remember, you are a home school and must make allowances for other children, phone calls, the doorbell, visitors, field trips, and other special events of educational interest, etc. None of these occurrences need to ruin your daily plans. Learn to have healthy flexibility.

9) *Do* have a family goal which keeps biblical priorities constantly before you. How can one know if he has arrived at his destination if he does not know where he is going? A family purpose or goal is your road map to success. Reveal what your priorities are and make your decision-making process becomes much easier.

10) *Do* associate with a local support group for fellowship and growth. After a settling-in period, ask what you can do for the group. Support groups are a cooperative effort.

11) *Do* keep good records. As covered earlier in this chapter, good record-keeping is a part of responsible home schooling. Ample aid is readily available.

12) *Do* expect home schooling to create changes in your routines and household. Obviously, when children are off to school from 7 A.M. to 3 P.M., Monday through Friday, moms will spend their time differently than if their children are home all day long. So expect a few things to change, albeit for the overall good.

Some Don'ts!

1) *Don't* make rash moves. Don't just yank your child out of school without planning and forethought. Give yourself time to proceed in the most effective and productive manner. The best time to withdraw your child is during the summer or between semesters. Don't be secretive and seclusive, but neither should you draw unnecessary attention to yourself or your child.

2) *Don't* rush out and buy expensive curriculum. Before you invest

161

in any curriculum, check out and familiarize yourself with the material other home schoolers in your area are using. Frequently you will find that you can obtain a very good curriculum without spending a great deal of money.

3) *Don't* be overly concerned about the legal aspects. Home schooling is legal in all fifty states. Know what your state laws are, but don't let them cause you unnecessary worry. According to the United States Constitution, selecting your child's education alternatives is a fundamental parental right.

4) *Don't* let your decision to home school be based on your child's acceptance of the idea. Many accept the idea immediately, but a few may require some time to adjust, especially those who are older when they start. Parents, not the children, have to give an account before God for what the child is learning. Sometimes a hard decision must be made over the selfish objections of a child in order to look after his overall good and welfare.

5) *Don't* expect your house to be perfect, especially if you have toddlers. It is unreasonable to expect your home to be the same before and after you home school. For those exceptions where it is the same, my hat's off to you. All the rest of you moms might have to lower your personal expectations of what can effectively be accomplished on school days.

Fathers, recognize that your wife is not a miracle-worker. Have an extra measure of tolerance for a wife who does the best she can. Be understanding and pitch in with the housework.

6) *Don't* get discouraged if others do not share your enthusiasm to home school. This is typical. Hence, the crucial reason to seek out and fellowship with other home schoolers.

EIGHT

Why Grandparents Should Support Home Schooling

In talking with scores of home schoolers across America I have discovered that grandparents have a big impact on home schooling—some positive, some negative. Grandparents of home schoolers can often do more to strengthen and encourage home educators than perhaps anyone else. Often they do not lend such support because they do not fully understand the reason and purpose of home schooling. In this chapter we want to look at ten reasons why grandparents should support those in their family who have decided to home school. Thus, I am writing this chapter as if speaking to grandparents.

If your son or daughter has chosen to home school, it was a decision which demanded very careful consideration. More than likely, it was a decision that didn't come easily. Estimates indicate that as many as one million children are home schooled in this country. The very fact that they have decided to go against the educational numbers and the complacent tide of social acceptance shows their devout courage and boldness. Their desire to keep their child home shows their parental devotion and self-sacrifice. Grandparents would do well to praise the priorities of offspring who show such concern and love for their children. Instead of pursuing the materialistic self-indulgence evident in much of modern society, your children have chosen to devote themselves to a very high calling. Many young people today are choosing not to have children because of the "bother and interference" they bring to their lifestyle. Others can't wait to shove them

163

off to kindergarten, and even preschool, to get them out from under their feet. The stalwart conviction of home educators shows their moral and spiritual backbone, which is a rare quality these days. In a hedonistic society whose hour of accountability is rapidly drawing nigh, home schoolers stand out as a value-centered elite.

How proud this should make the grandparents of home schoolers. Chances are, someone in your genealogical roots was home schooled with great success. You owe it to your son or daughter to consider the logic of the home schooling alternative. Below are ten reasons why grandparents should support their son or daughter's home schooling decision.

1) *You should support their decision because the education of American youth is still your responsibility.* No matter what your age or how long ago you graduated from school, the present generation is still your educational responsibility. Older Americans must help younger Americans experience quality learning. The future of this country rests in its young people. The strongest and most powerful army in the world is the army of youth, for there is not one position held in the world today that they will not hold tomorrow. Without your avid concern over our present educational crisis, the ideas our youth are embedded with today will one day surface in the form of unfair laws, burdensome taxation, and government interference. It has been said that "the hand that rocks the cradle rules the world." The question is, whose hand do you want it to be?

2) *You should support their decision if you believe in basic constitutional rights, which include such freedoms as religious exercise, speech and belief, privacy, and parental liberty.* America was founded on a solid constitutional base which thus far has given our citizenry the greatest freedoms of any country in the world. However, if these precious freedoms are stepped on or choked out, America will lose its greatness. If the rights of someone else is violated, it won't be long before yours are too. Abraham Lincoln once said, "The philosophy of our educational system of today will be the philosophy of our government tomorrow." Home schoolers merely want to exercise their constitutional rights of religious practice speech and belief, privacy, and parental liberty. It is to your advantage to see that these rights are not denied them.

Should the unthinkable time ever arrive when the constitutional rights of home instructing parents is violated, what an exceedingly grim day it will be. Not only would it manifest the massive erosion of fundamental American rights, but also the regrettable extent of governmental control in family matters. Should this ever occur, it is likely that persecution and interference into your private rights are not far behind.

3) *You should support their decision because you owe them an open-minded attitude toward educational alternatives.* The best American success stories have come from conscientious and innovative Americans who were given a fair chance. Did you ever embark on some new undertaking in life only to find yourself discouraged by closed-minded, negative-thinking people? Imagine how a home schooler must feel when he receives little or no encouragement from the ones he thought he could count on most—his family.

It is important that America maintains its rich tradition of educational options and choice. There is nothing wrong with free education. Free education, accessible to all, historically helped to make America strong. We can be proud of the concept of free schools. Nevertheless, free schools are not free at all if every child is compelled to attend. Authentic freedom crumbles when a single educational method is mandated. Our only freedom eventually becomes the freedom to compel—which is the ultimate tyranny.

It is a breach of liberty to standardize children by forcing them to accept instruction from a public institution only. Even as there is diversity in individual views and preferences, so there needs to be diversity in education. We must keep broad the range of individual freedoms, not the least of which is education. We must provide for self-determination. An education for all means an education by all. Thus, every person has an equal right to learn and instruct. Any government interference in this matter is a violation of human rights.

We must hold to pluralism in education—that there are more ways to a goal than one, that there is unity in diversity, that competition is healthy, that to monopolize is to stagnate, and that education should be a marketplace of opinions.

Do not take it as a personal insult if your son/daughter chooses to home school. They are not trying to depreciate the way you raised them or reject the manner in which they were schooled. Times have changed, and in some areas, not always for the better. What was once true about education is not necessarily true today. The point is, modern classroom education has not been achieving desirable results. Home schooling is one answer to the problem. Hence, do not take it as a personal affront to your own parentage.

4) *You should embrace their decision because your son/daughter need your support.* No one can give your son/daughter emotional, spiritual, and psychological support quite like you. You have a unique opportunity to do what no one else can. The reverse is also true. No one can cause more emotional and psychological hurt. Home schooling is a challenging task that requires love and support. As their lifelong parents, it is your proper role to give it.

5) *You should embrace their decision because your grandson/granddaughter needs your support.* Grandchildren need support too. They are keenly aware of any criticism of their parents and their home schooling decision, even though they may not let you know it. Usually home schoolers abide by their decision to home educate even if their parents disapprove. This being the case, why not make your grandchild's home schooling experience as pleasant as possible? Get involved and be a part of something exciting.

6) *You should support their decision because home education has effectively proven itself.* The academic track record of home schoolers is spectacular. In fact, they average about 30 percentile points higher on standardized academic achievement tests than do classroom students. In addition to their superior academic performance, home schoolers evidence more creativity, enthusiasm, family-centeredness, submission to authority, better manners, and display higher moral values. Who would deny that these are admirable qualities? So why knock a good thing, particularly when it works so well given half a chance?

7) *You should support their decision because you value the building of character and godliness in children.* Home schooling builds character, the kind of character found in great leaders and inventors. People like George Washington, Benjamin Franklin, Alexander Graham Bell, and Douglas MacArthur are a few of the long list of home schoolers. Character is what will set your grandchild apart from all the rest. Character is what will give him the ability to stand on his own two feet, to say no when he is asked to participate in something wrong. Character is that quality that gives him the ability to discern situations for himself and to make wise decisions.

Beyond that, home-schooled children are taught godliness.

How important is this to you? Do you want your grandchild brought up in the nurture and admonition of the Lord? If so, be cognizant of the fact that there is no better way to accomplish this than through home schooling. An emphasis on godly, Christian education is what gave early America her strength. One hundred four of the first 119 colleges and universities in America were founded by Christians. Harvard was 100 years old before it had any professors who were not also ministers. Dartmouth was started as a missionary outreach in Indiana, while Brown was the first Baptist College in America. Of the first 40,000 college graduates before the Civil War, 10,000 entered the ministry.[161]

8) *You should support their decision because it gives you a golden opportunity to participate in your grandchild's education.* Historically, grandparents have always been held in a place of high respect. They were looked up to and sought out for their sound wisdom, counsel, and advice. Much of this has been lost in our pleasure-seeking, me-first society. The elderly are shipped off to old folks' homes to be forgotten. Others have been persuaded by society that retirement is an end in itself. But home schooling attempts to bring back the wisdom and the teaching value of grandparents. The Bible says, "The glory of young men is their strength, gray hair the splendor of the old" (Prov. 20:29).

Help your grandchild discover your honor and splendor by allowing him to learn from your valued experiences in life and to treasure them in his heart. Perhaps you are well-equipped to teach sewing, canning, gardening, shop work, music, history, drafting, or science. The list is unending. Whatever talents and gifts God has given you can be passed on to your grandchildren. Furthermore, your son or daughter will appreciate your willingness to be a part.

9) *You should support their decision because you don't want your grandchild to be another clone of educational failure.* The dismal track record of public schools is another reason you should support home education. When one-third of our entire adult population reads very poorly or not at all, I think it's time we seriously examine our educational system. When science and math scores have shown a drastic drop over the past several decades, it is time that we take notice. How big a sign do you need to see the failure of public education? More importantly, why encourage your grandchild's participation in a system that doesn't work?

10) *You should support their decision because you love your grandchild*

and want his highest good. No one doubts your sincerity and love for your grandchildren. And here is the perfect opportunity to demonstrate it. Loving and responsible grandparents will support and encourage any viable avenue of education that will promote their grandchild's highest good, no matter how different it may seem.

Conclusion

When I speak of supporting your son/daughter, I do not mean passive acceptance and silent acknowledgement. The first way you can show support for home schooling is by reading up on the subject yourself. Find out everything you can about it. For starters, read this book in its entirety. Secondly, avoid making comparisons with other grandchildren, especially if the comparisons are negative in nature. Recognize that a home-schooled child is not perfect; home schooling just allows their character and personality the opportunity to develop to its fullest potential. Be careful not to discriminate or judge them differently, unequally, or with greater scrutiny. Thirdly, support involves showing a genuine interest in home schooling by your attitudes, mannerisms, facial expressions, and words. A good way you can show genuine interest is to ask your son/daughter how you can become involved.

NINE

How to Win Over Friends and Relatives to a Point of Understanding

Most home schoolers have friends and relatives that they have been working on, hoping they will become accepting of, or at least open-minded about, home schooling. In this chapter, we will consider ten time-tested, common sense techniques that will help facilitate that goal.

First, *pray for receptivity on the part of your listener.* I believe in the power of prayer. I believe prayer changes things. It even changes attitudes that we ourselves are powerless to change. From personal experience, I can testify that prayer has changed the hearts of my relatives who were at first closed to the idea. They didn't have their views turned around overnight, but God gave them the desire to listen with an open mind. Before you do anything else to win someone over, pray!

Second, *support your reasoning with God's Word.* Properly used, God's Word is a strong tool for winning over friends and relatives. One of the most important sales techniques is to appeal to a higher authority. I don't know of a higher authority than God. Explain how God's Word clearly establishes that the mental and spiritual development of children as a parent's highest priority. The Scripture, "Train up a child in the way he should go and when he is old he will not depart from it," was not given to public school teachers, but to parents. Parents are charged with this awesome responsibility and held accountable for their child's education. Scripture is replete with biblical injunctions to parents. Point out that educational duties may be delegated, but not the final responsibility for what children are taught. In light of God's Word, public and private school teachers are but proxies, surrogates, substitutes for those ultimately responsible—the parents.

Then explain that you have a conviction about home schooling based on God's Word. Even unbelievers, though they may reject the Bible, can respect strongly held convictions and personal beliefs. It's like the belief in personal honor held by many cultures. Americans may not always understand it, but they can empathize and even admire cultural convictions.

Third, *talk about your own mistakes first*. Talking about your mistakes first is one of the best ways to disarm your listener and share knowledge. You could say, "I used to think that education was the state's responsibility and never really had much to do with that part of my children's lives. But I have come to realize that I am held responsible for what my children learn or don't learn, so I view education a lot differently. That's when I first began to explore home schooling." You see, you have taken the first step to change that person's thinking without giving offense or arousing resentment.

Talk about your misconceptions too. "I used to think home schoolers were the weird fringe of society who hid their kids in a basement or a back room and let them play games or watch TV all day. But after I investigated the facts, I found that was not true. Most home educators are hard-working, committed to their children, and very serious about it." Disarm your listeners first by owning up to your initial but faulty appraisal.

Fourth, *don't argue with them*! There is only one way to get the best of an argument and that is to avoid it like the plague. If you argue with someone, nine out of ten times they will feel more firmly convinced that they are right. You can't win an argument! If you lose it, you lose. And if you win it, you lose. Why? Suppose you triumph over their arguments; you will feel great. But what about the person you're trying to win over? You make them feel ignorant and inferior. Losing an argument can damage a person's pride to such a degree that they concede your point but personally reject the solution. What have you accomplished then? There's an old saying, "A man convinced against his will, is of the same opinion still."

Also, be careful not to talk too much. A conversation dominated by one person is not really a conversation. It's a monologue. Once a customer came in a hardware store very interested in a particular lawn-mower. I watched as the salesman tried to sell him on the mower. He pointed out that the lawnmower had a steel deck and wheels. He told him about the easy start, emergency stop, and the nylon starter rope. The customer opened his mouth to ask a question, but, before he could, the salesman started in again exclaiming the virtues of the mower. As he did, I noticed the customer look frustrated. After ten minutes more of sales hype, the salesman stopped and said, "what do you think?" The customer said, "It sounds very nice. I'll take it." The salesman, barely acknowledging the sale, continued, "Oh, did I tell you about the warranty?" As the salesman rambled on once again, I saw the customer begin to lose interest. So he interrupted and said, "I'm sorry, but I've got to be going. I'll let you know." Then he left with disappointment on his face. The salesman had a sure sale but blew it with over zealousness and talking to much. Don't let that happen to you when you discuss home schooling. Part of the way to lead another person to a different conclusion is by being a good listener. Far too few people are good listeners. Many people are only interested in conveying their thoughts, knowledge, and wisdom.

Fifth, *show you care by respecting their opinion*. Home schoolers must guard themselves against arrogance, smugness, and conceit. It was once wisely said, "Be wiser than other people, if you can, but do not tell them so." Don't tell the person with your attitude, "I'm right. I know I'm right, and you're wrong." If the other person thinks public schools are the greatest thing since sliced bread, don't tell them they are crazy. Rather, respect their opinion and find out why they think that. You don't have to agree with them, just show you're interested in their thoughts and that you care. Keep their guard down by letting them know their opinions are worth something. If they make an erroneous assumption, don't laugh at them. Never laugh at a person's ignorance or lack of understanding about home schooling. Once I was having devotions with the family and read about how a king took his army to fight on the plain. My son asked, "Dad, how could they fight on an airplane?" I bit my lip to keep from laughing. Instead, I explained the meaning to him. Laughing would only have hurt his feelings and hindered further questions. Practice respecting another's opinion.

Sixth, *don't criticize how they are raising their children*. Nothing will raise a parent's ire faster than by criticizing how they are raising their children. If out of the blue you tell a person they need to take their children out of the public school and start home schooling, what you have done is to criticize their parental oversight. Want to get yourself in World War III? Tell them that if they really loved their children they wouldn't send their children to public school. You might as well kick a bear in the behind. Proverbs 18:19 says "a brother that is offended is harder to be won than a strong city."

Instead of criticizing them, find something positive to say. It may be something simple like "You seem like a sensitive and loving parent." It will open the door for you to present home schooling as a legitimate educational alternative. The best way to open their minds about home schooling without causing offense or arousing resentment is to avoid criticism. Then, indirectly call attention to their lack of information or myths they may have about home schooling.

By the way, grandparents sometimes reject the idea of home schooling because they feel you are showing lack of approval for the way they raised you.

Seventh, *don't be defensive!* Too many try to defend their decision to home school. Depending on who it is, you may choose to explain your reasons but don't become defensive. Your primary accountability belongs to God. There are many reasons people reject the idea of home schooling. Some criticize to appease their own complacency and lack of action. Some are not willing to make such a commitment. Some don't want to make the sacrifices like Mom giving up her full-time job. Many others will embrace home schooling if it is logically and lovingly explained to them. But a defensive attitude is a barrier to logical explanation. If they say, "You're depriving your children of opportunities—socialization, band, clubs, labs, etc." or "You should leave your children in public school as a witness," don't give an angry retort if you want to win them over.

Eighth, *steer your conversation to points of common agreement.* Never start any subject, much less the subject of home schooling, by discussing the things on which you differ. Talk about points on which you know they can agree with you. For example, their love for their children, having their child's best interest at heart, the need for more parental involvement, family time, and family interaction. Once you've laid the groundwork of things you agree on, new ideas and concepts will be much easier for them to accept.

Ninth, *preclude objections by politely answering questions before they arise.* Rather than waiting for someone to say, "Homeschoolers don't receive the proper socialization," or "Parents are not qualified to teach," preclude these objections by answering them before they arise. The best way to prevent a sticker in the foot is to pull the annoying weed out of your yard before you step on it. It is better to salt the sidewalk and porch than curse the ice after you slip on it. Say, "You know, there's been a lot of talk that parents aren't qualified to teach, but I've found that most are more concerned about results than they are about rhetoric. What about you?" What are they going to say? "I don't care about results!" No, they'll say results are important. Remind them that there are some thirty million functionally illiterate people in this country, and most of them did not come from home schooling. There. You've politely helped to preclude an objection before it arises.

Tenth, *help them become informed.* When you converse, concentrate on the facts. Good information is your best ally, so arm yourself with the facts. Ninety percent of misconceptions come from having ten percent of the facts. If you're not sure what the facts are, give them a copy of this book.

Conclusion

It is not difficult to treat a person with dignity and respect. By following a few common sense rules, you can win over friends and relatives to a point of understanding. There is one last point I want to make. It hurts when parents and friends do not understand and lend support, but don't be so naive as to expect everyone to. If everyone understood, got involved in their child's education the way the should, and acted on factual knowledge, we wouldn't have the current educational crisis we now have. Finally, remember that no matter how many facts you throw their way, your lifestyle is still your best advocate.

TEN

Reasons to Home School through High School*

First, *parents get to see the completion of their earlier home-school efforts.* While home schooling through grade school is better than not home schooling at all, the former can slowly create a dichotomized-value philosophy in your teenage children.

After Jesus picked the twelve to disciple, he finished the job. Jesus was so close to His disciples, He had little time to call His own. Like little children clamoring for the attention of their father, the disciples were always underfoot of the Master. For the disciples, class was always in session. Jesus knew that one living sermon was worth a hundred explanations. While Jesus did not neglect the masses, He took his private ministry, or discipling, very seriously. He actually spent more time with His disciples than with everybody else in the world put together. As the ministry of Christ lengthened into the second and third years, He gave increasingly more time to the chosen disciples, not less. Discipling to the end was so important to Jesus that during passion week He scarcely ever let His disciples out of His sight. Discipling unto the end was all-important to Him.

Something is lost when you turn the discipling of your children over to others. Home schooling through high school gives parents the opportunity to finish the discipling job they started. There is no higher calling on earth; no higher privilege or reward!

---

*The credit for the outlined points in this chapter belong to Elizabeth Smith who compiled them in 1991 for the Home School Legal Defense Association. The exposition of the points, however, is solely that of the author.

Second, *you can customize your child's education to provide motivation and development for his gifts and abilities. No one else will be able to provide the consistent and loving support in weak areas like you can.* It is a fact that no one will do for your son or daughter for pay what you will do for free, because the motivation is different. You know your teen's strengths and weaknesses better than anyone else in the world. Who could better custom-design their education to maximize their distinctive potential?

Third, *you can start higher education early.* You have the option of directing them to early college entrance.

While some teens may not be ready to enter college early, others are. Even public high schools cooperate with college-level programs of early entry. Or your child may want to enter an apprenticeship program. Home schooling in the teen years facilitates and optimizes your ability to prepare a highly motivated or gifted teen for these possibilities.

Fourth, *you can continue the family building process.* Teens continue to be impressionable. This is an invaluable time to cement all your family relationships. Home schooling builds an emotional integrity and a precious rapport between a child and parent like few things can. Going all the way through twelfth grade in home schooling will allow you to continue the family values building process started when they were young.

Fifth, *you can be sure your teens are learning if they are at home.* Studies have revealed that public high school students average only two hours and 13 minutes of academic work a day. Once a boy in eighth grade said to teacher, "I ain't got no pencil." His teacher said, "Now Johnny, that is not the way to say it. It's 'I don't have a pencil; you don't have a pencil; we don't have a pencil.' Now do you understand?" The boy quipped, "No, what happened to all them pencils?" There is a stark reality behind the humor that is not so funny. Our public educational system is in serious trouble. In many cases, children are not learning. I know something is very wrong with our educational system when I see parents filling out employment applications for their son or daughter so they can work at a fast-food restaurant.

When American public school students were asked to identify specific places on a map of the world, every other country except Italy and Mexico ranked higher than America. Among 18-to-24-year-olds, the United States finished last. It is estimated that 13 percent of American citizens are illiterate, approximately 30 million are functionally illiterate, and another 40-70 million are marginally literate.

Twenty-three percent of all adults and 40 percent of all minority youth are functionally illiterate. College board scores have dropped precipitously in the past several decades. The Educational Testing Service calls math scores by seventeen-year-olds "dismal." National Assessment of Educational Progress found that one-quarter of thirteen-year-olds cannot handle elementary math, and one-third of eleventh graders do not understand what their math teacher is talking about. Amazingly, some call this an education.

With a track record like this, you could never be sure what your teens are learning. But at home school, you know exactly where your children are. You know whether they are learning or not and what their strengths and weaknesses are. You see their work, know how much time they spend on it, and are able to supervise their progress. Furthermore, you know your teens will learn at home because you get to see the textbooks and even select them. You know what is in your teen's curricula!

Sixth, *you can continue to have influence over their peer relationships. Teen rebellion is not God's plan for the family.* Teen rebellion can certainly happen in the best of Christian families. But it is far more likely when parents lose the dominant influence over their children during their teen years. By home schooling your children through high school you retain that significant influence and irreplaceable time.

Seventh, *you can protect them from pressure to conform to what the other kids are doing. You won't need to spend time deprogramming.* When your teen is around peers a minimum of forty hours a week, his friends can plant more thoughts and ideas in his mind than parents and pastors can unteach on weeknights and weekends. The majority of their socialization comes from peer-group association, much of which is negative in nature and can affect them for life. When home schooling them is a viable alternative, why put your children through it? Plus, you won't have to worry about deprogramming.

Eighth, *home school is the best preparation for higher education. The education "style" is closer to college type instruction.* Scores of colleges and universities all across the country now accept home schoolers. Moreover, many prefer them and actually seek their matriculation. Why? Because they make good students and are well-suited for independent-style learning.

Ninth, *there is greater flexibility for work/study opportunities.* Since home-schooled students are not confined to the normal scheduling straitjacket typical of government schools, teens have the freedom to explore many work/study opportunities in their local community. Furthermore, fathers and mothers have the unique privilege of apprenticing their teens in their own occupation. It is an honor for parents who love their work to pass on their skills, trade, or knowledge to their teenagers. It helps give them a boost in life. I love to see sons and daughters going to work for and with Dad in his business, especially if it is a family business.

Tenth, *home educators have the best available curriculum and a greater selection.* Home educators can continue to eliminate poor learning methods like Outcome Based Education, anti-parent readers, evolutionary theory that is portrayed as fact, and many other curricular nuisances. School teachers and districts usually must confine their choices to what their state textbook committee allows. Home schoolers are free to choose from an abundant supply of all kinds of textbooks and publishers, both Christian and secular. Best of all, they are free to choose those that have good methodology and support a Christian worldview.

Eleventh, *public schools offer revisionist history and science that promote a humanistic perspective. The godly commitment of many great Americans has been deleted from public textbooks.* Public school texts are saturated in the humanistic perspective and delete the contributions of great, freedom-loving, Christian Americans. Modern public education has made an absolute hero out of the founder of humanism. It has lionized John Dewey as the father of progressive education.

Do you know what the heart of progressive education is? Listen to John Dewey, the father of American progressive education: "There is no God and there is no soul. Hence, there are no needs for the props of traditional religion. With dogma and creed excluded, then immutable truth is also dead and buried. There is no room for fixed, natural law or moral absolutes." You could have taken those words right out of the mouth of Adolf Hitler or Karl Marx. They happen to come from John Dewey and provide the very heartthrob of secularist public education for the last fifty years in this country. Is that the philosophy you want for your teen?

Twelfth, *the institutional method of public education is designed around "crowd control" and not learning. If and when teens learn it is usually a by-product of other priorities designed to maintain classroom order.* A Gallup poll showed that Americans regard lack of discipline as the number one problem in public schools.[162] Military wives have told me that their husband's military regimen and discipline is brought home from work and ultimately filters into their family life. The reverse is true of students in public high school—they bring home disrespect and lack of discipline. There are very few places we of us could work if businesses operated without order and discipline.

Many public school teachers are frustrated over the discipline problem. I'm reminded of the mother who went into her son's room to find out why he wasn't dressed for school. The son said, "I don't want to go to school." Mom asked, "Why?" The son replied, "For two reasons. The kids all hate me and the teachers all hate me." The mom snapped back, "Well you're going to school whether you like it or not." The son asked, "Why?" Mom said, "Two reasons; you're 42-years-old and you're the principal."

According to research reported in *Educators Newsletter,* 80 percent of students entering public school feel good about themselves and who they are. By the time they reach fifth grade, only 20 percent feel good about themselves. By the time they are seniors, only 5 percent. Furthermore, to control the crowd, students spend about sixty days each year receiving nagging and punishment. During the course of twelve years, the average public school student will be subjected to 15,000 negative statements. That's three times the number of positive statements. Is that the environment you want your teen in?

Thirteenth, *there will be a diversion away from the academic focus as well as spiritual priorities. Be aware of the many distractions that won't parallel your home life.* If you planted a garden from seed, spent two months watering and caring for it, would you abandon it to the weeds a few weeks before harvest? That would be silly, to say the least. If you put your child in public school at ninth grade, be advised and warned that there will be many distractions at school that will not correlate with the home life you maintained. Why not keep them at home?

Fourteenth, *young people will be thrown into things like preoccupation with boy/girl relationships, focus on clothes, and pressure to conform in appearance and music.* There are many dangers in modern, public coed education. The group message to individuals is dress, talk, and act the way we do or be ostracized. Why put your teen in an environment where they are constantly going to be on the moral defensive? Of course, people immediately raise the question, "We can't shelter our children forever, you know."

Certainly there is a measure of sheltering that takes place. Rightly so! Parents stand as a healthy and sober barrier between their teen and those things their son or daughter is neither emotionally nor physically strong enough to deal with. Every teen wants to feel attractive and accepted. Why heap the extra pressure of boy-girl relationships on top of it?

Public high school teens are under a perpetual siege by crude-talking students and sometimes even teachers. In public school one of the worst, most humiliating things you can call a teen today is a "virgin." Imagine your teen being publicly ridiculed as an inexperienced virgin. Every person wants to fit in. But do you want your teen to fit into an environment that is counter to your Christian views? Why subject your teen to being the oddball, the outcast, the black sheep of the worldly wise?

Add to this the condom-mania being taught in a coed milieu. Students are being asked in sex-education classes to practice unrolling condoms on bananas, cucumbers, and plastic sex organs. One modest student in Bellevue, Washington, felt uncomfortable saying the vernacular for various parts of male and female anatomy, so the teacher asked her to come to the front of the class and shout it out loud several times before all the students. Many schools have graphic instruction about sodomy under the guise of safe sex education. All of these things combined serve to morally lobotomize students.

Fifteenth, *vast amounts of time separated from the family will affect their relationship with you. We have all put a great amount of heart and time into the home-school years; we want those efforts preserved.* Children who are home schooled until sixth or eight grade and then put into public school are still vulnerable. Often a distancing between the teen and parent begins to slowly occur, and the blessed relationship you have built over their early years unfolds.

Sixteenth, *age/grade isolation or segregation inhibits socialization. Public school children are behind their home school counterparts in maturity, socialization, and vocabulary development, as demonstrated by available research.* As has already been pointed out, there is a common misconception that children need peer-group association in order to be properly socialized. But that is more myth than fact. Home schooled teens are not perfect, but their educational environment allows their character and personality to develop to its fullest Christian potential. Public school children are behind their home school counterparts in maturity, socialization and vocabulary development. On the other hand, research on self-concept by Dr. John Taylor demonstrates conclusively the superiority of socialization formed in a home school environment. In a survey of 45,000 home schoolers using the Piers Harris Children's Self Concept Scale, the premier testing instrument for measuring positive sociability, half of the home schoolers scored at or above the 91st percentile, which is 41 percent higher than the average conventionally-schooled child.[163]

A study by Dr. Larry Shyers compared home-schooled and conventionally-schooled children ages eight to ten in behavior and social development. These children were either solely home educated all their lives or had been solely schooled in the conventional classroom. His study found that home schoolers were not behind their conventionally-schooled peers in social development. More significant, using the Direct Observation Form of the Child Behavior Checklist instrument, Dr. Shyers found that home schooled children had consistently fewer behavioral problems. Traditionally-schooled children tended to be considerably more aggressive, loud, and competitive. Shyers attributes this to the fact that home schoolers tend to imitate their parent's behavior. Conversely, conventionally-schooled children tend to imitate the attitudes and behavior of their peers.[164]

My experience with a large number of home schoolers across our nation is that they relate better with children younger and older due to the blessed absence of age-segregation that is the norm in government schools. Moreover, most home schoolers I have met socialize quite well with their parents and grandparents. The generation gap is avoided. Why subject your teen to it by putting him back in public school?

Conclusion

If you home school through sixth or eighth grade, you have done a very good thing. There is not much difference in continuing on through high school. In fact, teens are more able than grade schoolers to learn and comprehend by independent study. If there are subjects you're not sure you can handle, it is easy to find a tutor in that area. The bottom line is, don't give up on a good thing. If at all possible, home school all the way through high school.

ELEVEN

Common Questions Asked about Home Schooling

All of the information in this chapter has been covered in greater detail throughout this book. However, it is written as a quick reference for those needing information or encouragement. It also might be used to present home schooling to others in a succinct manner. Below are short answers to some of the most commonly asked questions about home schooling.

1) *Why do families choose to home school?* The most common reason given by Christian parents is a conviction that it is God's will for them. They feel it is a return to a biblical model of education. Secondly, parents are concerned about their child's spiritual, moral, social, and academic well-being, and are cognizant of the public school track record in this area.

2) *Is it legal?* Home education is legal in all fifty states. Hundreds of thousands of children all over America, from kindergarten to the twelfth grade, are being home educated within the framework of the law. The constitutional right to employ home education is protected by numerous provisions of the United States Constitution, including freedom of religion exercise, freedom of speech and philosophic belief, the right to privacy, and the right to parental liberty. The state lacks any compelling interest in prohibiting or intrusively regulating home education. In many states, parents teach with complete freedom under the blessings of the law. Others comply in varying degrees with state regulations which govern the existence of a home school or the home school

as a private school. The Home School Legal Defense Association offers a free one-page summary of home school laws. Home schoolers need not fear state requirements. In fact, some of them are written for your legal protection with language suggested by the HSLDA—which is the home schoolers' best legal friend. Over the past few years, HSLDA has worked with resident home schoolers to help state after state liberalize their laws on home education. School districts that harass home schooling families find themselves, more often than not, in for a real surprise. There is a problem with encroachment of constitutional rights based in the First, Ninth, and Fourteenth Amendments. There will always be those uninformed people who love to create laws in their minds that simply do not exist. Then armed with these mental laws, they try to incite fear into the hearts of potential home schoolers. Don't listen to them, get the facts!

I believe God is on the side of the Christian home schooling movement as evidenced by the string of legislative and judicial victories over the years. State laws are continually being modified and revamped, mostly to the benefit of home educators.

3) *Are parents qualified to teach?* You do not need a teaching degree or certificate to qualify as a good teacher. You do need a loving concern for the overall development of your child's well-being and to simultaneously follow a few simple educational guidelines. You do not need to know everything in order to teach. Your example and enthusiasm in learning with your children will motivate and encourage them far more than striving to appear as if you know it all. God promises His wisdom in James 1:5-7 and assures you that He will supply your needs as you follow His leading, "If any of you lacks wisdom, he should ask God, who gives generously to all without finding fault, and it will be given to him."

Parents only need to be literate and committed to the home school process. Many home educators have nothing more than a high school diploma and a desire to teach their own, and yet, they have teaching success that is the envy of mass education. Based on the results of the public school system, I certainly wouldn't tout teaching degrees and certification as either an asset or a qualification. On the other hand, the academic track record of home schoolers is certainly worthy of public aggrandizement.

Parental tutoring is the biblical model for the education of children. Children are accountable to their parents who, in turn, are accountable to God. Mass education is at best a substitute for the principal educators, the parents. Since classroom-schooling has held sway for over a century in America, many parents have forgotten who is held responsible for their child's development. No school, public or private, can ever hope to do a better job of developing character and values quite like loving and devoted Christian parents. What kind of values can be taught a child in a public school where teachers must remain, as they call it "morally neutral?"

The teacher-certification label is of highly questionable value. Public teachers are parental, day-time surrogates who lack the qualifications for being the primary instructors of biblical truth upon which all knowledge is hinged. Proverbs 1:8-9 advises children, "Listen, my son, to your father's instruction and do not forsake your mother's teaching. They will be a garland to grace your head and a chain to adorn your neck."

Furthermore, it must also be remembered that sending a child off to parochial school also does not exempt parents from the divine charge in Deuteronomy 6 and Ephesians 6:1. Parochial schools cannot replace responsible, Christian parents when it comes to the teaching and mirroring of spiritual truth. Though they can choose to delegate their teaching responsibilities, the divine charge firmly rests upon parents.

4) *Will my child miss out on socialization?* This a common misconception. Popular opinion assumes that children need to extensively be around others their own age to be properly socialized. This dangerous assumption leads well-intentioned parents to false conclusions. So powerful is this psychological notion that many parents concede to the viability of academic instruction at home but keep their children in the public educational setting in order to help them develop and master their social skills. Sound research, however, lends little credibility to this socialization theory.

There are two types of socialization, positive and negative. Positive sociability builds responsibility, cooperation, kindness, fidelity, love, and bilateral trust. It molds a good self-image that delights in putting others first. Negative sociability is the result of coerced age-segregation and builds rivalry, contention, selfishness, peer-dependency, criticism, and derision. It molds a poor self-esteem that responds quickly to peer pressure.

Without a doubt, a loving, outreaching home environment is the best socializer a young child could possibly have. A home-schooled child tends to mix freely with all ages and not just a narrow age grouping. Home schoolers on average score higher than their conventionally-schooled peers in tests that measure both self-concept and sociability.

A young child learns good sociability primarily by watching and mirroring. Do you want your child to model after you or after his peers, after his teachers at school or his teachers at home? What kind of socialization do you want for your child, positive or negative? The evidence is overwhelming that shows where each kind is bred and nurtured.

5) *Are home-schooled children accepted in college and accredited schools?* Yes, they have been accepted in over 200 colleges and universities. Most colleges judge a child's academic competence based on his performance on college entrance exams such as the SAT and ACT. Home schoolers are being accepted into the finest institutions of learning. In many cases, home schoolers are prime admission targets of universities and colleges.

6) *Will my child miss out on field trips and extracurricular activities?* Not at all! If anything, he will enjoy more. In metropolitan areas, local home schooling families frequently join together for field trips. A few places our group has visited are the county courthouse to study about justice and law; historical sites to study about historical America; cultural events to study culture through art, plays, ballets; athletic events to study about recreation /sports; manufacturing plants to study how goods and products are made; police/fire departments to study how crime and fires are fought; public libraries to check out books and learn about library services; ranches and farms to learn how we get milk, butter, eggs, meat, etc; nature centers to study wildlife; airport/train stations to study transportation; and finally, television/newspaper offices to study how news is communicated.

These are but a few of the many field trips home schooling families engage in. Since these activities are often done as a family, they are a great deal more pleasurable and enriching. This in turn creates a better learning environment for your child.

7) *At what age should I begin?* It is very important to remember that learning readiness is not schooling readiness. Most children have a decided interest in learning from birth on. Many parents confuse an interest in learning with preparedness to start school. This is an unfortunate assumption. Children may be able to learn basic concepts, facts, and ideas without being able to emotionally han-

dle the demands and methods that are placed on them in a conventional educational setting. Many children are not ready for formal academic instruction until they reach the age of about eight. Home educators can start their child when they are sure they are ready. The key is not to do too much too early. That is the regrettable mistake of the education system right now. Take it easy! Enjoy your children and let them enjoy you. Use their day to day questions of curiosity as teaching and learning opportunities. In the early years especially, concentrate on character development.

8) *How advanced of a grade should I teach to?* Undertake the challenge a year at a time, endeavoring to teach as long as you can. There is no set rule or standard. Remember, even a few years of home education is better than none, especially in the early years. Many home-schooled children show marked elevation over their peers with just a couple of years of home tutoring. Some parents have the goal of teaching through sixth grade, some through junior high, and still others all the way through high school. The latter is preferable, though not absolutely necessary. Teach them as long as you can.

From a spiritual perspective, parents should have the goal of teaching until their child has demonstrated the self-evident maturity of being the salt and light of the world. By this I mean developing the ability to resist the strong peer-dependent tendencies inherent in mass education. I mean the ability to walk in the ways of God, firmly standing on biblical convictions in the face of social opposition and worldly enticements. These abilities primarily come with age-maturity and godly role modeling.

9) *How many children can I teach at home?* As many as you have. Some families home school as many as ten to twelve children simultaneously. And with great success, I might add. Responsible and organized parents can successfully and competently teach all of their children, so long as they have a strong, unswerving commitment and depend upon God as their source of strength.

10) *How much time does it take?* Home schooling takes time but not as much as you might think. Home tutoring is far more efficient than classroom instruction, hence it takes less time. You will not need to teach your child for six or seven hours a day! Not even conventional schools do that. Research shows that students are exposed to about two hours of "teacher talk" during a five-period day. And out of that, an average of seven minutes a day involves

teachers' responses to individual students.[165] It doesn't take much for home educators to exceed that unfortunate amount of one on-one communication. The consistency of private tutoring allows most home educators to accomplish an incredible amount of teaching in three to four hours a day, even less in the early grades. In this amount of time, most are easily able to supersede a conventional school in quality academic instruction.

Home schooling does require a commitment on the part of the parents. Part of that commitment requires an assessment of priorities. When you boil it all down, what are the most important things in life? Your career? Your house? Your hobbies? Your financial assets? Your personal entertainment? Or your children? Each needs to be placed in its proper perspective. Your children are with you but for a few short years, and then they are gone. The time you have to spend with your children is precious and numbered. Parents who are willing to commit themselves to the process will find home schooling both rewarding and within reach.

11) *Will my child listen to me and accept me as his teacher?* If your child listens and responds to your parental authority now, he will have little problem accepting you as teacher at home. However, if you have less respect and control over your child than you would like to have, the home school environment will be your best opportunity to regain it. In this book we have examined the ill effects of conventional classroom schooling and have seen that rebellion against parental authority is frequently a result. Peer dependency and growing anti-family attitudes in educational circles are believed to be eroding this traditional respect. As a home educator, you can reclaim and nurture this vital attribute.

12) *Should I defend my decision to home school before friends and family?* Some merely need to have home education logically explained to them. In that case, share whatever information or books helped you make your decision, like this one. Others with closed minds will never budge and will argue for the sake of arguing. Proverbs gives this advice: "Do not speak to a fool, for he will scorn the wisdom of your words" (Proverbs 23:9). In short, know your reasons, explain them to those to whom you feel it necessary but don't feel compelled to advertise your decision and defend it to every acquaintance.

From time to time you might be challenged or criticized for your decision to home school. Depending on who it is and the importance of your relationship, you may want to explain your reasons. This may be true in the case of immediate family and close friends. However, be very careful to what degree you defend your decision. Remember that your primary accountability belongs to God.

It is important for parents to know why they home school, but it is not important for them to spend all their time defending that decision to others. As you can see, there are many excuses people give for not home schooling. To satisfy their own lack of action, they will attempt to thrust these excuses onto you. Some may have an element of validity, many do not. It hurts when parents and friends do not understand and lend support but don't expect them to. If everyone understood, we wouldn't have our current public education crisis.

13) *What material is available?* There are many excellent Christian publishers who make teaching materials especially for home schoolers. Also, private Christian school texts can be adapted for home use. Some parents choose to teach exclusively from one publishing house. Others choose a publisher who they feel excels in a given subject, using, for example, one publisher for math, one for penmanship, one for reading, etc.

Research, common sense, veteran advice, and a little experience will give you the best guidance in choosing curriculum that is right for you. Under the "research" area, it is helpful to attend home school curriculum fairs and workshops, as well as to place your name on mailing lists of various curriculum publishers. An excellent resource guide in this area is Mary Pride's *The Big Book of Home Learning*. (There are several in the series corresponding to grade level).

Parents in local home schooling support groups will gladly give you curriculum suggestions based on their teaching experience. It is smart to listen to the advice of veteran home schoolers. At the same time, realize that there is no one curriculum that is right for every family. What may work well for someone else may not work well for you. Since you can always change, don't become overly bogged down in curriculum selection. It is more critical to home school with the proper motives, attitudes, and goals. Good textbooks are important, but love, kindness, organization and consistency are more important. Academics have great worth, but stressing values, character, and spiritual development have more.

14) *Should Christian children stay in school as a witness?* Unfortunately, the witness usually works in reverse. Children are usually influenced by the majority. Children are emotionally fragile and highly susceptible to being molded by a humanistic worldview. Children of all ages are morally and spiritually vulnerable to the values of their peers and teachers. If you put a good apple in a barrel of half-rotten ones, soon they all become rotten. Sickness is more contagious than health. If you put a pure white cotton ball in a bowl of ink, it's going to soak up the dark, black ink. In a negative environment, it doesn't take long for a child's innocence to be lost and his character defiled.

Children need to be given a strong biblical foundation so they can be effective as a witness and be able to defend their faith as they enter adulthood. If you were a missionary, would you want your first assignment to be among a tribe of cannibalistic headhunters? No, you would get your feet wet on a less hostile field. There are also times when we need to be like Joseph and run from evil. If Lot would have stayed away from the evil environment of Sodom, perhaps he wouldn't have lost his beloved wife. Please don't throw your lambs to the lions under the guise of being a witness.

15) *What are the biggest obstacles?* There are two big ones. They are:

Lack of Confidence It is not uncommon for new home schoolers to feel uneasy about teaching their own children. Suddenly being faced with multiple decisions like which curriculum, what teaching approach, setting up a schedule, and doubts about your ability to teach, all add to a lack of confidence. The good news is that it won't last. If you persevere, your confidence level will begin to mushroom.

Low Level Of Commitment: Home schooling should not be entered lightly. Without a high level of commitment, I can almost guarantee your home school will fizzle out. Don't consider home schooling merely out of convenience or because you have a friend who is doing it. The way to have a successful home school is to start with and maintain a high level of commitment.

16) *Who should not home school?* As a general rule, you should not home school unless both you and your spouse are in basic agreement about it and the atmosphere at home is relatively peaceful. If there is abnormal stress at home from a divorce filing, alcoholism, a contagious disease, mental illness, or any other highly

stressful event, home school should not be considered until the situation is resolved.

17) *How do I begin?* Before you do anything else, pray about it. Read this book thoroughly. Talk with the few veteran home schoolers. Then, if you are at peace with a decision to proceed, find out what the laws in your state are regarding home schooling. Next, pick a curriculum and comply with state laws regarding the removal of your children from public school. Finally, join a local support group and the Home School Legal Defense Association. Home schooling will take commitment, some godly prayer, and a little experimentation. But if you stay focused on the task, you will find it a great blessing to the whole family.

Parts of this chapter were sparked by *Home-School Questions and Answers,* a brochure by Sue Welch and Cindy Short (available from *The Teaching Home* phone number and address on page 193).

Appendix

Home School Resources

(This list is by no way comprehensive but will provide a good starting point.)

Magazines for Home Educators

1) *The Teaching Home,* 12311 NE Brazee, Portland, OR 97230. (503) 253-9633 (bi-monthly)
2) *Practical Homeschooling,* P.O. Box 1250, Fenton, MO 63026-1850. (quarterly)
3) *Home School Digest,* P.O. Box 575, Winona Lake, IN 46590. (quarterly)
4) *Homeschooling Today,* Box 956, Lutz, FL 33549
5) *Homeschooling Magazine,* 470 Boston Post Rd., Weston, MA 02193, (617) 899-2702

Home Schooling Video

1) *Home Schooling: A Foundation for Excellence,* Mission City Television, Inc., 326 Sterling Browing, San Antonio, TX 78232. (210) 490-4000. (A good visual introduction to home schooling.)

Book Clubs and Newsletters

1) Homeschooling Book Club, 1000 E. Huron, Milford, MI 48381. (810) 685-8773.
2) God's World Publications, P.O. Box 2330, Asheville, NC 28802-2330. (704) 253-8063. (A Christian current events paper in five graded editions K through Junior High)
3) *The Blumenfeld Education Newsletter,* P.O. Box 45161, Boise, Idaho 83711. (208) 322-4440. (Excellent advice and current information on the educational trends in America.)
4) *New Attitude Magazine,* 6920 S.E. Hogan, Gresham, OR 97080. (503) 669-1236 (oriented towards home school teens)
5) *American Information Newsletter,* 2408 Main St., Boise, Idaho 83702. (208) 343-3790. (A newsletter that gives a smorgasbord of current events from a variety of sources along with commentary.)

Home School Legal Protection

1) Home School Legal Defense Association, P.O. Box 159, Paeonian Springs, VA 22129. (703) 338-5600. In Canada contact HSLDA of

Canada, Box 42009 Lee Ridge P.O., Edmonton AB T6K 4C4, (403) 986-1566. (The author highly recommends membership in HSLDA! Don't stay home without it!)

Information on Home School Laws in Various States

1) *Home Schooling in the United States:* A Legal Analysis, by Christopher J. Klicka. (This book analyzes the home school legal atmosphere in all fifty states and United States territories. It is annually updated.)

Home School Information and Research Organizations

1) National Center for Home Education, P.O. Box 400, Paeonian Springs, VA 22129. (703) 338-7600 (The NCHE is an information and data gathering organization for home school leaders. Among other things, they prepare monthly mailings to state leaders, monitor hot legislative issues, coordinate conferences hosted by NCHE, and work as education consultants for HSLDA.)

2) National Home Education Research Institute, Western Baptist College, 5000 Deer Park Drive, S.E., Salem, Oregon 97301. (503) 581-8600. (NHERI conducts basic, data-gathering research, serves as a clearinghouse of information for researchers, home educators, attorneys, legislators, policy makers, and the public at-large. It is headed by Dr. Brian Ray).

Seminar on Home Schooling and Family Life

1) Ray Ballmann

We offer seminars on a variety of current topics of interest to the home schooling community:

- Beginning your home school
- Building an effective home school and family life
- Father involvement in the home school
- Understanding the effects of television in the home
- Biblical courtship vs. the Western custom of dating
- How to avoid home school burnout
- Reasons to home school through high school
- Home schoolers, the guardians of freedom
- Home schoolers response to Outcome-Based Education
- America's godly heritage and home schooling
- Why home schooling remains an attractive educational option
- Countering the socialization argument and rendering it meritless
- Principles that facilitate dynamic family leadership
- Guidelines for effective biblical parenting
- Time management for the home school—how to get more things done with and for the family.
- Principles for developing a godly family that impacts the world in a beneficial way

For information about scheduling a seminar in your area, contact:

Foundation For Family Development
Post Office Box 1267
Burleson, TX 76028
Phone: (817)-HIS-WORD (447-9673)
2) Gregg Harris
For information about scheduling a seminar in your area, contact:
Christian Life Workshops
Post Office Box 2250
Gresham, OR 97030
Phone: (503 667-3942)

Curriculum for Character Education

1) Character Foundation Curriculum, published by the Association of Christian Schools International, P.O. Box 4097, Whittier, California, 90607. (213) 694-4791 (Excellent material that can be used in conjunction with most curriculums. Also available are the character flash cards.)
2) Konos Character Curriculum, Konos Inc., P.O. Box 1534, Richardson, TX 75083. (214) 669-8337.
3) Character Sketches, Institute In Basic Life Principles, Inc., Box One, Oak Brook, IL 60521. (Though not specifically designed as a curriculum, it can serve as excellent resource material. They also have a family game entitled "Character Cues.") Those who enroll in the Advanced Training Institute International (also called ATII) receive a wealth of character training tools for home teaching use. For information, contact: ATI, Box One, Oak Brook, IL 60522-3001. (708) 323-7073.

Curriculum for Reading and Writing

1) Christ Centered Publications, Route 1, Box 620, Locust Grove, OK 74352. (800) 884-7858. (Distinctively biblical learning approach for the early ages. They also offer a math program.)
2) Sing, Spell, Read & Write, International Learning Systems, P.O. Box 16032, Chesapeake, VA 23328 (800)321-TEACH.
3) Alpha Phonics, Sam Blumenfeld, P.O. Box 45161, Boise, Idaho, 83711. (208) 322-4440
4) First Reader by Phyllis Schlafly, First Reader System Inc., P.O. Box 495, Alton, IL 62002. (800) 700-5228.

Curriculum Assessment Resources

The authors below provide extensive previews of the various curricula available to home schoolers and make recommendations.
1) *The Big Book of Home Learning* (volumes 1-4) by Mary Pride, published by Crossway Books. They can be obtained at your local Christian bookstore.
2) *Christian Home Educators Curriculum Manual* (2 volumes) by Cathy Duffy, published by Home Run Enterprises, 12531 Aristocrat Avenue, Garden Grove, CA. 92641.

Curriculum Publishers

Though there are many other good publishers, the following have proven effective and helpful to home schoolers worldwide. A more complete listing can be found in the curriculum assessment books mentioned above.

1) Alpha Omega Publications, P.O. Box 3153, Tempe, AZ 85280. (800) 821-4443.

2) Accelerated Christian Education School of Tomorrow, P.O. Box 14380, Lewisville, TX 75067-1438. (800) 925-7777.

3) KONOS, P.O. Box 1534, Richardson, TX 75083, (214) 669-8337.

4) Weaver Curriculum Series, 2752 Scarborough, Riverside, CA 92503,.(714) 688-3126.

5) Bob Jones University Press, Greenville, SC 29614. (800) 845-5731.

6) A Beka Books, Pensacola, FL 32523-1960. (800) 874-BEKA.

7) Rod and Staff, Hiway 172, Crockett, KY 41413. (606) 522-4348.

Newsletters For the Military

1) *Military Family Matters,* 2588 Prescott Circle West, Colorado Springs, CO. 80916-3139

2) *Christian Home Educators of Foreign Soil,* 1856 CSGP, PSC2 Box 8462, APO AE09012

Newsletters for the Handicapped

1) *National Handicapped Home School Associated Network,* 5383 Alpine Rd. S.E., Olalla, WA 98359 (206)857-4257

State Home School Support Organizations

The addresses below were current at the time of publication but are subject to change. If you find this the case, contact *The Teaching Home* listed under "Magazines for Home Educators" for the most current address.

1) *Christian Home Educators Fellowship of Alabama*
   Box 563
   Alabaster, Alabama 35007
   (205) 664-2232

2) *Alaska Private and Home Educators Association*
   Box 141764
   Anchorage, Alaska 99514
   (907) 696-0641

3) *Arizona Families for Home Education*
   Box 4661
   Scottsdale, Arizona 85261
   (602) 941-3938

4) *Arkansas Christian Home Education Assoc.*
   Box 4410

N. Little Rock, Arkansas 72116
(501) 758-9909

5) *Christian Home Educators Assoc.*
Box 2009
Norwalk, California 90651-2009
(800) 564-2432, (310) 864-2432 (out of state)

6) *Christian Home Educators of Colorado*
1015 S. Gaylord St. #226,
Denver, Colorado 80209
(303) 388-1888

7) *The Education Assoc. of Christian Homeschooler*
25 Field Stone Run
Farmington, Connecticut 06032
(800) 205-7844, (203) 677-4538 (out of state)

8) *Delaware Home Education Assoc.*
Box 1003
Dover, Delaware 19903
(302) 653-6878

9) *Florida At Home*
4644 Adanson
Orlando, Florida 32804
(407) 740-8877

10) *Georgia Home Education Assoc.*
245 Buckeye Ln.
Fayetteville, Georgia 30214
(404) 461-3657

11) *Christian Homeschoolers of Hawaii*
91-824 Oama Street
Ewa Beach, Hawaii 96706
(808) 689-6398

12) *Idaho Home Educators*
Box 1324
Meridian, Idaho 83680
(208) 482-7336

13) *Illinois Christian Home Educators*
Box 261
Zion, Illinois 60099
(708) 662-1909

14) *Indiana Assoc. of Home Educators*
1000 North Madison, Suite S-2
Greenwood, Indiana 46142
(317) 638-9600 ext 7000

15) *Network of Iowa Christian Home Educators*
Box 158
Dexter, Iowa 50070

(800) 723-0438, (515) 830-1614 (out of state)
16) *Christian Home Educators Confederation of Kansas*
    Box 3564
    Shawnee Mission, Kansas 66203
17) *Christian Home Educators of Kentucky*
    691 Howardstown Rd.
    Hodgensville, Kentucky 42748
    (502) 358-9270
18) *Christian Home Educators Fellowship of Louisiana*
    Box 74292
    Baton Rouge, Louisiana 70874
    (504) 642-2059
19) *Homeschooler of Maine*
    HC 62, Box 24
    Hope, Maine 04847
    (207) 763-4251
20) *Maryland Assoc. of Christian Home Educators*
    Box 3964
    Frederick, Maryland 21701
    (301) 663-3999
21) *Massachusetts Homeschool Organization of Parent Ed.*
    15 Ohio St.
    Wilmington, MA 01887
    (508) 658-8970
22) *Information Network for Christian Homes*
    4934 Cannonsburg Rd.
    Belmont, Michigan 49306
    (616) 874-5656
23) *Minnesota Assoc. of Christian Home Educators*
    Box 188
    Anoka, Minnesota 55303
    (612) 753-2370
24) *Mississippi Home Educators Assoc.*
    109 Reagan Ranch
    Laurel, Mississippi 39440
    (601) 649-6432
25) *Missouri Assoc. of Teaching Christian Homes*
    307 E. Ash St., #146
    Columbia, Missouri 65201
    (314) 443-8217
26) *Montana Coalition of Home Educators*
    Box 43
    Gallatin Gateway, Montana 59730
    (406) 587-6163
27) *Nebraska Christian Home Educators Assoc.*

Box 57041
Lincoln, Nebraska 68505-7041
28) *Home Education and Righteous Training*
Box 42264
Las Vegas, Nevada 89116.
(702) 593-4927
29) *Christian Home Educators of New Hampshire*
Box 961
Manchester, New Hampshire 03105
(603) 898-8314
30) *Education Network of Christian Homeschoolers*
65 Middlesex Rd.
Matawan, New Jersey 07747
(908) 583-7128
31) *New Mexico Christian Home Educators*
5749 Paradise Blvd. NW,
Albuquerque, New Mexico 87114
(505) 897-1772
32) *New York State Loving Education At Home*
Box 332
Syracuse, New York 13205
(315) 468-2225
33) *North Carolinians for Home Education*
419 N. Boylan Ave.
Raleigh, North Carolina 27603-1211
(919) 834-6243
34) *North Dakota Home School Assoc.*
4007 North State St.
Bismark, North Dakota 58501
(701) 223-4080
35) *Christian Home Educators of Ohio*
Box 262
Columbus, Ohio 43216
(800) 274-2436
36) *Coalition of Christian Home Educators of Oklahoma*
Box 471032
Tulsa, Oklahoma 74147-1032
37) *Oregon Christian Home Education Assoc. Network*
2515 NE 37th
Portland, Oregon 97212
(503) 288-1285
38) *Christian Homeschool Association of Pennsylvania*
Box 3603
York, Pennsylvania 17402-0603
(717) 661-2428

39) *Rhode Island Guild of Home Teachers*
Box 11
Hope, Rhode Island 02831
(401) 821-1546

40) *South Carolina Home Educators Association*
Box 612
Lexington, South Carolina 29071-0612
(803) 951-8960

41) *Western Dakota Christian Home Schools*
Box 528
Black Hawk, South Dakota 57718
(605) 787-4153

42) *Tennessee Home Education Assoc.*
3677 Richbriar Court
Nashville, Tennessee 37211
(615) 834-3529

43) *Home-Oriented Private Education For Texas*
Box 59876
Dallas, Texas 75229
(214) 358-2221

44) *Utah Christian Homeschoolers*
Box 3942
Salt Lake City, Utah 84110

45) *Christian Home Educators of Vermont*
2 Webster Avenue
Barre, Vermont 05641-4818
(802) 476-8821

46) *Home Educators Assoc. of Virginia*
Box 1810
Front Royal, Virginia 22630
(703) 635-9322

47) *Washington Assoc. of Teaching Christian Homes*
N. 2904 Dora Rd.
Spokane, Washington 99212
(509) 922-4811

48) *Christian Home Educators of West Virginia*
Box 8770
South Charleston, VA 25306
(304) 776-4664

49) *Wisconsin Christian Home Educators*
2307 Carmel Ave.
Racine, Wisconsin 53405
(414) 637-5127

50) *Homeschoolers of Wyoming*
Box 926

Evansville, Wyoming 82636
(307) 237-4383
51) *Christian Home Educators of the Caribbean*
Palmas Del Mar Mail Service
Box 888-Suite 273
Humacao, Puerto Rico 00791
(809) 852-5284

Station Listings for "Home School Heartbeat Radio" Broadcasts:

Alabama
Centreville WBIB-1110 AM 9:30 A.M.
Dothan WVOB-91.3 FM 11:05 A.M.
Enterprise AFRN-90.5 FM
Montgomery WLBF-89.1 FM 11:40 A.M.
Opelika WJHO-1400 AM 7:55 A.M.
Sheffield AFRN-89.9 FM

Arizona
Lake Havasu City KNLB-91.1 FM 12:40 P.M.

Arkansas
Arkadelphia AFRN-91.9 FM
Blytheville AFRN-91.5 FM
Crossett AFRN-91.7 FM
El Dorado AFRN-91.9 FM
Forrest City AFRN-91.5 FM
Jonesboro AFRN-90.5 FM, KNEA-970 AM
Mena KENA-1450 AM 9:35A.M.
Pocahontas AFRN-91.1 FM
Warren AFRN-91.3 FM

California
Angwin KCDS-89.9 FM 11:30 A.M.
Burney-Redding KIBC-90.5 FM 12:12 P.M., 5:02 P.M.
Rosamond KAVC-105.5 FM 4:00 P.M. Sundays
Santa Maria KGDP-660 AM, KGDP-95.7FM
Stockton KCJH-90.1 FM 11:45 P.M.

Colorado
Breen KLLV-550 AM 3:40 P.M.
Denver KPOF-910 AM 8:45 P.M.
Grand Junction KJOL-90.3 FM 10:55 A.M. Saturdays
Johnstown KHNC-1360 AM

Florida
Ft. Lauderdale WAFG-90.3 FM
Ft. Walton Beach WPSM-91.1 FM 10:20 A.M., 12:50 A.M.
Gainesville WJLF-91.7 FM 1:20 P.M.
Jacksonville WAYR-AM 3:00 P.M.

Madison WMAF-1230 AM 12:15 P.M.
Palm Bay WEJF-90.3 FM 12:05 P.M.
Pensacola WVTS-610 AM 1:45 P.M.
Punta Gorda WVIJ-91.7 FM 2:45 P.M., 11:30 P.M.
Sarasota WKZM-105.5 FM 12:30 P.M.
Starke WTLG-88.3 FM 8:39 A.M.
Tallahassee WLOR-1120 AM 8:30 A.M.

Georgia
Atlanta WFTD-1080 AM 11:50 A.M.
Dublin AFRN-91.9 FM
Macon WJTJ-91.3 FM 4:15 P.M.
Valdosta WAFT-101.1 FM 3:30 P.M.
Waycross AFRN-91.9 FM

Hawaii
Hilo KFSH-97.1 FM 7:20 A.M.
Honolulu KLHT-1040 AM 8:00 P.M.

Idaho
Boise KFXD-580 AM

Illinois
Mt. Vernon AFRN-91.3 FM
Olney WPTH-88.1 FM 7:31 A.M., 4:46 P.M.

Indiana
Ft. Wayne WFCV-1090 AM
Indianapolis WBRI-1500 AM 5:03 P.M.
  WXIR-98.3 F 6:25 A.M.
Jeffersonville WZCC-1570 AM 7:15 A.M.
  WXLN-105.7 FM 12:00-1:00 P.M.
Salem WSLM-1220 AM and 98.9 FM Mornings

Iowa
Sioux City KTFC-103.3 FM 6:25 A.M.
Sioux Rapids KTFG-102.9 FM 6:25 A.M.

Kansas
Emporia KNGM-91.9 FM 2:00 P.M.
Ft. Scott KVCY-101.7 FM 12:30 P.M.
Goodland KGCR-107.7 FM 2:15 P.M.
Great Bend AFRN-819.7 FM
Hays AFRN-89.7 FM
Kansas City KLJC-88.5 FM 9:15 A.M.
Medicine Lodge KREJ-95.9 FM 8:57 A.M.
Topeka KBUZ-90.3 FM
Wichita KCFN-91.1 FM

Kentucky
Ashland AFRN-91.1 FM
Campbellsville AFRN-91.7 FM
Danville WDFB-1400 AM and 88.1 FM 3 times daily

Louisville WZCC-1570 AM 7:15 A.M. and 12:00-1:00 P.M.
McDaniels WBFI-91.5 FM
Somerset WTHL-90.5 FM

Louisiana
Lafayette KSJY-90.9 FM 12:20 P.M.
Ruston AFRN-88.3 FM

Maine
Freeport WMSJ-91.9 FM 10:45 A.M., 1:45 and 6:45 P.M.

Maryland
Baltimore WRBS-95.1 FM 9:55 P.M. Thursdays
Braddock Heights WJTM-88.1 FM 3:15 P.M. Tues.and Thurs.
Denton WKDI-840 AM 12:50 P.M.
Princess Anne WOLC-102.5 FM 3:30 P.M.

Massachusetts
Boston Songtime Radio
Quincy WEZE-1260 AM Weekends

Michigan
Albion WUFN-96.7 FM 6:53 A.M.
Gaylord WPHN-90.5 FM 7:30 P.M.
Hancock WMPL-920 AM 12:25 A.M. and 3:03 P.M.
Kingsford WEUL-98.9 FM 11:18 A.M. and 4:18 P.M.
Marquette WHWL-95.7 FM 12:18 and 5:18 P.M.
Traverse City WLJN-89.9 FM 11:30 A.M.

Minnesota
Duluth WWJC-850 AM 8:45 A.M. and 1:30 P.M.
International Falls KBHW-99.5 FM
Pequot Lakes KTIG-100.1 FM 2:55 P.M.
Worthington AFRN-88.1 FM

Mississippi
Cleveland WDFX-98.3 FM
Columbus AFRN-91.9 FM
Forest WQST-92.5 FM
Jackson WQST-92.5 FM 1:15 P.M.
Kosciusko WJTA-91.7 FM 4:15 P.M.
McComb WAKK-1140 AM 3:30 P.M.
Natchez AFRN-91.1 FM
Starkville AFRN-88.9 FM
Tupelo WAFR-88.3 FM 1:15 P.M.
West Point AFRN-96.9 FM

Missouri
Kansas City KLJC-88.5 FM 9:15 A.M.
Kennett KFRN-91.5 FM
Mexico KJAB-90.1 FM 1:13 P.M.
Neosho KNEO-91.7 FM
Springfield KLFJ-1550 AM 11:30 A.M.

Nebraska
Dakota City KTFJ-1250 AM 5:30 P.M.
Omaha KCRO-660 AM
Scotts Bluff KCMI-96.9 FM 11:25 A.M.

Nevada
Las Vegas KNLB-91.9 FM 12:40 P.M.
Reno KRCV-630 AM

New Mexico
Clovis AFRN-91.1 FM
Hobbs KKKK-98.3 FM 12:28 P.M.

New York
Cape Vincent WMHI-94.7 FM 12:24 P.M.
Houghton WJSL-90.3 FM 12:24 P.M.
Rochester WASB-1590 AM
Syracuse WMHR-102.9 FM 12:24 P.M.
Webster WMHN-89.3 FM 12:24 P.M.

North Carolina
Asheville WGCR-720 AM 4:15 P.M.
   WKJV-1380 AM
Durham WRTP-1530 AM 11:15 A.M.
Mocksville WDSL-1520 AM 3:30 P.M.
New Bern AFRN-88.5 FM
Statescille WAME-550 AM 12:15 P.M.
Tryon WTYN-1160 AM 3:30 P.M.
Winston-Salem WSMX-1500 AM

Ohio
Castalia WGGN-97.7 FM 1:55 P.M.
Cincinnati WAKW-93.3 FM 7:58 P.M.
Cleveland WCCD-1000 AM 11:25 A.M.
Columbus WRFD-880 AM 2:30 P.M.
Conneaut WGOJ-105.5 FM 7:25 A.M.
Lancaster WFCO-90.9 FM 8:40 P.M.
Steubenville WSTV-1340 AM 2:30 P.M.
   AFRN-88.9 FM
Toledo WJYM-730 AM 8:55 A.M.
Zanesville WCVZ-92.7 FM 10:00 A.M. and 5:30 P.M.

Oklahoma
Ada AFRN-88.7 FM
Elk City KPDR-88.3 FM 1:41 and 11:16 P.M.
Enid KBVV-91.1 FM 8:15 A.M.and4:30-5:00 P.M.
Oklahoma City KQCV-800 AM 3:26 P.M.
Sand Springs KTOW-1340 AM 7:20 A.M.
Tulsa KCFO-970 AM 2:00 and 8:30P.M.

Oregon
Coos Bay KYTT-98.7 FM 9:00 A.M.

Springfield KORE-1050 AM 3:47 P.M.
Pennsylvnia
Bedford WBFD-1310 AM 12:10 P.M.
Lancaster WDAC-94.5 FM 12:30 P.M.
Lebanon WADV-940 AM 9:10 A.M.
Phillipsburg WPHB-1260 AM 11:40 A.M.
Sellersville WBYO-88.9 FM
Warminster WRDV-89.1 FM 6:00 P.M.
Windber WFRJ-88.9 FM 11:15 A.M.
Rhode Island
Portsmouth WJFD-90.7 FM
South Carolina
Beaufort WAGP-88.7 FM 9:30 A.M.
Greenville WMUU-94.5 FM 2:30 P.M.
WLFJ-89.3 FM; WTBI-91.7 FM
Spartanburg WTYN-1160 AM 3:30 P.M.
Tennessee
Ardmore WLSV-1110 AM 8.30 A.M.
Bristol WHCB-91.5 FM 4:35 A.M. and 4:45 P.M.
Chattanooga WDYN-89.7 FM 12:05 P.M.
Church Hill WMCII-1260 AM 6:25 A.M.
Cookeville WWOG-90.9 FM
Dayton WREA-1520 AM 3:30 P.M.
Jackson AFRN-88.1 FM
Mcmphis WCRV-640 AM 4:00 P.M.
WGSF-1210 AM
Shelbyville AFRN-91.3 FM
Springfield WDBL-94.3 FM
Texas
Amarillo KPDR-88.5 FM 1:41 and 11:16 P.M.
AFRN-90.7 FM; KRGN-103.1 FM 6:55 P.M.
Austin KIXL-970 AM 3:55 P.M.
Big Springs KKKK-103.9 FM 12:28 P.M.
Borger KPDR-88.1 FM 1:41 AND 11:16 P.M.
AFRN-91.5 FM
Canadian KPDR-88.1 FM 1:41 and 11:16 P.M.
Farwell KIJN-92.3 FM 10:20 A.M.
KIJN-1060 AM 10:20 A.M.
Giddings KOKE-101.7 FM 8:20 P.M.
Houston KTEK-1110 AM 7:21 A.M.
Humble KSBJ-89.3 FM 1:20 P.M.
Jacksonville KBJS-90.3 FM 12:28 P.M.
Levelland AFRN-91.1 FM
Lufkin KSWP-91.9 FM 1:21 P.M.
Midland KKKK-99.1 FM 12:28 P.M.

Pampa KPDR-91.9 FM 1:41 and 11:16 P.M.
   AFRN-90.9 FM
Plainview KWLD-91.5 FM 2:00 P.M.
Texarkana KHSP-1400 AM 6:40 A.M.
Waco KBBW-1010 AM 6:00-7:00 A.M. and 5:00-6:00 P.M.
Wheeler KPDR-90.5 FM 1:41 and 11:16 P.M.
Wichita Falls KMOC-89.5 FM 1:31 P.M.

Utah
St. George AFRN-88.7 FM

Virginia
Amherst WAMV-1420 AM 9:00-11:00 A.M.
Arlington WAVA-105.1 FM 8:30 P.M.
Cambridge WPEX-90.9 FM
Chase City WMEK-980 AM
Martinsville WPIM-90.5 FM 2:12 and 4:10 P.M.
New River Valley WPIN-90.5 FM 2:12 and 4:10 P.M.
Pulaski WPUV-1580 AM 7:15 A.M.
Roanoke WPIR-91.3 FM 2:12 and 4:10 P.M.
Warrenton WPRZ-1250 AM 4:23 P.M.
Winchester WTRM-91.3 FM 2:15 P.M.

Washington
Spokane KUDY-1280 AM 5:29 P.M.
   KTFL-101.9 FM

West Virginia
Bluefield WPIB-90.9 FM 2:12 and 4:10 P.M.
Huntington WEMM-108 FM 5:06 P.M.
Charelston WJYP-100.9 FM 10:55 A.M.

Wisconsin
Lancaster WJTY-88.1 FM 12:30 P.M.
Miladore WGNV-88.5 FM 12:20 P.M.
Milwaukee WVCY-107.7 FM 12:30 P.M.
Suring WRVM-102.7 FM 3:03 P.M.
Tomah WVCX-98.9 FM 12:30 P.M.

Wyoming
Casper KCEB-91.1 FM 8:20 A.M.

Notes

Home Schooling: The Return to a Biblical and HIstorical Model of Education

1. Raymond and Dorothy Moore, *Home-Style Teaching* (Waco, Texas: Word Books, 1984), p. 201.
2. Letter to the Secretary, Dept. of Education, from Dr. Raymond Moore, April 18, 1985, p. 1.
3. "The CQ Researcher", published by Congressional Quarterly, Inc., Vol 4, No. 33, Sept. 9, 1994, p. 788.
4. Urie Bronfenbrenner and Maureen A. Mahoney, *Influences of Human Development* (Hinsdale, IL, Dryden Press, 1975), pp. 497-499.
5. John Whitehead, et. al., *Home Education and Constitutional Liberties* (Westchester, IL: Crossway Books, 1984) p. 22:Report of the Governor's Task Force on Compulsory Education, State of Iowa, Des Moines, IA—Nov.,20, 1985) p. 10.

Is Home Schooling For You?

6.. *United States Supreme Court Reports: Lawyers' Edition*, Second Series (Rochester: Lawyers Co-operative Publishing Co.,1973), p. 35.
7. Mel and Norma Gabler, *What Are They Teaching Our Children?* (Wheaton, IL., Victor Books, 1985), p. 88.
8. Paul C. Vitz, *Censorship: Evidence of Bias in Our Children's Textbooks* (Ann Arbor, Mich.: Servant, 1986), n.p.
9. Stanley Coopersmith, *The Antecedents of Self-Esteem*, (San Francisco: Freeman and Company, 1967), pp. 164-166.
10. Raymond and Dorothy Moore, *Home Grown Kids* (Waco, Texas:Word Books, 1981), p. 39.
11. Ibid.
12. "A Study of Schooling: Some Findings and Hypotheses," *Phi Delta Kappan*, March 1983.
13. Raymond and Dorothy Moore, *Home Style Teaching* (Waco, Texas:Word Books, 1984), p. 156.
14. Raymond and Dorothy Moore, *Home Grown Kids*, pp. 32-33.
15. David Elkind, *The Hurried Child* (Reading, Mass,: Addison-Wesley Publishing Company, 1981), p. 157.

Public Education: Retarding America and Imprisoning Potential

16. Jonathan Kozol, *Illiterate America* (Garden City, N.Y.: Anchor Press/Doubleday, 1985), pp. 8,9.

17. Jonathan Kozol, *Illiterate America,* p. 16.

18. "16th Annual Gallup Poll of Public's Attitudes Toward the Public School, " *Phi Delta Kappan,* Sept. 1984, p. 24.

19. William Jasper, "Not My Kids," *New American* May 19, 1986, p. 47.

20. Phyllis Schlafly, *The Phyllis Schlafly Report,* Vol.26, No. 10, May 1993.

21. Ibid.

22. Jonathan Kozol, *Illiterate America,* p. 16.

23. "Young People Are Getting Dumber" *Dallas Morning News,* August 26, 1971.

24. 5 May 1983, Congressional Record, S6060.

25. "Another Study Says Schools Are in Peril," *Washington Post,* July 21, 1983.

26. Sally Reed, *NEA: Propaganda Front of the Radical Left* (Alexandria, VA.: NCBE, 1984), p. 25.

27. Ibid.

28. "Dispatches," Hollywood, CA, July 29, 1994.

29. Mel and Norma Gabler, *What Are They Teaching Our Children?* (Wheaton, IL.: Victor Books, 1985), p. 34.

30. Samuel L. Blumenfeld, *NEA: Trojan Horse in American Education* (Boise, Idaho:Paradigm Company, 1984), p. 211.

31. "Johnny Can't Count—the Danger for the U.S.," *U.S. News and World Report,* September 15, 1982, p. 46.

32. "A New Test Begins for America's Schools" *U.S. News and World Report,* September 9, 1985, p. 63.

33. Tim Bovee, "If Johnny Can't Learn, Maybe Teacher Didn't," *Washington Times,* 16 July 1991, A1.

34. "SAT Scores Decline," *Teacher Magazine,* November/December 1991, 21.

35. Sam Blumenfeld, *The Blumenfeld Education Letter,* April 1994, Vol 9, No. 4, #92, 1-2.

36. Ibid.

37. *The Wall Street Journal,* October 12, 1993.

38. Samuel L. Blumenfeld, *NEA: Trojan Horse in American Education, p. 103.*

39. Sam Blumenfeld, N.E.A.: Trojan Horse In American Education Boise,, p. 2.

40. John Whitehead et. al., *Home Education and Constitutional Liberties* (Westchester, IL, Crossway Books, 1984) p. 22: Report of the Governor's Task Force on Compulsory Education, State of Iowa, Des Moines, IA—November 20, 1985) p. 10.

41. Sam Blumenfeld, *The Blumenfeld Education Letter,* Vol. 9, No. 11, #99, Nov. 1994, p. 5.

42. Ibid.
43. Mel and Norma Gabler, *What Are They Teaching Our Children?*, p. 20.
44. Paul Copperman, *The Literacy Hoax* (New York: William Morrow and Company, 1978), 79.
45. *The Wanderer,* November 18, 1993.
46. Mel and Norma Gabler, *What Are They Teaching Our Children?*, p. 56.
47. *American Information Newsletter,* Vol.III, No.2, Feb. 1993, p 1. (In this issue the editor, Lawrence Dawson, summarizes data gathered from *The Gabler Newsletter,* Dec. 1992).
48. Mel and Norman Gabler, *What Are They Teaching Our Children?*, 53.
49. "Help! Teacher Can't Teach!," *Time* June 16, 1980, p. 54.
50. "The Valedictorian" *Newsweek,* September 6, 1976, p. 52.
51. Paul Copperman, *The Literacy Hoax,* pp. 103-105.
52. "Remedial R's Aid Many Freshman," *Washington Times,* 7 August 1991, A6.
53. Paul C. Vitz, et. al., "Religion and Traditional Values in Public School Textbooks: An Empirical Study," (study pursuant to a grant contract from the National Institute of Education, Department of Education), pp. 70-71.
54. "Secular Humanism in the Dock," *Newsweek,* October 27, 1986, p. 96.
55. Ibid, p. 96.
56. Phyllis Schlafly, *Child Abuse in the Classroom,* p. 85.
57. Ibid., p. 312.
58. Mel and Norma Gabler, *What Are They Teaching Our Children?*, p. 66.
59. Ibid.
60. *Education Reformer,* Alton, Illinois, March 1994.
61. Kim Painter, "Fewer Kids Save Sex for Adulthood," *USA Today,* March 5, 1991., p. 1D-2D.
62. Barrett Mosbacker, *Teen Pregnancy and School-Based Health Clinics* (Washington, D.C.: Family Research Council of America, Inc.), p. 1.
63. House Select Committee on Children, Youth and Families, Teen Pregnancy: What Is Being Done? A State-By-State Look, December 1985, p. 378.
64. *Family Planning Perspectives,* 12, No. 5, September/October 1980, p. 229.
65. *Schools Without Drugs* (Washington, D.C.: U.S. Department of Education, 1986), p. 5.
66. "*Teen Drug Abuse* Up, Study Says," Fort Worth Star-Telegram Dec. 13, 1994, p. A1.
67. *Schools Without Drugs,* p. 5.
68. Ibid, p. 8.

69. Verne Faust, *Self-Esteem in the Classroom* (San Diego, Calf.:Thomas Paine Press, 1980), p. 41.
70. Mel and Norma Gabler, *What Are They Teaching Our Children?* p. 101.
71. Ibid., p. 86.
72. Ibid, p. 102.
73. Ibid, pp. 179-180.
74. Phyllis Schlafly, *Child Abuse in the Classroom*, pp. 368, 371.
75. "Home Schooling: Up From the Underground," *Reason Magazine*, April 1983, p. 26.
76. Urie Bronfenbrenner, *Two Worlds of Childhood: U.S. and U.S.S.R.*, (Simon & Schuster-New York, 1970) pp 97-101; Moore, Raymond, et. al., "When Education Becomes Abuse: A Different Look at the Mental Health of Children," *Journal of School Health*, February, 1986.
77. Janet Kizziar and Judy Hageforn, *Search for Acceptance: The Adolescent and Self-Esteem* (Chicago: Nelson-Hall, 1979), p. 2.
78. Dorothy C. Briggs, *Your Child's Self-Esteem: The Key to Life* (Garden City, N.Y.: Doubleday, 1970), p. 20.
79. "Home Schooling: An Idea Whose Time Has Returned," *Human Events*.
80. "Restoring Order to the Public Schools," Phi Delta Kappan, March 1985, p. 490.
81. Mel and Norma Gabler, *What Are They Teaching Our Children?* pp. 21-22.
82. "Annual Study Shows 3 Million Crimes on School Campuses," National School Safety Center News Service, Pepperdine University, California, October 1991.
83. "Restoring Order to the Public Schools," *Phi Delta Kappan*, March 1985, p. 490.
84. David Elkind, *The Hurried Child* (Reading, Mass,:Addison-Wesley Publishing Co., 1981), p. 155.
85. Survey of NEA K-12 Teacher Members 1985 (National Education Association, Professional and Organizational Development/Research Division: 1985), p. 18
86. "Most Teachers in Poll Cite Low Pay, Consider Quitting," Fort *Worth Star-Telegram*, Nov. 12, 1986.
87. Emily Post, *The New Emily Post's Etiquette* (The Emily Post Institute, Inc., 1975), p. preface.
88. Phyllis Schlafly, *Child Abuse in the Classroom*, p. 113.
89. *The Evangelical Methodist*, volume 73, number 6, June, 1994, p.7.
90. *Midnight Messenger*, Clackamas, OR, May/June 1994.
91. Samuel L. Blumenfeld, *NEA: Trojan Horse In American Education*.
92. "U.S. Teachers Held Hostage by the N.E.A.," *Human Events*, Sept. 7, 1985, p. 12.
93. "A Religion for a New Age," *The Humanist*, Jan/Feb. 1983.

94. Kim Painter, "Fewer Kids Save Sex for Adulthood,", 1D-2D.

95. "Remedial R's Aid Many Freshman,", A6.

96. *Journal of the American Family Association,* March 1992, Tupelo, MS, 13.

Why Home Schooling Is the Best Alternative

97. Raymond and Dorothy Moore, *Home-Spun Schools* (Waco, Texas: Word Books, 1982), pp. 10-11.

98. "Handbook for Texas Homeschoolers," by Home-Oriented Private Education, 1994, p. 6.

99. "Why Parents Should Enroll Their Children in a Christian School," *Christian School Comment,* 14, No. 6.

100. Timothy Dwight, Yale University President, 1795-1817.

101. John Whitehead et. al., op cit., p. 17; Unpublished letter from J.R. McCurdy, Education Administrator for Manitoba, Canada, to Texas Home School Coalition, dated July 4, 1986; Moore, op. cit., p. 372; Unpublished letter from J.W. Rogers, Attendance Counselor for Ontario, Canada, to Texas Home School Coalition, dated May 30, 1986: Iowa Task Force Report, op. cit., p 28: "Compulsory Schooling and Nontraditional Education," *E.C.S. Issuegram* No. 12, p. 2 (Education Commission of the States—August, 1985).

102. Whitehead et. al., op, cit., p. 17.

103. Whitehead et. al., op, cit., p. 17.

104. Edward Gordon, "Home Tutoring Programs Gain Respectability", *Phi Delta Kappan,* February 1983, pp. 398-399.

105. "1994 Rollups Basic Battery" Iowa Tests of Basic Skills, results obtained from the National Center for Home Education.

106. Dr. Brian Ray, "A Nationwide Study of Home Education: Family Characteristics, Legal Matters, and Student Achievement." (Seattle, Wash.: National Home Education Research Institute, 1990), 53-54.

107. "Home Schoolers Beat National Average on Achievement Tests," *Home School Court Report,* Vol. 7, No. 5, September/October 1991, 18.

108. Fed Up With Schools, More Parents Turn To Teaching at Home," *The Wall Street Journal,* May 10, 1994.

109. National Center For Home Education, Paeonian Springs, Virginia, 1990.

110. Dr. Brian Ray, "Marching to the Beat of Their Own Drum," A study by the Home School Legal Defense Association, 1992, p. 7.

111. "The School at Home," *Moody Monthly,* March 1984, pp. 18-19.

112. Ibid., p. 19.

113. *The CQ Researcher,* published by Congressional Quarterly Inc., Vol. 4, No. 33, Sept. 9, 1994, p. 773.

114. Kirk McCord, *Home Education: Is It Working,* Booklet published by Home Oriented Private Education for Texas, 1994, p. 5.
115. *The CQ Researcher,* Vol. 4, No. 33, Sept. 9, 1994, p. 773.
116. "Handbook for Texas Homeschoolers," by Home Oriented Private Education, 1994, p. 6.
117. SusanSaiter, "Schooling in the Home: A Growing Alternative", *New York Times,* April 14, 1985.
118. *The CQ Researcher,* Vol. 4, No. 33, Sept. 9, 1994, p. 772.
119. List compiled by Home School Legal Defense Association, July, 1994.
120. "Home Schooling: Up from the Underground," *Reason Magazine,* pp. 23-24.
121. *Webster's New Collegiate Dictionary* (Springfield, Mass.: G & C. Merriam Co., 1973), p. 748.
122. Dr. Linda Montgomery, "The Effect of Home Schooling on Leadership Skills of Home Schooled Students," *Home School Researcher* (5)1, 1989.
123. *Harvard Education Letter,* May-June 1993.
124. "Comparison of Social Adjustment Between Home and Traditionally Schooled Students," doctoral dissertation by Dr. Larry Shyers, University of Florida's College of Education, 1992.
125. Larry Shyers, "Comparison of Social Adjustment Between Home And Traditionally Schooled Students," abstract of dissertation presented to the graduate school of the University of Florida, May 1992.
126. Thomas C. Smedley, M.S., "Socialization of Home Schooled Children: A Communication Approach," thesis approved for MS in Corporate and Professional Communication, Radford University, Radford, Virginia, May 1992.
127. "New Research on Sociability," *The Parent Educator and Family Report,* 4, No. 3 (May/June 1986), p. 1.
128. J. Gary Knowles and James A. Muchmore, "We've Grown Up and We're OK: An Exploration of Adults Who Were Home-Educated as Children," paper presented at annual meeting of American Educational Research Association, April 1991. Authors are education professors at the University of Michigan.
129. Urie Bronfenbrenner and Maureen A. Mahoney, *Influences of Human Development* (Hinsdale, IL: Dryden Press, 1975), p. 491.
130. Shirley C. Samuels, *Enhancing Self-Concept in Early Childhood* (New York: Human Science Press: 1977), p. 34.
131. "Research and Common Sense: Therapies for our Homes and Schools," *Teachers College Record,* Winter 1982, p. 366.
132. John Bowlby, *Deprivation of Maternal Care* (New York: Schocken Books, 1966), pp. 15-29.
133. James Dobson, *Hide and Seek,* (Old Tappan, N.J.: Fleming Revell, 1974), p. 38.

134. Robert H. Schuller, *Self-Esteem: The New Reformation* (Waco, Texas,: Word Books, 1982), p. 17.

135. Verne Faust, *Self-Esteem in the Classroom*, p. 61.

136. Nathan Pritikin, *The Pritikin Promise* (New York: Pocket Books, 1983), p. 10.

137. First National Conference on Youth Fitness, 1984.

138. Raymond and Dorothy Moore, *Home-Grown Kids* (Waco, Texas: Word Books, 1981), pp. 37-38.

139. Ibid., p. 23.

The "How" of Home Schooling

140. *United States Supreme Court Reports: Lawyer's Edition,* Second Series (Rochester: Lawyer's Co-operative Publishing Co., 1973), p. 24.

141. "Marching to the Beat of a Different Drum", Home School Legal Defense Association, p. 5.

142. H.W. Byrne, *A Christian Approach to Education* (Grand Rapids: Zondervan Publishing House, 1961), pp. 97-99.

143. Charlie W. Shedd, *Time For All Things* (Nashville, TN.:Abingdom Press, 1972), pp. 13-94. (Elements of the author's thoughts on time management were gleaned from parts of this book.)

144. J. Richard Fugate, *What The Bible Says About...Child Training* (Garland, Texas: Aletheia Publishers, Inc., 1980), pp.65-69.

145. Ibid, pp. 65-69.

146. Ibid.

147. Ibid.

148. Cathy Duffy, *Christian Home Educators' Curriculum Manual-Elementary Grades,* (Garden Grove: Home Run Enterprises, 1992), p. 8.

149. *The CQ Researcher,* published by Congressional Quarterly Inc., Vol. 4, No. 33, Sept. 9, 1994, p. 773.

150. "A Report of the Working Group on the Family," *The Family—Preserving America's Future,* p.41.

151. Ibid.

152. Bob Larson, *Family Issues* (Wheaton, IL.: Tyndale House, 1986), p. 257.

153. Ibid.

154. James Dobson, *The Impact of TV on Young Lives,* pamphlet (Pomona, CA:Focus on the Family, 1983), p. 3.

Why Fathers Should Be Involved in the Home School

155. Robert Coleman, *The Master Plan of Evangelism* (Old Tappan, NJ:Fleming H. Revell), pp. 33,41,43.

156. Michael Farris, elements of key note address given at the national homeschooling convention in Portland, OR, 1988.

157. Ibid.
158. Ibid.
159. Ibid.

How to Begin

160. *Washington Post,* July 2, 1990.

Why Grandparents Should Support Home Schooling

161. *The Evangelical Methodist,* Vol. 73, No. 2, Feb. 1994, p. 6.

Reasons to Home School through High School

162. "16th Annual Gallup Poll of the Public's Attitude Towards the Public School," *Phi Delta Kappan,* Sept. 1984, p. 25.
163. "New Research on Sociability," *The Parent Educator and Family Report,* 4, No. 3 (May/June 1986), p. 1.
164. "Comparison of Social Adjustment Between Home and Traditionally Schooled Students," doctoral dissertation University of Florida's College of Education, 1992.

Common Questions Asked about Home Schooling

165. "A Study of Schooling: Some Findings and Hypothesis," *Phi Delta Kappan,* March 1983, p. 467.

Select Bibliography

Adams, Jay. *Back to the Blackboard*. Phillipsburg, N.J.: Presbyterian and Reformed, 1982.

Blumenfeld, Samuel L. *How to Start Your Own Private School, and Why You Need One*. Boise, Idaho: Paradigm.

_____. *How to Tutor*. Milford, Mich.: Mott Media, 1977.

_____. *Is Public Education Necessary?* Boise, Idaho: Paradigm.

_____. *NEA: Trojan Horse in American Education*. Boise, Idaho: Paradigm, 1984.

_____. *The New Illiterates*, Boise, Idaho: Paradigm.

_____. *The Retreat From Motherhood*. Boise, Idaho: Paradigm.

Brooks, Barry, Tim Lambert, Hank Tate, Patti Moore, Philip May, Donna Harp, *Handbook For Texas Home Schoolers*, Austin: TX.: HOPE, 1994.

Byrne, H. W. *A Christian Approach to Education*. Milford, Mich.: Mott Media, 1977.

Chall, Jeanne. *Learning to Read: The Great Debate*. New York: McGraw-Hill, 1967.

Christian Liberty Academy. *Class Legal Manual*. Prospect Heights, Ill.: Christian Liberty Academy.

Copperman, Paul. *The Literacy Hoax*. New York: William Morrow and Co., 1978.

Damerell, Reginald G. *Education's Smoking Gun: How Teachers' Colleges Have Destroyed Education in America*. New York: Fareundlich Books, 1985.

De Jong, Norman. *Education in Truth*. Phillipsburg, N.J.: Presbyterian and Reformed, 1969.

Dobson, James. *Hide or Seek*. Expanded and updated ed. Old Tappan, N.J.: Revell, 1974.

Duffy, Cathy, *Christian Home Educators' Curriculum Manual— Junior/Senior High*, Garden Grove, CA.: Home Run Enterprises, 1991.

Elkind, David. *The Hurried Child*. Reading, PA.: Addison-Wesley, 1981.

Farris, Michael P., *The Homeschooling Father*, Paeonian Springs, VA.: Michael P. Farris, 1992.

———. *Where Do I Draw the Line*, Minneapolis, Bethany House, 1992.

———. *Constitutional Law for Christian Students*, Paeonian Springs, VA.: HSLDA, 1991.

Falwell, Jerry. *Listen America*. New York: Bantam.

Flesch, Rudolf. *Why Johnny Still Can't Read: A New Look at the Scandal of Our Schools*. New York: Harper & Row, 1983.

Foundation for American Christian Education. *The Bible and the Constitution of the United States of America*. San Francisco: Foundation for American Christian Education.

Fugate, J. Richard. *What the Bible Says About Child Training*. Tempe, Ariz.: Aletheia, 1980.

Gabler, Mel and Norma. *What Are They Teaching Our Children?* Wheaton, Ill.: Victor, 1985.

Hall, Verna M. *The Christian History of the Constitution of the United States of America*. San Francisco: Foundation for American Christian Education, 1960.

Holt, John. *Freedom and Beyond*. Boston, Mass.: Holt Associates, 1984.

———. *Teach Your Own: New and Hopeful Path for Parents and Educators*. New York: Delta, 1986.

Iserbyt, Charlotte. *Back to Basics . . . or Skinnerian International Curriculum*. Upland, Calif.: Barbara Morris Report, 1985.

Klicka, Christopher, *The Right Choice: Home Schooling*. Gresham, Oregon: Noble Publishing Associates, 1992.

———. *Home Schooling in the United States: A Legal Analysis*, Paeonian Springs, VA.: HSLDA, August, 1994.

Kozol, Jonathan. *Illiterate America*. Garden City, N.Y.: Anchor Press, 1985.

LaHaye, Tim. *The Battle for the Mind*. Old Tappan, N.J.: Revell, 1983.

———. *The Battle for the Public Schools*. Old Tappan, N.J.: Revell, 1983.

Macaulay, Susan Schaeffer. *For the Children's Sake*. Wheaton, Ill.: Crossway, 1984.

May, Phillip. *Which Way to Educate?* Chicago: Moody, 1975.

Mayberry, Maralee, J. Gary Knowles, Brian Ray, Stacy Marlow, *Home Schooling: Parents As Educators*, Thousand Oaks, CA.: Corwin Press, Inc., 1995.

Moore, Raymond S., and Dorothy Moore. *Better Late Than Never*. New York: Readers' Digest Press.

———. *Home-grown Kids*. Waco,Tex.: Word, 1981.

———. *Homespun Kids*. Waco, Tex.: Word, 1982.

———. *Home-style Teaching*. Waco, Tex.: Word, 1984.

Nuttal, Clayton L. *The Conflict: The Separation of Church and State*. Schaumburg, IL.: Regular Baptist Press, 1980.

Pride, Mary. *The New Big Book of Home Learning—Vol 1, Getting Started.* Wheaton, IL: Crossway, 1990.

_____. *The New Big Book of Home Learning—Vol. 2, Preschool and Elementary.* Wheaton, IL: Crossway, 1991.

_____. *The New Big Book of Home Learning—Vol 3, Teen and Adult.* Wheaton, IL: Crossway, 1991.

_____. *The New Big Book of Home Learning—Vol 4, Afterschooling.* Wheaton, IL: Crossway, 1990.

_____. *Schoolproof,* Wheaton, IL: Crossway, 1988.

_____. *The Way Home: Beyond Feminism, Back to Reality.* Wheaton, IL: Crossway, 1985.

_____. *All The Way Home,* Wheaton, IL: Crossway, 1989.

Ray, Brian. *Marching to the Beat of Their Own Drum,* Paeonian Springs, VA.: HSLDA, 1992.

Reed, Carl. *Our Reeds Grow Free.* Amarillo, Tex.: Owen Haney Press.

Reed, Sally. *NEA: Propaganda Front of the Radical Left.* Alexandria, Va.: NCBE, 1984.

Shackelford, Luanne, Susan White, *A Survivors Guide to Home School,* Wheaton, IL: Crossway, 1988.

Schaeffer, Francis A. *A Christian Manifesto.* Wheaton, Ill.: Crossway, 1981.

Schindler, Claude, Jr. and Pacheo Pyle. *Educating for Eternity.* Wheaton, IL: Tyndale.

Schlafly, Phyllis, ed. *Child Abuse in the Classroom.* Alton, IL: Pere Marquette, 1984.

Slater, Rosalie J. *Teaching and Learning America's Christian History.* San Francisco: Foundation for American Christian Education, 1965.

Sommer, Carl. *Schools in Crisis: Training for Success or Failure?* 2nd ed. Houston, Tex.: Cahill, 1984.

Trumbull, H. Clay. *Hints on Child Training.* New York: Charles Scribner's and Sons.

Vitz, Paul C. *Censorship: Evidence on Bias in Our Children's Textbooks.* Ann Arbor, Mich.: Servant, 1986.

Wade, Theodore E., Jr., et al. *The Home School Manual: For Parents Who Teach Their Own Children.* 5th ed. Auburn, Calif.: Gazelle, 1993.

Whitehead, John W *The Separation Illusion.* Milford, Mich.: Mott Media.

Whitehead, John W and Wendell R. Bird. *Home Education and Constitutional Liberties.* Wheaton, IL: Crossway, 1984.